I0015051

The AS/400 & IBM i Pocket SQL Guide

QuikCourse: IBM i SQL By Example

by Brian W. Kelly

*– A Comprehensive Book of IBM I SQL examples &
information for the new SQL Developer –*

Contains AS/400 and IBM i SQL Concepts, Coding Examples & Exercises.
This book is based on The AS/400 Database DB2/400 and the excellent
Kelly Consulting QuikCourse™ SQL education modules.

**LETS GO !
PUBLISH**

Contains significant reference material, how-to's, and insightful tutorials.

BRIAN W. KELLY

Published by: LETS GO PUBLISH!
Brian P. Kelly, Publisher
P.O Box 621
Wilkes-Barre, PA 18703
info@letsgopublish.com
www.letsgopublish.com

Library of Congress Copyright Information Pending
Book Cover Design by Michele Thomas

ISBN Information: The International Standard Book Number (ISBN) is a unique machine-readable identification number, which marks any book unmistakably. The ISBN is the clear standard in the book industry. 159 countries and territories are officially ISBN members. The Official ISBN For this book is:
978-0-9982683-0-9

The price for this work is : $25.99 USD

10	9	8	7	6	5	4	3	2	1

Dedication

To my wonderful wife Patricia, and our loving children, Brian, Michael, and Katie as well as the greatest pack of brothers and sisters, aunts and uncles, cousins, nieces and nephews that any person could ever hope to have in just one life.

Acknowledgments

I would like to thank many people for helping me in this effort.

I would first like to thank my immediate family, starting with my lovely and dear wife, Patricia. Again, as I offer in all my books, my wife Patricia is my source. She is the person who keeps me alive and sane and well in more ways than can be mentioned. She is the glue that holds our whole family together. Besides that, she keeps getting better looking as the years go by, and I love to see her wonderful face every day in my life. Her daddy, a wonderful man in his own right, Smokey Piotroski, called his little girl Packy as a nickname. Though Stash is now with the Angels, I love that name and the person who wears it and I still use it to address my little Packy. God gave me a gift that keeps me going. Thank you Packy for all you do to keep me and our whole family well and mostly, thank you for the smile that you always put on my face.

I would also like to thank my twenty-year-old daughter, Katie, who is still my little baby doll. Kate helps me in any way she can. Even more than that, her sweet voice and her accomplished guitar playing gets the muse racing as my fingers pound the keyboard. Katie is starting to feel better now and we thank God for that but it still is not easy for her. She is on her way to being OK. I thank my Katie for she will always be Daddy's Little Girl. I love you very much. A special thank you also goes to Dr. Patrick Kerrigan, who is working his way up the list in record time. Dr. Patrick comes to the job with the abilities of Hippocrates and the patience of Job. He has left no stone unturned in helping Katie through her illness.

Thanks also go out to my twenty-three-year-old son, Michael, who more than made the deans list in his last semester at King's College this year as he received his B.S. Degree in Accounting. Michael had very good LSATs and his academic record was more than enough for him to be accepted in Law School and he will be beginning his three year trek this month. I am always happy to have my youngest son close by so I am going to miss him very much.

I also thank my twenty-four-year-old son, Brian, who just knocked 'em dead in Law School and graduated Magna Cum Laude. Brian spent most of this summer taking courses in preparation for the Bar Examination, which he took last week. He thinks that he did very well and that he'll be getting permission to practice soon. After a short break, Brian will be starting a clerkship. Congratulations Brian, you make us very proud. Mom and I are very proud of all of our children and we thank each of them for their work in academia and their efforts on our behalf.

Thanks also to the extended family who are always there to lend a helping hand. Barb, Kim & Dave, Dawn, Cindy & Dave Boyle, Megan and Sean are some of the most wonderful family in my life. And dad Joe, with the angels, always gets his plugs in. Thanks also to Melissa and Paul Sabol and their new baby boy Paul IV.

Accomplishments often materialize because of a strong friendship infrastructure. I am pleased to have a number of great friends. Among them is my longtime best friend Dennis Grimes, who is always there to help, though he may think everything I write sounds the same. Professor Grimes is on the faculty with me at Marywood University and he is a CIO for Klein Wholesale. He is very talented and very helpful. I selected his comments about Chip Wars as a cover quote. Barbara Grimes, Patricia Grimes Yencha, Elizabeth (Wizzler), Mary the PhD., Denyse back from the U.K., Grandma Viola, and Grandma Gert also pitch in whenever the opportunity arises. Dennis helps me in whatever way I ask, especially when

I am stuck. I really appreciate all you do for me "D." Thank you.

The busiest guy on all of my book projects, besides myself, is always Joe McDonald. Joe is the businessman in our publishing venture, and in that, he's all business. Joe is the former Publisher of the Scranton Tribune/Scrantonian Newspaper. So he's got the right background to make sure everything is A-OK! I promised Joe that my next book was going to be non-technical as we moved the publishing business to Children's books and third party authors. Joe assures me that after this book, he will have the courage to lead me to the children's side of the business where our next book is scheduled to be The Adventures of Eddy (The Dog) written by Joe's Grandson. Soon, it will be on the bookshelves of America. My thanks also go to Peg McDonald for making sure that Joe is always ready for action.

Of course, the long list of helping hands contains lots of names: Gerry Rodski and Joyce, Jeanne and Farmer Joe Elinsky, John and Carol Anstett, Grandma Leona and Grandma Annie (from Mayflower), Carolyn and Joe Langan, Bob & Cathy Wood, Karen and Al Komorek, Bonnie and George Mohanco, Becker and Robin Mohanco, Lilya, Josh, and Alaina Like Mohanco, Bob and Nettie Lussi, Kim and Ruth Borland--- they are all there when needed.. Other helping hands include Dr. Lou and Marie Guarnieri as well as Mary and Cindy Guarnieri, whose hands have been indispensable.

I can't forget Mike and Frannie Kurilla & Frankie and Tony, Jerry and Hedy Cybulski, Linda DeBoo and Bob Buynak, Joe, the Chief, LaSarge, John and Susan Rose, and Dave and Nancy Books. Thanks also to Dr. Rex Dumdum from Marywood-- my academic mentor. Special thanks also to the E.L. Meyers Class of 1965 (40th reunion this year) for some early training in the art of writing.

And don't let me forget Patricia's parents, Arline and Stanley Piotroski, who continue to guide us in our lives. Cathy and Marty Piotroski, Dr. Susan Piotroski and Dr. Mitch Bornstein, Matt and Allie, Dr. Stan Piotroski, Carol Piotroski, Sister Marlene, Justin and Katie, Merek, MacKenzie, Myranda, Erin, Ralph Harvey, Lynn, and Scott Piotroski, Pierre Le Kep. The Kelly parents -- Ed and Irene also provide guidance from upstairs as well as direct intervention as needed; Anna Maye, Nancy and Angel Jim Flannery (Leland (No K) Zard), Renee (Bean), Jimmy (Jim Bob), Bridget, Mary (MeeWee), Danny, Michael (McPike) , Ken (La Rue), Jen, Angel David Davidow (Brunoch Zard), Stephen (P.Q. Whoozer), Matthew(M.Q. Peph), Bailee Roo, Viva La Vieve, and Billiard Peph, Joe and Rosalee, Raymond and the real Sparkey. Mary and Bill Daniels, Liz (Weezler), Bri, Meg (Gledeebaigledee), Bill Jr (Billdog) ., Vicky, Sophia (Chubby Cheeks,) Elise (La Leese), Diane and Joe Kelly, Tara and Col, Ed and Eudart Kelly, Eddie, John, and Robert. Bill Rolland- Notre Dame's # 1 Fan and master of accommodations, Bill Kustas, Bill & Helen Kush, Steve and Shelly Bartolomei, Keith and Dorie Zinn, Cheryl Danowski, Ricky, Joane, Briana and Eric Bayer, and of course the great musical cutter Harrison Arthur and his friend Harry Heck Jr. More thanks to Judy Jones and Jerry Reisch and Judy Judy Judy Seroska.

Going back to the top of the list of helpers is my wonderful and huge pack of cousins. The list begins with the Uncles and Aunts, many of whom are now Angels. Uncle Nick and Aunt Emma McKeown, Dave and Kathleen Conklin, Rita and Frank DeRiancho, Joan and Tom Nelson, Aunt Ruth and Uncle Joe McKeown, Kathy and Joe McKeown Jr., Aunt Louise and Uncle Jimmy McKeown, Patsy, Danny and Jerry McKeown, Nina and Jim Brady, Jimmy Brady, Tommy and Mary Rowan, Arlene and Richard May, Little Tommy Rowan, Helen and Joe Drexinger, and all the other cousins, uncles & aunts who can't make it to the special muse event every summer in Montrose.

Of course, there's Uncle Johnny Kelly, Aunt Catherine and Leonard Lamascola, Aunt Mary Kelly, Sharon, Maureen, Jud,

Pat Jr., and Tommy Kelly. Red Cloud is also on the list for his due diligence in writing postcards.

In the special care category, Dr. Lou has been making sure that my bones are aligned properly for years. So that I can give those speeches with a bright smile, I got some big help from Dr. Lou Kicha the Great and his highly competent team of professionals at Aspen Dental-- John Cicon, Carol Kephart, Nicole Arnone, Anita Florek, and the tooth architect, Mary Lou Lennox. Thank you all very much.

Special acknowledgments to Steven Dressler and Howard Klein, the top management team at Klein Wholesale Distributors in Wilkes-Barre, PA, who use chip technology to the fullest. Their vision, foresight, and execution have brought Klein to the enviable position of being the third largest candy and tobacco wholesaler in the United States.

Various members of the Klein development staff offered information over the time in which this book was written. In alphabetical order, by first name, the Klein team includes: Barb Chaderton, Bill 'Curly' Kepics, Cindy Dorzinsky, Cindy Goodwin, Dennis Grimes, Eric Priest, Jeff Massaker, Jerry Reisch, Joe Byorick, Joe Rydzewski, John Robbins, Paula Terpak, Rod Smith, and Rosalind Robertson.

I would also like to thank Nancy Lavan, our sponsor at Offset Paperback, our printer. She continually encourages us in our writing and publishing efforts. Chris Grieves, our new customer service person has made working with the printing process an easy task. Special thanks go to Michele Thomas, who takes ideas and makes wonderful images from them, such as this wonderful cover.

To sum up my acknowledgments, as I do in every book that I have written, I am compelled to offer that I am truly convinced that "the only thing you can do alone in life is fail." Thanks to my family, good friends, and a helping team, I was not alone.

Table of Contents

Preface:

This is a learn by example guide for AS/400 and IBM i SQL-based application development

Finally, there is a Pocket Developer's Guide for AS/400 and IBM i SQL database development. Yes, it is in big pocket guide form and it is tutorial in nature. You'll be pleased with all the valuable explanations and examples. You won't want to put down this comprehensive guide to learning AS/400 and IBM i SQL now that you've got your hands on it. This book is 20 years overdue.

In today's IT landscape, most shops support heterogeneous systems with numerous client and server PCs, and even Unix boxes. Ironically, all of these non-IBM i platforms, from the smallest to the largest have one thing in common in the relational database area. They all use SQL as their data language.

That's a big change in the database landscape. Nobody even tries to deny that SQL is now the industry data / query language standard. IBM backs SQL 100%. Not many know that IBM invented SQL. It was the groundbreaking work of IBM engineers Donald D. Chamberlin and Raymond F. Boyce in the early 1970s.

A quick look at the SQL function list for the latest version of IBM i gives a good indication that SQL will have an even more important role in the IBM i future. IBM has been chipping away at all the little things and the annoying things over the years so that SQL is no longer a lesser function cousin on AS/400 and IBM i systems compared with DDS.

It certainly is not yet the time to throw in the DDS towel but the new SQL functions are more and more compelling with each release. So, today, it makes little sense for an IBM i professional to not be on board by warming up to SQL – at least for functions that return sets of data.

This Guide has an example for just about every type of common SQL function you can imagine—from creating tables & views to performing simple and complex selections, column and scalar functions, sub-queries, all the way to unions and joins.

Author Brian Kelly designed this book to show you how to use SQL by working with rich examples that you'll use over and over again. Additionally, for each example, there is the explanation you need to get a head start on being an SQL guru.

This is the first book to hand to your new developers and it is a natural for the veteran development team. More importantly, rather than seeing Oracle as the only database taught at your local Community Colleges, Colleges, and Universities, finally there is an up-to-date SQL Guide as the right sized text to use as a teaching vehicle for a modern IBM i database course.

Both entry level and existing programmers will enjoy the easy to read, down home style of this pocket guide. The book also gives a general notion of how file systems work and / or how DBMS systems tick to get you started in learning SQL

Even if you are new to AS/400 and IBM i, and you want to understand how to use SQL for DDL for functions that you might have used IBM's OPNQRY tool, you can learn all you need right from this pocket book. It is written in a way which assumes very little prior database knowledge.

There is no CD with this book as the examples help you create your own databases with SQL.

Go ahead and leaf through this book now. You'll see it is chocked full of examples. Many screen shots are included so you can play SQL right along with your AS/400 or IBM i server.

Who Should Read this book?

New programmers, existing programmers, supervisors, operation personnel, advanced end users and even IT management should all read this QuikCourse on SQL IT managers today are looking for ways to educate their staff in SQL. The fact is that many information requirements can be met with just a few SQL DML statements.

Database knowledge and SQL can save a wealth of high level language (HLL) coding. Look no further. If you plan to train operations people or PC people as AS/400 developers, or you want to help your staff better understand the marvels of the IBM i SQL, this is the right book.

With all of the smart, yet sometimes clueless PC technicians running around every business and institution, there are many who would appreciate the opportunity to learn the IBM i SQL interface to the native database. These people would do well in the IT Department if redeployed. This book can be all you need to move them off the mark.

While many larger AS/400 and IBM i shops may have had SQL on their boxes for some time and may have even used it to solve some business problems, more and more IBM i shops are now taking the plunge to SQL. Even smaller IT shops have SQL on their machines since it is bundled with Express systems. There are not many IBM i departments out there anymore that are disenfranchised from the SQL data / query language environment.

IBM thinks the time is now for SQL and Big Blue has said many times that SQL is its strategic database language. In fact IBM built a new Query Engine on the IBM i just for SQL and it is substantially better and faster than the classical query engine. Though IBM does not recommend a wholesale abandonment of DDS, it is certainly the right time for a good look at SQL. And there is no better way to do that than to learn it by example.

If you've always wanted to be able to tell your team what you know about database and SQL on the AS/400 and IBM i, but you did not have the time, I've done it for you. I've said what you would have said if you had the time to say it Moreover, the folks at LETS GO PUBLISH think you'll like what you would have said.

Consider creating a home-made SQL knowledgeable programmer with some nice database knowledge. It may be a good deal for you and for your company.

As you may know, there typically is no DB Administrator position in AS/400 shops. The database job is up to you - the AS/400 and IBM i Application Developer. Though rich in content, IBM's reference manuals are not built to teach you. They are for reference. There is too much in IBM's manuals to learn from but they are great references. This Pocket Guide for SQL uses a different approach. It is your teaching / learning vehicle to SQL. It is your new tool to help you solve programming problems efficiently with SQL coding—rather than having to work harder building program code.

The Step Often Forgotten

It helps to remember that before anybody can work on their first program in your shop, they have to understand the AD environment and the tools that are in the shop's development kit. The next thing they need to know is how the database works. That's how we once taught formal development and database courses. First the AD tools; then the database. By supplying sample databases and plenty of SQL examples in this QuikCourse, this pocket guide can prepare your team to effectively engage the AS/400 and IBM i database with the SQL language without spending thousands on computer based training or classroom education.

When prospective developers learn the AD tools, and the database with SQL, they can then move on, to learning or using, an AS/400 / IBM i programming language, such as RPG/400, ILE RPG (RPGIV), or even COBOL. Unfortunately, most IT shops do it the other way around. The student is sent to programming school or assigned to a real project long before he or she learns the IBM i operating system, the system's essential AD tools, SQL, and the database. This book can help you get things done in the right sequence.

I wish you well in your database endeavors, and I hope to see you again reading another Lets Go Publish Pocket Guide.

Brian W. Kelly
Wilkes-Barre, Pennsylvania

About the Author

Brian W. Kelly retired as a 30-year IBM Midrange Systems Engineer in 1999. While with IBM, he was also a Certified Instructor and a Mid-Atlantic Area Designated Specialist. When IBM began to move its sales and support to Business Partners, he formed Kelly Consulting in 1992 as an IT education and consulting firm. Kelly developed numerous AS/400 professional courses over the years that range from soup to nuts.

He has written 89 books with better tha half of them on advanced IT topics. He has also written hundreds of articles with many about current IT topics. These include articles for The Four Hundred, Midrange Computing, Showcase, News/400, AS/400 Systems Management, AS/400 Internet Expert, Computer Business News, Search400, and others. Kelly has also developed and taught a number of college courses and recently retired as a member of the Business / IT faculty at Marywood University in Scranton, Pennsylvania, where he also served as IBM I technical advisor to the IT faculty.

Chapter 1   What is a Database?

The Database Concept

Since SQL depends on there being a relational database management system (RDBMS) on the server in order to use all of its features, let's define the notion of database and look at a number of databases, both old and new to put the relational database as used by SQL in perspective. In the later chapters of this book we delve deeper into database theory and we discuss the physical and logical structure of the files that are produced by SQL and the native database language on the IBM i. The first step in defining the notion of database is to define the elusive term, data.

The word data is the plural of the Latin word, datum, which simply means something given. However, for the word to make more sense in computer systems, it is often defined as one or a series of unorganized facts. The word data, despite its origins is not always treated as a plural noun in English. More and more scientists and researchers think of data as a singular mass entity like information, and most people now follow this in general usage. So, data is actually now used as the singular and plural.

The term "raw data" is used to differentiate the notion of data from the notion of information. The term "raw" accentuates the idea of the unorganized nature of the facts. Information, a term often misused in place of data, means data organized for decision making. Through processes such as classification, sorting, and manipulation acting on database structures, data becomes information.

A database then is an organized collection of data necessary to perform a task which, as a by-product creates information. Related data fields are grouped together to form a record. Similar records are grouped together into a file. One or more related data files are grouped to form a database. What is Database Management?

Database management is the process of managing data. It is the underlying software which enables the database to function. Some of the basic capabilities for database functionality are often provided through the native data management portion of the operating system, upon which the database software is built. The rest is provided by the database software itself. Data management is needed to provide organization, access, and control of the data that is stored in a computer system.

Besides being a necessary component of a database, database management provides benefits by providing and maintaining structures, enabling data actions, and enforcing data rules. It is substantially more productive for a given computer to perform functions with the database than for a programmer to code the same functions in every program that uses the database.

Data Organization

Data organization facilities in a database must provide for a flexible data structure which meets the organization's application needs, yet can adapt to changing business requirements. Additionally, a database should be able to handle ad hoc requests for information as a by-product.

Data Access

Data access facilities in a database determine how you get at the data. They provide the ability to retrieve data, format data, and sequence data. It is through this software that the database is able to provide its data services to other constituent parts of the computer system, as well as to user programs.

Data Integrity

Data integrity control facilities in a database are also very important. They provide data independence from programs and assure the maintenance of data integrity such that, among other things, all database fields contain the correct data types.

Data Control

When referring to SQL, the term data control most often refers to the notion of security. Through the SQL Data Control languages (DCL), for example security officers are able to grant and revoke authority of users to see or manipulate data within a database.

What If There Were No Database?

Without a database, there is no flexible data structure, and data access is done by application programs. Security and control are provided by programmers through their individual programming efforts (very costly and time consuming, inconsistent, and not very secure). Additionally, without a database, many more programs need to be written. For example, something as simple as a new data selection would need to be programmed.

Therefore, without a database, each reordering and each new selection increases the programming backlog. Another common example of how data bases help operations is when a change is required to a file's record layout. Without a database, input and output definitions must be hard coded into all programs which need to access the file. Thus, even a simple change to a record layout, such as a field addition or field deletion, or even a field change in field length or an attribute means that each dependent program must be changed.

In summary, programs written without the help of a database, must do lots more work, and thus they contain more lines of code, are more expensive to build, are slower to develop, and are more difficult to maintain. Overall, they are not a good deal for the long term. Besides the impact on programmers, systems without database make it very difficult for end users to construct queries that depend on the availability of data definitions to end users.

DBMS Types: Function and Structure

Since all of the features of SQL work only with relational databases, we will forego any major description of the other database types. But it is a worthwhile exercise to identify and briefly explain the other forms.

Just like everything else that you encounter in life, there are many types of databases. Moreover, there are also a number of ways to classify databases. The two most popular ways to classify databases today are by function and by structure (data model). Let's look first at function.

Databases Characterized by Function

Database experts have classified two major forms of functional databases. These are as follows:

- ✓ Operational Database
- ✓ Analytical Database

Operational Databases

Let's first look at operational databases. In another word, operational databases are also known as production databases. This means that these databases are used in the normal computer processing of the business. So, if the company takes orders, sends out bills, collects money, and keeps track of all its finances, the databases used to store all of this valuable data are known as operational / production databases. Through the normal operations of the business, these databases are updated and maintained by the computer applications in support of business functions.

In simple English, operational databases let you actually change and manipulate the data. You can modify data in any way that is necessary. For example, you can add data, delete data, or even change the data.

Because these applications process business transactions, a more recent term to describe these databases has been fashioned -- Online Transaction Processing (OLTP) databases. These databases then are the master, transaction, and archive data repositories for operational data.

Analytical Databases

One of the problems with operational data is that it is designed to support operations and, though the data is quite valuable for decision making, it is not formatted well for end user access. Ironically, one of the problems that database implementation was supposed to solve is data redundancy. However, the recommended way today of providing databases that are shaped for informational purposes v. operational purposes is to construct analytical databases. These databases in most cases do not use the typical relational structure. Instead, the data is built into a data warehouse and the type of functional database that is ideal for this is called an On Line Analytical Processing (OLAP) database.

So, these OLAP databases are primarily used to keep track of statistics, rather than to record operational events as they occur. They are most often read-only, meaning that you can only retrieve and view data, but you can't modify the data in any way. OLAP databases keep track of important data and make it readily available for further analysis for information queries.

The data in an OLAP database gets updated by systems processes that take the operational data and reformat it for analytical use.

For example, the company's sales data can be read and analyzed to determine how and when more products are sold. The analytical databases hold much more descriptive information about important data in the company that it is easier for management to access the data in an ad hoc manner to gain information on the fly.

Data Bases Characterized by Function / Model

Another way of classifying databases is by the way the data is structured within the database itself. You might ask, so, what's a data model? A simple answer is that it is the intangible form in which data is stored. It is kind of like the internal structure of a database. However, data models have often been just theoretical ideas that are made practical through implementation. They are abstract concepts that you cannot touch. Data models are used to describe how the data is stored and retrieved in a database. Now, let's list and discuss a few of the types of data models so you see what they are all about.

These are the most popular types of database management systems (DBMS):

Flat file model
Hierarchical model
Network model
Relational model
Object-oriented database model
Object database model
Client / server database model
XML database model
Dimensional database model

The earliest databases were flat-file, hierarchical, and network oriented. In general terms, these types of database organizations and management systems are far more complex and less flexible than a relational database management system (RDBMS). Moreover, both the hierarchical and the network models rely on address pointers being embedded in database records making the navigation of the database and the maintenance of the database structure an effort of major consequence for DB administrators and programmers.

The other five models listed above are more recent additions to the list. In one way or another, these five are additions and combinations to address the need for more function. In most cases, they use the relational model as their base. Each of these are generally described below and the relational model and its implementation on the IBM IBM i is further explained in the later chapters of this book.

Flat-file Database Model:

The flat-file data model is the model that was used before databases were invented in the 1970's. Thus, it can be argued that such models are used by the old paper-based databases. In this system, data was stored in numerous data files. There were no links captured within the files so any relationships that the data had in common, such as a customer file and an order file, were not stored in the files.

The files were not linked, so programs had to be used to bring the data from multiple files together. Good programmers were able to emulate the linkage functions of good database systems but it was far more difficult to do than with database systems designed to provide this function.

Because file systems were very dependent on the speed of the systems of the day, data would often be repeated in more than one file so that the system would not have to access multiple files to provide data for programs. In many ways this created an environment in which there was significant redundancy. The problems with these original "flat-file databases" inspired scientists and mathematicians to find a way to link files so that they would not be repetitive, and that the database work could be done in the database rather than in each program.

Hierarchical Database Model

One of the arguments for relational database was always that, unlike a hierarchical style database, its model was based in sound mathematics. The hierarchical database is not based on a mathematical model, but rather a database implementation called the Information Management System (IMS) developed in the early 1970's by IBM.

The hierarchical database model made many improvements over the flat file approach to help get rid of the repetitiveness of flat files and other shortcomings. Although it was somewhat successful, it did not completely succeed. Redundant data was still needed in the hierarchical databases.

The most noted issues with hierarchical databases always include these:

Each file relates only to one above or below
No lateral links
Requires repeat data
Hard to search (query)

A hierarchical database consists of a series of databases that are grouped together to resemble a family tree as seen I Figure 1-1.

Figure 1-1 Hierarchical DB Model

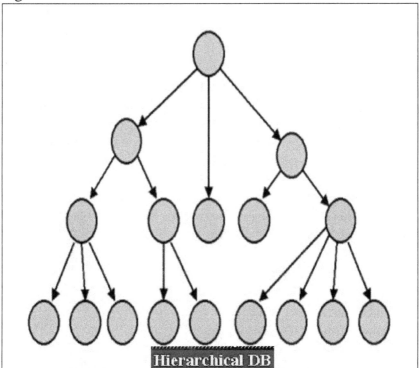

Hierarchical DB

Each of the circles in the diagram represents one database. The top circle in the hierarchical model is called the "parent." The databases under it are called "child" databases. One "parent" can have many "children," but a "child" can only have one "parent." The child databases are all connected to the parent database via hard links in the records called "pointers." This arrangement created a nightmare for programmers. For example, to access child records from a parent, a programmer had to devise navigational programming algorithms to read the disk pointers and then access the next record in the pointer chain until the potentially lengthy chain was complete.

So, to get to a child database in the hierarchical database model, the programmer had to first go to the parent database, after navigating all the levels above the parent. Notice in the diagram above that the child databases on the same level are not connected. This makes it even tougher to use this style database. It presents a problem in the hierarchical database model and makes searching for data (running queries) extremely difficult.

Another problem is that data cannot be entered into the child databases until data has been added to the parent database. So, the reality is that the hierarchical database model reduced data redundancy, but it created its own share of new problems. Because there were so many issues with the new database technologies of the 1970's, large companies hired expensive database administrators, who learned the software and were able to assist the company in using this new technology (for the 70's) – the hierarchical database as well as possible.

Network Database Model

The network database model was designed to solve the issues identified as being caused by the hierarchical "model, and it did. For example, it allowed for links between the child databases. This not only helped reduce redundant data, but it also makes searching for data much easier than the hierarchical model. So network databases provided the following:

Improvement over hierarchical
Each file with multiple owners
Still can't relate files to each other

Figure 1-2 Network DB Model

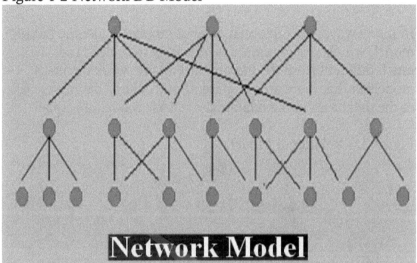

There are plusses and minuses in the list. A major plus of the network database model is that while in the hierarchical model a child database can only have one parent, in the network model, a child database can have more than one parent! But, there never were many other reasons to choose the Network Model. If it had solved all the problems, there would be no more models to study. But, it did not. In fact, it brought its own share of problems to the forefront. Network databases were simply difficult to operate and maintain. You needed bona fide database experts to successfully use these databases. It was difficult for the general public to use network databases for real-life applications. So, they were short lived.

Relational Database Model

The relational database model is a real model based on mathematics (relational algebra and tuple calculus)

The relational database model became extremely popular because it solved most of the problems presented by the hierarchical and network database models.

In many ways, the relational database model is like the flat file model, which at a minimum is very easy to understand. It is much different from the hierarchical and network database models in that there are no "parent" and "child" databases. All of the databases in the relational database model are equal.

Figure 1-3 Relational Model

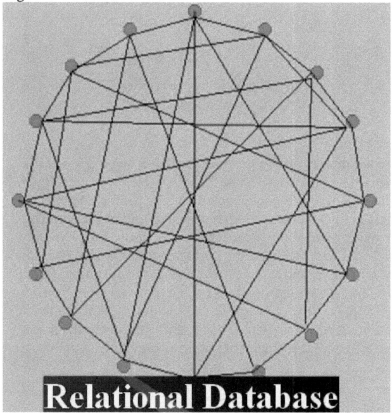

Just as with the "flat file model," data can be stored in any number of separate databases. Unlike The flat file model, however, these databases can be linked by "key" fields which are managed by the DBMS. A key field is a field or set of fields that is found in all the other databases that are being brought together. All of the databases can be used to hold different types of data.

For example, let's suppose that we have a customer address book, which was once a "paper-based database." If we were to use the relational database model, then we could store all of the data in separate databases. One database could hold a company's address; another could hold the company phone number, etc. However, all of the databases might have one field that is the same like, for example, customer number.

Relational database technology makes it far easier to search for and extract data from databases. It is also very efficient and easy to use. Though it is as easy to understand as a flat file system, it has many facilities not found in these primitive file organizations. One might conclude from this that it is no wonder why this database model is so popular! And, one would be correct in that conclusion.

Object-Oriented Database Model

In the 1990's with the advent of multi-media, spatial engineering data and repositories of all kinds, the traditional notion of data and databases no longer applied. Databases were originally designed to store text and numeric values, and there were no special features to store photos, sounds, videos, and all sorts of graphics and other renderings. To meet these needs, special purpose companies evolved to build and market what were called object-oriented database models.

These models let databases store and manipulate not only text, but also sounds, images, and all sorts of media clips! They were extremely useful, but they never really became mainstream. Soon, as the major relational vendors realized this facility was necessary, they began to add new data types into the relational model so that besides traditional data, the non-traditional could be stored and made available.

Object Database Model

Over the last several years this object oriented notion has been further applied to database technology. From the demands for more facility and a structure that better matches some of the new object oriented progrmaming languages, a new type of database built on the "object database model" has been developed. The purpose for this database model is to bring the database world and the newest application programming world closer together.

Just as in object programming systems, object databases are beginniing to introduce key ideas, such as encapsulation and polymorphism, into the world of databases. It is far beyond the scope of this book to describe this phenomenon in any more detail.

Client/Server Database Model

With the proliferation of personal computers, the Internet is now one of the most popular usages of a computer. Besides the phenomenon of client server on a PC and a server model in which the client runs the application and fetches data from a network server, the databases used for the Internet and the WWW are often referred to as client server.

In many ways, the database structure for client server is the same structure that we have described as relational. The difference is not in structure but in use. Regardless of whether the program runs natively on a PC or comes in from a Java applet, or is initiated as a servlet, many applications today are written as if the database is not located on the system making the data request.

For example, assume that you pull down a menu from one of your vendors that permits you to see all of the transactions that you have completed in the past month. You pick the function that you want from a little menu that might be driven by html or xml and it goes ahead and calls a Java servlet from a servlet server such as WebSphere. Since java does not have any notion of native database access, it uses a special client server interface known as Java Database Connectivity (JDBC) to access the database. With companies sporting hundreds of Internet servers, this is a good technique since the database can be moved from system to system with minimal changes to servlets since the servlets do not expect the database to be resident on the same machine as the database. So, the servlet as a client fetches data from a database server which more than likely stores its data in relational format.

XML Database Model

Over the last several years, more and more advances have been made in the XML database area. Like HTML, xml is a tag level language that many of us have used or at least seen when we click the view source item on our browsers. XML databases contain a definition of the data within the data itself and this makes the use of XML as portable as any database that has ever been developed. XML databases are often linked to client server databases over the internet to permit xml forms and local databases to easily update the relational databases in the back end. From the early successes with XML, some key ideas are being integrated into the established relational products.

The objective of XML databases is to remove the traditional divide between documents and data, allowing all of an organization's information resources to be held in one place, whether they are highly structured or not. Whether this idea will be achieved in practice is for the future to determine. But XML databases are here today and the links that are being built with traditional relational databases have made working with data on the Web substantially easier.

Dimensional Database Model

Though we suggested earlier in this chapter that OLAP databases were used for analytical processing, the structrure of many OLAP databases is implmented in what is called the dimensional model. This model is a specialized adaptation of the relational model used to represent data in data warehouses in a way that data can be easily summarized using OLAP queries.

A dimensional model separates data into measures, those things that a user needs to track, count and upon which otherwise perform analysis. The dimensions are the "factors" that contribute to the value of a measure, such as the customer to whom you sell, the products that you sell, the locations in which you sell and the time periods in which you operate. Dimensions have hierarchies, reflecting the way in which you group and aggregate dimension members. They also have attributes, allowing you to filter and make selections. Dimensions and measures are eventually brought together into logical containers affectionately known as cubes.

In the dimensional model, a database consists of a single large table of facts that are described using dimensions and measures. Many aspects of business activities can be well described using dimensional data. Take sales for example. How many dimensions of sales are there? The answer is that hopefully there are as many as you need. Using the many dimensions of sales, for example, there is value to knowing sales by customer, product, channel, promotion, time etc. Of course country, state, salesman, and territory may also be valid data sales dimensions. The dimensional database notion is thus used to provide information to users who have a need to understand data over multiple dimensions.

Relational DB
The idea of a relational database was conceived and published by Edgar Frank (E. F.) Codd, who is known historically as Ted

Codd of IBM's Almaden Center in San Jose. His work was highlighted in the ACM Journal during the 1970 time frame. It was titled: "A Relational Model of Data for Large Shared Data Banks." A co-worker at IBM Almaden, Don Chamberlin, is credited as being the co-inventor of the SQL language.

Codd's idea was to create a database system, simple in concept, yet founded in sound mathematical principles.

Benefits of a Database Management System (DBMS)

Database management systems of all varieties provide certain benefits to their users. The generic benefits of all database software are as follows:

Figure 1-4 Features and Benefits of an RDBMS

Feature	**Benefit**
Data Sharing	Many simultaneous users of the same data
Data Currency	Changes to data reflected immediately in all sequences
Data Security	Data guarded by the DBMS
Data Backup/Recovery	Facilities built into DBMS
Programmer Productivity	Standardization of data definitions. Database does record selection /ordering. Less duplicate work

Chapter Summary

A database is a set of computer files used to store business data. Database Management is the software function that enables you to create databases, insert, add, or update its contents. A database comes with facilities and commands to provide for data organization, data access, and data control while assuring data integrity.

Without a database, programming and end user tasks would be much more difficult since data would have to be described by programmers and administrators before it could be used.

Databases can be characterized across two different categories: function and structure. The two types of functional databases are operational databases and analytical databases.

Data Bases characterized by function are referred to as database models. The first four models on the list below have been used for many years whereas the last five are more recent entries into the world of database. The list of database models includes the following:

- **Flat-file Database Model**
- **Hierarchical Database Model**
- **Network Database Model**
- **Relational Database Model**
- **Object-Oriented Database Model**
- **Object Database Model**
- **Client/Server Database Model**
- **XML Database Model**
- **Dimensional Database Model**

There are number of features in all databases that provide the "can't live 'without' benefits. These features include the following

- **Data Sharing**
- **Data Currency**
- **Data Security**
- **Data Backup/Recovery**
- **Programmer Productivity**

Key Chapter Terms:

ACM Journal
Analytical database
Attribute
Chamberlin, Don
Client server database
Codd, Ted
Data access
Data backup/recovery
Data control
Data currency
Data integrity
Data manipulation
Data models
Data organization
Data security
Data sharing
Database
Database management
DBMS types
DCL
Dimensional database
Dimensional model
Field addition
Field change
Field deletion
Flat file model
Hierarchical model
Information

IMS
Java applet
Java servlet
Network database model
Object database model
Object-oriented database model
OLAP
OLTP
Operational database
Pointer
Programmer productivity
Programs
RDBMS
Record
Relational
Relational model
Servlet
Servlet server
Structures

Exercises

1. Is it less or more difficult to program an IBM i environment with a database than to ignore the database and use program definitions?

2. What is the earliest form of database model used in the 1960's and 1970's before database?

3. Which database model carries has the definition of the data along with he data?

4. What are he advantages and disadvantages of a database?

5. The database language used for data control is?

6. A Java program that runs on the server? Client?

7. What is database management?

8. Why is the relational model superior to the other models?

9. Which database model is based on relational algebra and tuple calculus?

10. Describe the major differences between the hierarchical and network databases compared to the relational DB?

Chapter 2   Distributed Relational Databases with SQL Underpinnings

What Is a Distributed Database?

In addition to host specific SQL implementations, there are a number of distributed database protocols that depend on the SQL language to provide the database command language function.

A distributed relational database consists of a set of tables and other objects that are spread across different but interconnected computer systems. Each computer system has a relational database manager, such as DB2 UDB for IBM i to manage the tables in its environment. The database manager software facilities communicate and cooperate with each other in a way that allows a given database manager to execute SQL statements on another computer system.

Distributed relational databases are built on formal requester-server protocols and functions. This is client server without necessarily having a PC workstation. An application requester supports the application end of a connection. It transforms a database request from the application into the correct communication protocols suitable for use in the distributed database network. These requests are received and processed by a database server at the other end of the connection. Working together, the application requester and the database server handle communication and location considerations, so that the application can operate as if it were accessing a local database.

A picture is worth a thousand words. The chart in Figure 2-1, courtesy of IBM shows the many distributed database protocols that can be used today with an IBM i.

Figure 2-1 Multi-platform connectivity to IBM i

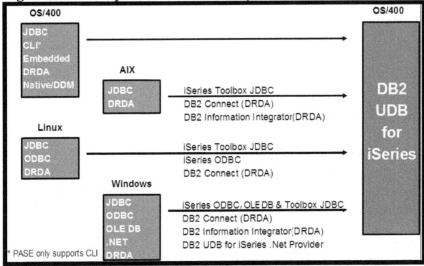

Distributed Database Architectures and Protocols

Some of the most important protocols that are used in this distributed database environment are as follows:

- ✓ DRDA -- Distributed Relational Database Architecture
- ✓ JDBC --   Java Database Connectivity
- ✓ ODBC -- Open Database Connectivity
- ✓ DB2 Connect
- ✓ DB2 UDB CLI (Call Level Interface)
- ✓ Embedded Dynamic SQL

What is DRDA?

DRDA stands for Distributed Relational Database Architecture. It is a set of protocols, or rules, that enable a user to access distributed data regardless of where it physically resides. As a distributed architecture, when protocols are implemented accordingly, it provides an open, robust heterogeneous distributed database environment. DRDA provides methods of coordinating communication among distributed locations. This allows applications to access multiple remote tables at various and separate locations and has them appear to the end user as if they are a logical whole, existing on one system.

To better understand DRDA, a distinction should be made, however, between the architecture and the implementation. DRDA describes the architecture for distributed data and nothing more. It says how things should be done. It defines the rules for accessing the distributed data, but it does not provide the actual application programming interfaces (APIs) to perform the access. So DRDA is not an actual program, but is more like the specifications for a program.

In this light, it helps to know that when a DBMS is said to be DRDA-compliant, all that is implied is that it follows the DRDA specifications. For example DB2 UDB for IBM i and all other platforms is a DRDA-compliant RDBMS product.

Benefits of DRDA

DRDA was designed to function with platform-specific extensions to SQL and one of its major advantages is that static SQL (See Chapter 9) can be used with DRDA.

DRDA is just one architecture for supporting distributed RDBMS. Of course, if you are a DB2 user, it is probably the only one that matters.
The biggest benefit provided by DRDA is its clearly stated set of rules for supporting distributed data access. Any product that follows these rules can seamlessly integrate with any other DRDA-compliant product. Since all DB2s are compliant with

DRDA, it follows that all IBM systems and non-IBM systems with DB2 UDB can talk to each other using this architecture. Furthermore, DRDA-compliant RDBMSs support full data distribution including multi-site update. The greatest advantage, however, is that it is available today, and that is one of the reasons why many vendors are jumping on the DRDA-compliance bandwagon.

What is JDBC?

DB2's Java support includes JDBC (Java Database Connectivity), a vendor-neutral dynamic SQL interface that provides data access to your application through standardized Java methods. JDBC is similar to DB2 CLI (defined below) in that you do not have to precompile or bind a JDBC program. As a vendor-neutral standard, JDBC applications offer increased portability. An application written using JDBC uses only dynamic SQL.

JDBC can be especially useful for accessing DB2 databases across the Internet. Using the Java programming language, you can develop JDBC applets and applications that access and manipulate data in remote DB2 databases using a network connection. You can also create JDBC stored procedures that reside on the server, access the database server, and return information to a remote client application that calls the stored procedure.

The JDBC API, which is similar to the CLI/ODBC API, provides a standard way to access databases from Java code. Your Java code passes SQL statements as method arguments to the DB2 JDBC driver. The driver then handles the JDBC API calls from your client Java code.

Java's portability enables you to deliver DB2 access to clients on multiple platforms, requiring only a Java-enabled web browser, or a Java runtime environment.

What is ODBC?

ODBC (Open Database Connectivity) is a standard application programming interface (API) for accessing data in both relational and non-relational database management systems. It is used outside of the Java world. Using this API, database applications can access data stored in database management systems on a variety of computers even if each database management system uses a different data storage format and programming interface.

ODBC is a standard database access method developed by the SQL Access group (now part of X/Open) way back in 1992, so it has been around long enough to be good. The goal of ODBC is to make it possible to access any data from any application, regardless of which database management system (DBMS) is handling the data. ODBC was one of the earliest client server DB protocols used successfully to support client PC code accessing server databases.

ODBC manages data access by inserting a middle layer, called a database driver, between an application and the DBMS. The purpose of this layer is to translate the application's data queries into SQL-like commands that the DBMS understands. For this to work, both the application and the DBMS must be ODBC-compliant -- that is, the application must be capable of issuing ODBC commands and the DBMS must be capable of responding to them. Since version 2.0, the ODBC standard supports the ANSI standard SAG SQL.

What is DB2 Connect?

For DB2 clients on a LAN, a DB2 Connect server enables access to data that is stored on mainframes and IBM i systems. DB2 Connect provides transparent access to host or IBM i data through the standard architecture (DRDA) for managing distributed data. DRDA enables applications to establish a fast connection to mainframe and IBM i databases without expensive mainframe or IBM i components or proprietary gateways.

Although DB2 Connect is often installed on an intermediate server machine to connect DB2 clients to a mainframe or IBM i database, it is also installed on machines where multiple local users want to access the mainframe or IBM i servers directly. For example, DB2 Connect may be installed on a large machine with many local users.

DB2 Connect may also be installed on a Web server, Transaction Processing (TP) monitor, or other three-tier application server machines with multiple local SQL application processes and threads.

What is DB2 UDB CLI (Call Level Interface)?

The DB2 UDB Call Level Interface (CLI) is a callable Structured Query Language (SQL) programming interface that is supported in all DB2 environments except for mainframes (DB2 UDB for zOS and OS/390(R) and DB2 Server for VSE and VM.) It is basically a callable SQL interface. It is implemented as a WinSock application program interface (API) for database access that uses function calls to start dynamic SQL statements.

DB2 UDB CLI is an alternative to embedded dynamic SQL. The important difference between embedded dynamic SQL and DB2 UDB CLI is how the SQL statements are started. On the IBM i, this interface is available to any of the ILE languages.

DB2 UDB CLI also provides full Level 1 Microsoft Open Database Connectivity (ODBC) support, plus many Level 2 functions. For the most part, ODBC is really a superset of the ANS and ISO SQL CLI standard.

What is Embedded Dynamic SQL?

An application that uses an embedded SQL interface requires a precompiler to convert the SQL statements into code. Code is compiled, bound to the database, and executed. However, there is a way using a feature known as PREPARE, to write your programs so that parts of the SQL statement (such as the item you are searching for can be supplied during execution rather than having to be pre-coded for the precompiler)

How Does Embedded SQL Compare to DB2 UDB CLI?

In contrast to embedded dynamic SQL, a DB2 UDB CLI application does not require precompilation or binding, but instead uses a standard set of functions to execute real SQL statements and related services at runtime.

This difference is important because, traditionally, precompilers, such as those provided for RPG and COBOL on IBM i have been specific to a database product. This is not good for portability. It effectively ties your applications to that product. On the other hand, DB2 UDB CLI enables you to write portable applications that are independent of any particular database product. This independence means that a DB2 UDB CLI application theoretically at least does not have to be rewritten recompiled or rebound to access-different database products. An application selects the appropriate database at runtime.

Despite these differences, there is an important common concept between embedded dynamic SQL and DB2 UDB CLI: DB2 UDB CLI can execute any SQL statement that can be prepared dynamically in embedded SQL. This is guaranteed because DB2 UDB CLI does not actually execute the SQL statement itself, but passes it to the DBMS for dynamic execution.

Chapter Summary

A distributed relational database is one that is distributed on multiple like or unlike computer systems. So that all IBM DB2 database products would have no trouble working with remote DB2 databases on IBM or non-IBM systems, IBM defined an architecture or set of detailed specifications and rules for how this could be accomplished. IBM called its architecture Distributed Relational Databases Architecture or DRDA for short. Any database vendor can choose to implement the DRDA standard and some have done so. When this happens and the vendor holds to the specifications, the resulting product can communicate with all of the IBM systems as well as non-IBM systems running DB2.

ODBC is another of these architectures and actually provides the rules for how diverse databases can talk to one another. In addition to databases ODBC supports flat file systems.

JDBC is very much like ODBC but it runs only in systems that support he full range of Java programming.

DB2 Connect and the DB2 UDB CLI are IBM implementations of DRDA. Embedded dynamic SQL is a facility that gives some of the benefits of purely dynamic SQL while still having the precompiler disadvantages of embedded static SQL.

Many Solutions – One SQL Language

Though there are many solutions to accessing distributed databases from / or to an IBM i, all of the solutions depend on SQL as the language within the protocol wrappers that actually deliver the data. So, there are really no ODBC experts or JDBC experts or an expert in any distributed DB protocol who does not have a solid background in SQL. Even if DDS (native AS/400 DB access facility) does it for you internally on the IBM i, once you get off the island or the island must connect to the world, you'll find the friendly face of SQL behind all of these protocols.

Key Chapter Terms

Application requester
Database server
DB2 clients
DB2 Connect
DB2 UDB CLI
DB2 UDB for IBM i
DBMS
DDS
Distributed database
Distributed Relational Database
DRDA
Embedded Dynamic SQL, 2, 4
IBM systems
Java programming
JDBC
JDBC API
Non-IBM systems
ODBC
Open Database Connectivity
OS/390
Precompiler
PREPARE
RDBMS
Relational
SQL statements
Structured Query Language
Transaction processing

Exercises

Use this chapter or look up information on the Web to answer the following:

1. What is an application requester?

2. How does a distributed database differ from a local database?

3. What purpose does the PREPARE SQL statement perform?

4. In what ways does the DB2 UDB for IBM i database support distributed relational database?

5. What is the difference between Embedded SQL and embedded dynamic SQL?

Chapter 3   What is SQL?

Powerful Database Development Language

SQL stands for Structured Query Language. This IBM-Invented database language however is far more powerful than its name suggests. Though, as its name suggests, it is very useful for database queries, SQL has powerful facilities built within the language for the creation, control and manipulation of a relational data base. In addition to providing tools to create and control database artifacts, the major manipulation facilities that are built into the SQL language are as follows:

Select data from a database
Insert data to a database
Update data in a database
Delete data from a database

Query as the middle name for SQL does not mean that SQL should be thought of only as a query tool. SQL is an application development tool that is used for the following:

Query via Query Manager
Data definition via Data Definition Language (DDL)
Data manipulation via Data Manipulation Language (DML)
Data control via Data Control Language (DCL)

As you will see as we go back in time to the origins of SQL, it was designed using mathematical set theory as its basis. Therefore, SQL is best for "set at a time" processing as opposed to single record level access.

Unlike normal programming languages in which the developer must control all aspects of data access, SQL does not expect the programmer to have to understand how SQL is going to go ahead and do its thing. Instead of how, the developer merely tells SQL what to do and SQL obliges. There are not long instructions sequences. Just about all major functions occur within one command.

With SQL, a developer has tools that include full data definition facilities. Therefore, with SQL commands, the developer can build, maintain, secure, and delete database objects in the form of Schemas, Tables, Views, and Indexes. With full data manipulation facilities, the developer can retrieve, update, insert, and delete records in database tables or IBM i physical files. With full data control facilities using SQL Grant and Revoke commands, the SQL developer can grant access and authorization or revoke such privileges.

Why SQL in the First Place?

With the native database language on the AS/400 and IBM i being the Data Description Specification language or DDS, IT professionals in these shops have not had to look too far to find very rich function in DDS to satisfy their database needs. DDS clearly has been key to System/38 and AS/400 database success over the years. So, it is fair to ask why an AS/400 developer would use SQL.

"No man is an island, entire of itself; every man is a piece of the continent, a part of the main…" This famous passage by John Donne (1573-1631) fits in here someplace. The fact is that regardless of how powerful DDS continues to be, SQL is the standard relational database language for the rest of the universe. It is the standard language for DB serving.

The IBM i is an island of sorts. Though a very rich, bountiful, and self-sustaining island, in the total land of IT, it is an island nonetheless. Those of us who willfully inhabit the island, however, unlike Gilligan, the Professor, the Captain, and Mary Ann do not have to exist only on the island. Yes, the IBM i is like no other machine and yes, IBM has bestowed on it and its predecessors a plentiful and powerful data language known as DDS. For ten years before the AS/400 was announced, while the rest of the world were honing their SQL skills, inhabitants of the System/38 island were doing just fine with DDS as their data language. In fact, most still are doing fine with DDS.

When SQL was made available for the AS/400, the former System/36 users mostly were indifferent since many avoided database use even with DDS. Moreover, both System/36 and System/38 shops had a hard time believing there was value in paying for a data language for a free and integrated database that had its own highly functional free data language. So, most chose not to buy the AS/400 SQL from IBM. In many ways, the isolation of a large part of the IBM i community from SQL came about because this group felt that IBM had not given them a compelling reason to buy the language. DDS worked fine.

Now, in the first decade of the 21st century, things have really changed. Most IBM i shops support heterogeneous systems with numerous client PCs, even server PCs and many have Unix boxes. Ironically, all of these non-IBM i platforms, from the smallest to the largest have one thing in common in the relational database area. They all use SQL as their data language. That's a big change in the database landscape.

In my home area of Northeastern Pennsylvania, I now see a number of small AS/400 shops, who had not found a convincing reason to switch to IBM's model 8XX IBM i, moving or planning to move to a new IBM i Express Model. The small AS/400 shops are now re-enfranchised for affordable IBM software with the low cost IBM I systems which just happen to come with SQL, free of charge with the Express bundle. Many larger AS/400 and IBM i shops have been adding SQL over the years. However, even with SQL on the system, none of my clients have replaced DDS and none expect to any time soon. They have been using SQL on the AS/400 and IBM i as mostly a sidebar database language. Overall, many IBM i shops now have or will be getting SQL but few have used SQL extensively because of the good job DDS has done for them.

HAS SQL's Time Come with IBM i?

There is another reason why it may be time for SQL. IBM has said many times, especially recently that SQL is its strategic database language. In fact IBM invested in its own recommendation over the last five years as the company introduced a new Query Engine on the IBM i (IBM i/OS) specifically for SQL. Though the old (classical) query engine still exists and is used for many things including OPNQRYF, this new engine is substantially better and faster than the classical query engine.

Big Blue has already introduced and will continue to introduce newer and more powerful strategic database facilities that will not be available in the DDS environment. I would hope that IBM tempers this posture somewhat in the future, considering that its install base has yet to arrive where it is leading them. Moreover for those who do not have SQL, it is still not free and nobody can use a product that company management will not permit them to acquire We can add to this the AS/400 community's low propensity to change before it believes it is time.

Historically AS/400 heritage users such as the former System/36 community and the AS/400 RPG community have resisted IBM's call to major change before they were ready. Look no further than the problems IBM has had over the last few years in moving its RPG base to Java. So, I would hope and I expect that IBM will relent and continue to offer advanced function in DDS because Big Blue is smart and it does not need a Java-like revolt coming from its IBM i DDS constituents.

Moreover, neither IBM nor I are suggesting that the IBM i community abandon DDS for SQL anytime soon. However, I happen to agree with IBM that based on all the other systems out there that exclusively run SQL as their database language, It is good for IBM i shops to become adept at SQL sooner, rather than later.

Right now, regardless of whether DDS can do it all for you on the IBM i, it still makes lots of sense to learn SQL for all the other platforms that you must service in one way or another. Nobody can deny that SQL is the industry data / query language standard. Clearly IBM backs it 100% and if you take a look at the SQL functional enhancements list for V5R4 that percentage is actually increasing. So, today, it makes little sense for an IT professional to be an island or to exist only on the island. This is not Java. It's not perfect yet for a IBM i shop, but it may very well be necessary for one reason or another. One thing is for sure. Today even for a IBM i shop, it is professionally appropriate to become well versed in SQL.

IBM SQL / Relational Database Leadership

Though Oracle was the company that first publicized the capabilities of relational database, the Oracle founders had gotten much of their information from a paper produced by the late Dr. Edgar Frank (Ted) Codd ((1924-2003), Dr. Codd almost single-handedly defined the whole notion of relational database while working for the IBM Corporation in the IBM San Jose Research Lab in California.

In June 1970 he published an article called 'A relational model of data for large shared data banks', which appeared in the ACM (=Association for Computing Machinery) magazine, Vol. 13, No. 6, pp. 377-387. Dr. Codd's objective was to create a system in which you could query the database tables using

English like commands. His research and this article laid the foundations of the theory of relational databases.

Codd's Vision

Dr. Ted Codd saw a relational database as something that was perceived externally as a table of rows and columns. Since the notion of tables and columns fit in well with the mathematical notion of relational algebra and relational calculus, Codd was able to show that a number of functions that would be useful to manipulate data could be proven with mathematics. Just as matrix functions in math, Codd saw great similarities with the idea of a relational database. Both required operations on sets of data. Operating on asset of data at a time was new to the computer industry. It was not the typical method of the day for accessing data -- one record at a time through programming.

The language that Codd roughed out would need to provide operations for sets of data. Additionally, Codd demanded that the database be free from implementation details. In other words, the user would specify what they wanted to do to the database or receive from the database but the user would not specify how the system was to deliver the function. Theoretically, this would enable internal relational functions to be implemented differently on the same or different systems as long as they provided the same result.

April 18, 2003 - Ted Codd Passes Away

On April 18, 2003, Ted Codd passed away. He left behind a true legacy as an IT industry pioneer. As we have been discussing, Codd was the inventor of the relational model of data and the concept he proved is today responsible for the multibillion-dollar relational database industry

One of Ted Codd's good friends and peers in the relational database field, Chris Date, a DB Guru in his own right took the time to write a brief tribute to Dr. Codd. It was published by the Intelligent Enterprise on April 25, 2003.

http://www.intelligententerprise.com/. I have taken the liberty
of including several paragraphs from CJ Date's tribute to Ted
Codd since Codd's passing is historically significant to the
entire database industry. Moreover, Date's words are very
compelling about this true pioneer and exceptional scientist,
who revolutionized the computer world in 1970 with his
conception of the relational database.

Ted Codd was a genuine computing pioneer. He was also an
inspiration to all of us who had the fortune to know him and
work with him. He began his career in 1949 as a programming
mathematician for IBM on the Selective Sequence Electronic
Calculator. He subsequently participated in the development of
several important IBM products, including its first commercial
electronic computer (IBM 701) and the STRETCH machine,
which led to IBM's 7090 mainframe technology. Then, in the
1960's, he turned his attention to the problem of managing large
commercial databases — and over the next few years he
created, single handed, the invention with which his name will
forever be associated: the relational model of data.

The relational model is widely recognized as one of the great
technical innovations of the 20th century. Codd described it
and explored its implications in a series of research papers —
staggering in their originality--which he published throughout
the period 1969-1979. The effect of those papers was twofold:
They changed for good the way the IT world (including the
academic component f that world in particular) perceived the
database management problem; and they laid the foundation
for an entire new industry, the relational database industry,
now worth many billions of dollars a year. In fact, not only did
Codd's relational model set the entire discipline of database
management on a solid scientific footing, it also formed the
basis for a technology that has had, and continues to have, a
major impact on the very fabric of our society. It is no
exaggeration to say that Ted Codd is the intellectual father of
the modern database field.

Codd's supreme achievement with the relational model should not be allowed to eclipse the fact that he made major original contributions in several other important areas as well, including multiprogramming, natural language processing, and more recently Enterprise Delta (a relational approach to business rules management), for which he and his wife were granted a US patent.

The depth and breadth of his contributions were recognized by the long list of honors and elected positions that were conferred on him during his lifetime, including IBM Fellow; elected ACM Fellow; elected Fellow of the Britain Computer Society; elected member of the National Academy of Engineering; and elected member of the American Academy of Arts and Sciences. In 1981 he received the ACM Turing Award, the most prestigious award in the field of computer science.

He also received an outstanding recognition award from IEEE; the very first annual Achievement Award from the international DB2 Users Group: and another annual achievement award from DAMA in 2001. Computerworld, in celebration of the 25th anniversary of its publication, selected him as one of 25 individuals in or related to the field of computing who have had the most effect on our society. And Forbes magazine, which in December 2002 published a list of the most important innovations and contributions for each of the 85 years of its existence, selected for the year 1970 the relational model of data, by E. F. Codd.

Proven by Math

Along with the use of "relational algebra," IBM's Dr. Ted Codd introduced a few other important notions including "tuple calculus" and "domain calculus" to the relational model. This provided a declarative database query language based on math principles for this data model. It thus formed the inspiration for the database query languages QUEL and SQL of which the latter, though far less in accordance to the original relational model and calculus, is now used in almost all relational database management systems as the ad-hoc query language. QUEL was developed as a query language for the groundbreaking relational database project that became known as Ingres. The project was spearheaded by the University of California, Berkeley, under the able sponsorship of Professor Michael Stonebreaker, one of the most influential relational database management system experts of all time

While Dr. Michael Stonebreaker was off developing QUEL, the original 1970 CODD article had laid the groundwork for a query language that would be finished by others in IBM. While IBM was testing and testing its System/R and its SQL languages, it still had no product to announce. Ironically, it was Honeywell that introduced the first commercial SQL based product in June 1976.

SQL and IBM

Donald D. Chamberlin, and Raymond F. Boyce, two other IBM employees took the mathematical work that Codd had laid out and invented the English keyword-oriented language that today is known as SQL. Chamberlin and Boyce published papers on SQL in 1974, at about the same time the IBM Company began its famous relational database project

The project from which SQl was born was called System/R within IBM and besides the underlying relational database management system; one of the other deliverables from the effort was the "query language" that IBM originally named SEQUEL for Structured English Query Language. When the language was fully implemented, IBM was looking for even more capability and the company completely rewrote it in 1976–1977 to include multi-table and multi-user features. IBM briefly named the new version "SEQUEL/2," but then re-named it "SQL" for legal reasons. The acronym SEQUEL was found to be a trademark held by a company in the UK

Deficiencies of Hierarchical and Network Databases

Unlike the popular hierarchical and networking database methodologies of the 1970's, relational database was actually designed based upon the sound mathematical theories of Ted Codd. The hierarchical "model" and the networking "models" were never mathematically proven. They were implementations of how somebody determined a database should be structured. So, it is easy to see how relational DB theory has endured and prospered over the years and its future continues to be bright. The rest of this book will show you how to learn and how to use SQL in your IBM i shop.

Codd knew that with a proven mathematical theory as the basis for the database system that he designed, he could avoid the limitations, pitfalls, and anomalies inherent in hierarchical, networking, and other pointer-oriented database implementations.

Relational Technology Is the Best

Relational database software and its natural language SQL have since been a godsend to the industry. It combines the ease-of-use and ease-of-implementation characteristics of record-oriented file systems with the structural and productivity features of database technology. There are no embedded pointers. Files are brought together (joined) in structured views, external to the files themselves, based on relationships formed by SQL among the data elements (fields). Programmers need not know the implementation details in order to access the data. There is no complex navigation required for access.

For example, a customer record can be "joined," or linked, to an order record using the respective customer number fields in both files. The files are "combined" when the join fields have an equal "relationship." The database software uses the defined SQL relationship to create a virtual link between the two files.

In essence, they are logically united. When accessed, the database presents a new "joined" record view of the projected fields that is different from the record layouts of any of the based-on files.

What Can SQL do?

On systems with IBM i, the SQL "language" allows anyone with a computer terminal or an emulated Telnet device to interactively access and use relational databases. Developers can also embed SQL in high level language programs such as RPG and COBOL. Though anybody can learn to do it, as a query and data manipulation language, interactive SQL is not designed for end users. It is extremely powerful and with proper or accidental authority an end user can create major havoc with the IBM i.

SQL uses about 30 simple "English like" commands such as Create Table, Grant, Select, and Update to operate the database. For example, the SQL command shown below could be used to select all database records in the "Eastern" region.

SELECT * FROM SALES WHERE USRegion="Eastern"

IBM Provides a Database Referee

Although SQL can be used interactively by simply typing in commands like this, the SQL language is tricky for non-programmers to learn. One of the major benefits of SQL is that it provides a more or less standard way to access and use database systems from a variety of vendors, including IBM. For example, the SELECT statement listed above would work exactly the same on IBM i, Power Systems with Unix or Linux, Oracle, Sybase, DB2, Ingres, or any other SQL based database on any host machine.

In 1985, when the great database wars were well underway, IBM's offerings included its integrated S/38 relational database, SQL/DS for DOS mainframe systems and DB2 for large MVS mainframe systems. Oracle, and Ingres were out there dueling it out with IBM at the same time for customer favor. To help matters, Dr. Codd decided to referee the contest by publishing a list of 12 rules that concisely define an ideal relational database. These rules have provided a guideline for the design of all relational database systems ever since. Many, if not all of the rules, when implemented, are deployed in practice via SQL commands.

Unfortunately or maybe fortunately, Dr. Codd was a tough taskmaster. I had the privilege of hearing him speak at a Data Base Colloquium along with Dr. Michael Stonebreaker and Chris Date, another DB guru in San Francisco in the mid 1980s. There was no question that Codd felt all of his rules should be implemented. Despite what is theoretically possible, to date, not one commercial relational database system fully conforms to all 12 rules. The rules, therefore, represent the ideal relational implementation.

There was a time in the mid 1980's through the mid 1990's that database vendors and industry analysts kept scorecards on how feature rich, after the hype, the various DB offerings stacked up against the rules. In essence they rated each commercial product's conformity to Codd's rules. Codd's rules no longer mean as much as in the 80's and 90's but they continue as a goal for purity in relational database system implementations.

I have included Codd's 12 database rules in this introductory chapter along with a simplified description of each rule. There is plenty written about these rules on the Internet if you need additional information. For those rules that have been noticeably difficult for vendors to implement over the years, I have included an indicator as to what level of implementation might be found on the IBM i.

Codd Rule 1: The Information Rule
All data should be presented to the user in table form – rows and columns – regardless of the underlying structure

Codd Rule 2: Guaranteed Access Rule
All data should be accessible without ambiguity. This can be accomplished through a combination of the table name, primary key, and column name.

Codd Rule 3: Systematic Treatment of Null Values
A field should be allowed to remain empty.

Codd Rule 4: Dynamic On-Line Catalog Based on the Relational Model A relational database must provide access to its structure through the same tools that are used to access the data. The IBM i implementation uses a system wide catalog in library QSYS2 as well as schemas in user libraries.

Codd Rule 5: Comprehensive Data Sublanguage Rule
The database must support at least one clearly defined language that includes functionality for data definition, data manipulation, data integrity, and database transaction control. System/38 and AS/400 for years depended on an IBM-invented non-standard language called DDS. Today, all commercial relational databases including the IBM i use forms of the standard SQL (Structured Query Language) as their supported comprehensive DB language. IBM i continues support for DDS.

Codd Rule 6: View Updating Rule
Data can be presented to the user in different logical combinations, called views. Each view should support the same full range of data manipulation that direct-access to a table has available. In practice, providing update and delete access to logical views is difficult and is not fully supported by any current database. IBM i permits many views to be updated. Join Views are not updatable in any language yet. IBM i engineers have been saying that the database is staged for

update views for many years but the update facility has not come to the product.

Codd Rule 7: High-level Insert, Update, and Delete
Data can be retrieved from a relational database in sets constructed of data from multiple rows and/or multiple tables. This rule states that insert, update, and delete operations should be supported for any retrievable set rather than just for a single row in a single table. Most implementations support this rule.

Codd Rule 8: Physical Data Independence
The user is isolated from the physical method of storing and retrieving information from the database. Changes can be made to the underlying architecture (hardware, disk storage methods) without affecting how the user accesses it. IBM i, with its single level storage notion has always implemented this rule.

Codd Rule 9: Logical Data Independence
How a user views data should not change when the logical structure (tables structure) of the database changes. This rule is particularly difficult to satisfy. Most databases rely on strong ties between the user view of the data and the actual structure of the underlying tables. With IBM i, if an attribute in a based-on file changes, then the view must change

Codd Rule 10: Integrity Independence
The database language (like SQL and DDS) should support constraints on user input that maintain database integrity. This rule is not fully implemented by most major vendors. At a minimum, all databases do preserve two constraints through SQL.

* No component of a primary key can have a null value. (see rule 3)

* If a foreign key is defined in one table, any value in it must exist as a primary key in another table. IBM i has implemented sophisticated referential integrity constraints.

Codd Rule 11: Distribution Independence
A user should be totally unaware of whether or not the
database is distributed (whether parts of the database exist in
multiple locations). This rule is especially difficult to
implement. Though it may not take much effort to change
from local to remote databases, it is not transparent.

Codd Rule 12: Nonsubversion Rule
There should be no way to modify the database structure other
than through the multiple row database language (like SQL and
DDS). Most databases today support administrative tools that
allow some direct manipulation of the data structure. Tools
such as DFU and DBU on IBM i violate this rule.

The publication of Codd's original set of rules resulted in a
considerable amount of relational database research done in the
early 1970s. By 1974, IBM had finished its prototype of a
relational database called System/R. This project , completed
in 1979, had two significant accomplishments. It proved the
viability of the relational data model and the SQL language was

No Patent on RDBMS or SQL

As noted above, IBM did not patent its ideas for relational
database. Instead, the company through Codd, Chamberlin,
Boyce, and others proudly published their theories for all to see
long before IBM products emerged. IBM engineers were not
the only ones watching. Another group of engineers who had
read about IBM's work and who were closely watching the
System/R project realized relational databases' potential and
formed a company named Relational Software, Inc.

Though Honeywell may have been first with SQL, they did not
exploit their lead and never built a recognizable relational
RDBMS upon which to run SQL. So, in 1979, Rational
Software took the lead and produced the first commercially
available relational database management system and

implemented SQL as its query language. They called the product Oracle. Later they called the company Oracle. Soon after, Larry Ellison Oracle's CEO became a billionaire.

IBM did not even have clear sailing with SQL. Even this IBM-invented language SQL had some competitors – most notable was QUEL, used by the Ingres RDBMS. During the early 1980's, Oracle and Ingres's provider, Relational Technology, Inc., slugged it out on the commercial market before Ingres lost and QUEL effectively disappeared in 1986. To survive, Ingres adopted SQL as its query language. I

BM followed up its successful System/R research project with its own first relational product, the IBM System/38, which was not beaten by much to market by Oracle. Then IBM introduced SQL/Data System (SQL/DS) and later its ultimate champion. Database 2 (DB2). With IBM's weight behind a relational database product with SQL, the IBM version of SQL became the de facto standard. In the mid 1990's IBM renamed the AS/400 integrated relational database as DB2/400 so now all IBM boxes support DB2. Again in 2000, IBM renamed its database as DB2 Universal Database or DB2 UDB.

Support for Database and SQL Standards

SQL is now an ANSI (American National Standards Institute) standard computer language for accessing and manipulating database systems. In this standard, SQL statements are used to retrieve and update data in a database. SQL as a language drives database programs such as MS Access, DB2, Informix, MySQL, SQL Server, Oracle, Sybase, etc.

Unfortunately, there are many different dialects of the SQL language, but to be in compliance with the ANSI standard, they must support the same major keywords in a similar manner (such as SELECT, UPDATE, DELETE, INSERT, WHERE, and others).

Note: Most of the SQL database programs also have their own proprietary extensions in addition to the SQL standard!

Since the late 1980's, many relational database management systems have come to market – all supporting SQL as their primary language. It is a given Then, after it became apparent that relational databases were not a passing fancy, and not really wanting IBM to dictate the shape of the language, ANSI (American National Standards Institute) began work on creating a standard definition. Today's ANSI SQL standard is based mostly on IBM's implementation, with a considerable amount of additional defined features ANSI was so forward looking that their "SQL2" standard contains a prescription of features that are not yet implemented by any major database vendor.

The European technical community also got in the act in preparing its own standard for SQL. The X/OPEN group has already assembled standards for a UNIX-based portable application environment. Their standards play a major role in Europe. As luck would have it, ANSI and X/OPEN do not agree one everything. Several features differ between the X/OPEN and the ANSI/ISO standards. Most implementations so far use the ANSI/ISO standards including IBM's DB2 systems (IBM i et al), Microsoft SQL Server, Oracle, Informix, and Sybase. Now that IBM owns Informix, the DB scenario is even more interesting but since Informix does not run under OS/400 or IBM i/OS,.most IBM i shops are unaffected.

The intention of standardization, of course is to have all database implementations support the same code. Although an ANSI standard for SQL was adopted in 1986, and later revised in 1989, many DB vendors had already implemented their products by then and it would have been too costly to wholesale change the specifications. Therefore, even today, almost twenty years after the first standards attempts, no commercial SQL product exactly conforms to the ANSI spec.

Each product has a slightly different dialect of the SQL language and almost all DB vendors have added non standard extensions to the standard SQL language.

Just like there are dialects of human languages that make one group not completely understand another, the SQL dialects are basically similar but yet, incompatible in their detail. Therefore, it is very difficult for any vendor to write applications software using a standard SQL that runs with all versions of SQL server databases. However, the standardization situation is improving and over time, more and more applications will be able to work with more and more SQL servers. In the meantime some vendors have designed and written their SQL code to make it possible to allow for minor differences in SQL dialects. Obviously adding to the implementer's burden is not in the best interests of the database vendor community so things should be changing for the better.

Today's SQL Standards

The American National Standards Institute (ANSI) standardized SQL in 1986 (X3.135) and the International Standards Organization (ISO) standardized it in 1987. The United States government's Federal Information Processing Standard (FIPS) adopted the ANSI/ISO standard. In 1989, a revised standard known commonly as SQL89 or SQL1, was published.

A disturbing fact about the standards from 1989 is that because of conflicting interests from commercial vendors, much of the SQL89 standard was intentionally left incomplete. In fact, many features were labeled implementer-defined, which is code word for no standard. In order to strengthen the standard, ANSI revised its previous work with the SQL92 standard ratified in 1992 (also called SQL2). This standard addressed a number of weaknesses in SQL89 and set forth conceptual (future) SQL features which at that time exceeded the capabilities of any existing RDBMS implementation. The

SQL92 took about six times the amount of paper to print than its predecessor.

As a result of the original disparity, the standards authors defined three levels of SQL92 compliance: Entry-level conformance (only the barest improvements to SQL89), Intermediate-level conformance (a generally achievable set of major advancements), and Full conformance (total compliance with the SQL92 features).

More recently, in 1999, the ANSI/ISO released an updated standard called SQL99 -- also called SQL3. This addresses more of the advanced and previously ignored areas of modern SQL systems, such as object-relational database concepts, call level interfaces, and integrity management. SQL99 replaces the SQL92 levels of compliance with its own degrees of conformance: Core SQL99 and Enhanced SQL99.

What is IBM i Database and SQL Conformance?

To develop and run SQL on an IBM i, there are two components necessary. These are the following

Two Components to AS/400 SQL

1. DB2 UDB for IBM i - DB2/400 Database Manager

This is the AS/400 integrated database. It is a part of every AS/400, and IBM i. It supports the newer, faster SQL engine and its parser and run time support also supports many advanced database / SQL APIs.

2. DB2 Query Manager and SQL Development Kit for IBM i LICPGM (5722-ST1)

This is a product that is separately orderable with the AS/400 and IBM i. With its Express IBM i 520 models, for the past two years, IBM has included the SQL toolkit with each new system. The toolkit brings development capabilities to the IBM i/OS environment with the following features:

- ✓ IBM Query Manager
- ✓ IBM ISQL (Interactive SQL) interface
- ✓ SQL Precompilers
- ✓ Other features

As noted previously, SQL is the standard query language for systems outside of AS/400 environment. Moreover, SQL is beginning to catch on such that many shops are getting the product and they are doing some new AS/400 DB development work with embedded SQL!

The DB2 UDB database running under IBM I/OS, along with the V5R3 SQL Development Kit do a nice job of conformance with standards as attested by the following list:

Note: V5R4 is the newest version of AS/400 SQL facilities and it conforms even better and offers additional advanced facilities. There are also some nice additions for using SQL in an RPG environment.

AS/400 Standards Met

- ✓ ISO (International Standards Organization) 9075: 1992, Database Language SQL -Entry Level
- ✓ ISO (International Standards Organization) 9075-4: 1996, Database Language SQL - Part 4: Persistent Stored Modules (SQL/PSM)
- ✓ ISO (International Standards Organization) 9075: 1999, Database Language SQL - Core
- ✓ ANSI (American National Standards Institute) X3.135-1992, Database Language -- SQL - Entry Level

✓ ANSI (American National Standards Institute) X3.135–
4: 1996, Database
✓ Language SQL - Part 4: Persistent Stored Modules
(SQL/PSM)
✓ ANSI (American National Standards Institute) X3.135-
1999, Database Language -- SQL - Core

Chapter Summary

SQL was invented by IBM and it stands for Structured Query
Language. SQL has powerful facilities built within the
language for the creation, control and manipulation of a
relational data base. In addition to providing tools to create
and control database objects, SQL has many tool which a
developer can use to gain productivity in application
development

SQL provides the ability to create databases to select, insert,
update and delete records from its database tables. Though
IBM i users have their own native database, the fact that SQL is
a standard language for database and many of the non-IBM
systems installed in IT shops use SQL as a primary database
language , more and more IBM i shops are beginning to learn
SQL and deploy it for specific applications.

Dr. Ted Codd, an IBM Fellow and employee for many years
invented relational database in IBM's labs in Southern
California. IBM permitted Ted Codd and others to publish
their scientific works in the prestigious technical publications of
the day. It was a personal honor for an IBM employee to be so
recognized by prestigious journals. A few of the journal's avid
readers took Codd's ideas and beat IBM to market with a
relational database product. Oracle is the biggest name from
today as well as Ingres.

In 1985, at a time when imposters were entering the relational
DB field, Ted Codd was compelled to codify 12 rules of

relational database to separate the true believers from the imposters. These rules have provided a guideline for the design of all relational database systems ever since. Many, if not all of the rules, when implemented, are deployed in practice via SQL commands.

Codd's relational theories were proven by math and as the implementations caught up to the design, relational database worked as well as the math proved that it would. IBM has continued its SQL leadership and basically controls the standard in a de-facto manner, though there are formal standards bodies such as ANSI and X/OPEN which publish database standards for the industry at large.

The IBM i as the successor to IBM's first relational database system, the System/38 conforms very nicely to all of the many industry standards for relational database and SQL.

Key Chapter Terms

SQL Development Kit
AS/400 standards
Attribute Authority
Boyce, Raymond,
Catalog,
Chamberlin, Don,
Codd, Ted
SQL99
Data Manipulation Language
Data Control Language
Data Definition Language,
Data Description Spec
Database language
DB2 Query Manager
DB2 UDB for IBM iDCL, 1
DDL
DDS
DML
Guaranteed Access Rule,
Information Rule

Exercises

Use this chapter or look up information on the Web to answer the following:

1. What is SQL?

2. Why would an IBM i native database developer want to use SQL?

3. Who invented relational database?

4. Who invented SQL?

5. On the theoretical side, what was the big difference between relational databases and its predecessors?

6. What two branches of mathematics did Ted Codd use to perfect the relational database theory?

7. What can SQL do?

8. Why did IBM not patent SQL?

9 How many rules did Ted Codd create and why did he create them?

10. What standards organizations are involved in SQL today?

11 What are the two components of database on the IBM i?

12. To what level does the IBM i conform to database standards?

Chapter 4   SQL Concepts & Facilities

Is SQL an End User Tool?

When you first look at SQL, each statement makes a lot of sense, and it would be reasonable to conclude that a sharp knowledge worker (end user) in an organization ought to be able to use the SQL tool independently of the IT department. At first brush, you might even look at SQL as a query language for end users. However, it is not.

It would be a big mistake for any organization to forget that SQL is designed for IT professionals. Depending on the IT job function, some IT people might never need to use SQL. Based on the IT function, there would necessarily be a difference in the level of use and the knowledge required. The types of positions in an IT shop that would depend on SQL as a tool include the following:

- ✓ Application developers
- ✓ System programmers
- ✓ Database administrators

One of the leading IBM i database gurus for the past twenty years or more is a former IBMer, Skip Marchesani. Skip goes way back with the IBM i product line. In fact, Skip was one of a number of IBM instructors who conducted IBM internal System/38 database education classes in the 1979 / 1980 time period, even prior to the machine becoming generally available. I am proud to say that I was an eager-to-learn student in Skip's System/38 classes.

I mention Skip in this section because I have what is almost an exact quote (shown below) from him about his perception of end user involvement in SQL. It is very telling:

"Putting SQL in hands of end users is like giving a razor blade to a 3 year old to cut pictures out of magazines ...Who gets to clean up the mess?"

AS/400 ANSI SQL Advanced Facilities

There is a whole lot more than just a query engine in SQL. In addition to the basic database facilities expected in any database language, such as table and view creation with DDL, and query and update capabilities supplied by DML, and authority supplied by DCL, the SQL language provides the most advanced facilities available for the IBM i database. For example, the following advanced database functions are provided in the database and usable through the SQL interface:

Declarative Referential Integrity

This integrity constraint provides the ability for developers to define integrity relationships to be enforced at the database level, rather than the program level. The DB2 UDB for IBM i implemented via SQL provides support for the following actions when the defined integrity rules are attempted to be broken:

NO ACTION
RESTRICT
CASCADE
SET NULL
SET DEFAULT

Triggers

Triggers are also implemented via the SQL language and the DB2 UDB database. When you have defined that certain actions need to occur when and if certain database values change, you implement that function with "Triggers."

Without triggers, you code these actions into all the programs that touch a database. And, as you know, in most shops, there are many programs that cause updates to the same database. That's where DB Triggers help out. When a certain action occurs on the database as a result of an insert, or update, or a delete, a trigger fires and a program that you write gets control. In this program you can code whatever has to be done to protect your business at that time.

For example, one of my clients has an order entry program that was purchased many years ago. The software company no longer supports it and will not provide the source code. They want this client to buy their new version but the client is unwilling. DB Triggers are a way of getting into the logic of a program even if you do not have the source. In my client's case, by law they are prohibited from selling certain products in certain jurisdictions. If they violate the law, they could lose their license to do business within a particular state.

Having their backs to the wall, the best solution for them was to write an order entry trigger program that analyzed the DB update to the order file before it was made. In this way, the client company was able to send the order taker a message and not permit the bad line item to be written to the transaction database.

Stored Procedures

Stored procedures consist of compiled code residing on an intelligent database server such as the DB2 UDB for IBM i. The major purpose of stored procedures is to reduce the processing burden on the client side of client server as well as to reduce the communication interactions time. These precompiled SQL routines (and other languages such as RPG and COBOL on IBM i) are stored on the IBM i.

When implemented, they provide major advantages for client server and intelligent Web processing. The major benefit is that the application performs better since the server code is precompiled and because there is minimal back and forth action over the network between the client and the server. Additionally, because the code is on the server, one set of code can be reused for as many clients as necessary.

SQL Basic Facilities

In addition to the advanced facilities noted above, SQL is rich in the type of ease of use capabilities that are necessary to support relational databases from the simple to the complex.

Table Facility

First and foremost, SQL provides a table facility that enables a prompted, intuitive interface for the following functions:

- ✓ Defining databases
- ✓ Populating databases with rows
- ✓ Manipulating databases.

Table Editor

SQL also provides a table editor that makes it easy for you to perform the following functions against rows in table data that is structured in row and column format:.

- ✓ Access
- ✓ Insert
- ✓ Update
- ✓ Delete

Query Facility:

With the Query facility, SQL permits you to interactively define queries and have results displayed in a variety of report formats including the following:

- ✓ Tabular
- ✓ Matrix
- ✓ Free format

For those readers who have a IBM i background, you will notice that SQL brings with it its own naming scheme that is significantly different from corresponding native objects. See table 4-1 for specifics

Figure 4-1 The SQL Name Game

SQL Name	IBM i Name
Database	System Name
Entity	File
Table	Unkeyed Physical File
View	Unkeyed Logical File
Row	Tuple or Record
Column	Attribute or Field
Index	Keyed Logical File
Collection	Library w/ SQL info objects
Schema	Library w/ SQL info objects
Log	Journal
Isolation Level	Commitment Control Level
Tablespace	Not needed in DB2/400
Storage group	Single Level Storage

Basic SQL Data Definition Language

Let's start our examination of the SQL language by doing
something simple such as constructing a query against a table
that already exists in our database. This will help us quickly get
a flavor for the conciseness and power of the SQL language
syntax. Suppose we have never even defined an SQL table but
on the IBM i, there is a file defined and in use by the accounts
payable application. It's name is Vendorp. It is a physical file
and it contains data about vendors. It was created using DDS
years ago.

For our simple purpose let's say that it contains just four fields -
- a vendor number (field name VNDNBR), vendor name (field
name NAME), the class of the vendor (field name VNDCLS),
and the balance owed to that vendor (field name BALOWE).

Sample SQL Table – Mini-Vendorp

As you recall from Chapter 3, a relational database is a
database that is perceived by its users to be a collection of tables
(and nothing else but tables). An SQL table is defined as a
series of rows and columns where each row represents a record
and each column represents an attribute of the records
contained in the table. With that as a backdrop, let's look at
our first table in Figure 4-2 after it has been populated by just a
few records:

Figure 4-2   SQL, The Basics -- Table - VENDORP

```
          +---------------------------------+
          |VNDNBR NAME           VNDCLS BALOWE|
          | |
          | 001   IBM               01    250 |
ROW       | 034   ROBIN COMPANY     04    153 |
---->     | 049   JIM STUDIOS       06      0 |
          | 058   LOAD MACHINERY    05      0 |
          | 195   AMERICAN CO       20    100 |
          | 226   H H COMPANY       20    863 |
          ?---------------------------------+
            |
                COLUMN
```

This simple table in Figure 4-2 with data gives the notion of rows and columns as used by SQL.

Creating Table/File with CRTPF and DDS:

Now, that we have a general idea of a file/table, let's say that we are going to start all over with Vendorp, since we left out too many fields to make it worthwhile altering the table. The native coding in DDS for this new, enhanced Vendorp file is shown in Figure 4-3. Notice we added quite a few more fields to the Vendorp physical file. The list of fields in Figure 4-3 is actually the DDS for the Vendorp file. If we were to issue a create physical file command (CRTPF) against this set of DDS, we would create a database object named Vendorp in a to-be specified library. A library on the AS/400 is like a big directory that helps us organize objects.

Figure 4-3 DDS for Expanded Vendorp File Definitions

```
   FMT PF  .....A..........T.Name++++++RLen++TDpB..
            *************** Beginning of data ******
   0001.00      A          R VENDRF
   0002.00                   VNDNBR        5S  0
   0003.00                   NAME         25
   0004.00                   ADDR1        25
   0005.00                   CITY         15
   0006.00                   STATE         2
   0007.00                   ZIPCD         5   0
   0008.00                   VNDCLS        2   0
   0009.00                   VNDSTS        1
   0010.00                   BALOWE        9   2
   0011.00                   SRVRTG        1
            ***************** End of data *********
```

In line 1 (sequence # 1) of the DDS specifications, as you can see, in Figure 4-3, we defined the record format with a name of VENDRF. In high level programming languages (HLL), such as RPG and COBOL, many of the file operations such as read and write are directed at the record format name as opposed to the file name in flat file systems. When the program that references a database file such as Vendorp is compiled, some of the high level language compilers, especially RPG/400 require that the DB file's record format name is different from the name of the file. When tables are created with SQL, the default record format name is always used and for its own reasons, IBM has selected the name of the file for the record format name in SQL database table objects. This creates issues when trying to use SQL created database objects in existing high level programs.

IBM wrote a whole book (Redbook) on considerations for moving to an SQL-only environment and because DDS and SQL's capabilities are not completely the same, this book is helpful if you choose to make the move to SQL from DDS. The Redbook name is Modernizing IBM eServer IBM i Application Data Access -A Roadmap Cornerstone. The Redbook site is www.redbooks.ibm.com. From there, search for some words in this title, and you can download this valuable IBM manual.

In line 2 of Figure 4-3, we defined the vendor number field named as VNDNBR. RPG/400 demands that no more than 6 character field names be used so many IBM i databases are defined with very short names as you can see in the figure. The number five on the line says the field length of VNDNBR is 5 and the S data type stands for unpacked decimal. This means that this field takes 5 positions of storage in the disk record. The zero at the end of the line says that the field is numeric with zero decimal places.

Contrast this with the BALOWE field in line 10. There is no S. But there is a 2 in the decimal positions column. This says that the field is numeric, just as VNDNBR, but without the S for data type, it defaults to a packed decimal data type. Therefore, for the nine positions defined, with packed decimal, this large numeric field can be stored in just five positions in the disk record. That's the nature of packed decimal as a data type. It saves space.

Now, look at the NAME field as defined in line 3 of the DDS. It is barebones, meaning the name NAME, and the field length of 25 are the only two pieces of information specified for this field. This coding means that this field is character or alphanumeric as IBM likes to call it. If a DDS line has no decimals specified, that means the field being defined will hold character data. When read in a program, no mathematical operations can be performed against character data.

Now, let's take the same file as defined in DDS and define it in SQL. SQL tables become physical file objects on IBM i after they are created – with either DDS or SQL. The command to create a table in SQL is Create Table. The full SQL coding for the Vendorp table is shown in Figure 4-4.

Figure 4-4 Creating a Tables/File with SQL

```
CREATE TABLE SQLBOOK/VENDORP
     (VNDNBR       NUMERIC(5,0)      NOT NULL,
      NAME         CHAR(25),
      ADDR1        CHAR(25),
      CITY         CHAR(15),
      STATE        CHAR(2),
      ZIPCD        DEC(5,0),
      VNDCLS       DEC(2,0),
      VNDSTS       CHAR(1),
      BALOWE       DEC(9,2),
      SRVRTG       CHAR(1))
```

Unlike DDS, the SQL data definitions for creation of a table begin after the command to create them, not in a separate screen panel or program. As you can see in Figure 4-4, the SQL statement Create Table starts the processing command. It is going to create the table name specified after the word "Table." So following the Create Table, you specify the schema / collection (SQLBOOK) in which the table will be created, immediately followed by the name of the table that is being created (Vendorp).

After the Create Table Name, the rest of the SQL statement provides the data definition. The first element in the data definition is the field name. This is followed by the data type. Notice that the signed decimal data type from DDS has an equivalent in SQL. In SQL this is the NUMERIC data type. The packed decimal data type from SQL (no type specified with decimals specified) also has its equivalent, as the DECIMAL or DEC data type. Finally, in this example, though there are many data types in SQL, the last data type in this example is CHAR type, meaning character. This is the equivalent of no decimals specified and no data type specified for a field in DDS.

Basic SQL Data Manipulation Language

As noted in Chapter 3, SQL's Data Manipulation Language (DML) has four basic functions provided by four different SQL statements. You may recall these are as follows:

- ✓ Select data from a database
- ✓ Insert data to a database
- ✓ Update data in a database
- ✓ Delete data from a database

Now that we have a database defined, let's assume for the next set of basic examples that we took it all the way. The Vendorp table is created and it is pre-loaded with the data necessary to execute the following examples. The first examples are simple Selects, followed immediately by Insert, Update, and Delete examples.

Basic SQL Select Statement

The verb, Select is the query verb in SQL. Whenever you use this verb, you can perform any of the many RDBMS functions such as projection, selection, intersection, join, etc. as defined by Ted Codd.

Let's start with the most basic example of select. The three parts to a basic select are as follows:

Command	Function
Select	Select verb starts the statement
[colums]	[* for all or column names to select]
From:	From clause specifies the library and
table	

When we want to select all of the columns and all of the rows, the select statement in its most simple is shown below

```
Select *
From SQLBOOK/vendorp
```

This brings back all of the columns and all of the records in a memory table and it displays the result table if the user is in interactive mode. If this is executed in a program, it brings the whole table into the memory of the program.

Let's bring back the rows that we explored in Figure 4-2 above.

Select
VNDNBR, NAME, VNDCLS, BALOWE
From SQLBOOK/vendorp

This command provides four fields from the Vendorp table across all of the rows.

Now, if you refer to the data (6 records) in Figure 4-2 above, let's add a row constraint with the SQL Where Clause. Let's display only those vendors whose class value VNDCLS is 20.

Here is what this looks like

```
Select
VNDNBR, NAME, VNDCLS, BALOWE
From SQLBOOK/vendorp
Where VNDCLS = 20
```

The results of the query from this mini database in Figure 4-5.

Figure 4-5 SQL, Basics -- Table – VENDORP VNDCLS 20

```
        +----------------------------------+
        |VNDNBR NAME         VNDCLS BALOWE|
ROW     | 195    AMERICAN CO    20    100  |
---->   | 226    H H COMPANY    20    863  |
        ?----------------------------------+
        |
        |
                      COLUMN
```

Let's say you add the fields from Figure 4-4 to the file and that
you add a few more records. If you run the same Select Query
again, you will see results such as those shown in Figure 4-6:

Figure 4-6 Result of Projection and Selection with Larger File

```
                            Display Data
                                   Data width . .
Position to line  . . . .         Shift to column  .
....+....1....+....2....+....3....+....4....+....5....+..
VENDOR   NAME                     VENDOR    BALANCE
NUMBER                            CLASS     OWED
   40    SCRANTON INC               20       250.00
   44    J B EQUIP INC              20        50.00
   48    DENTON AND BALL            20     3,500.00
   26    B MACHINERY                20     1,495.55
   28    C ENGRAVING CO             20       100.00
   30    D CONTROLS                 20       900.25
   32    I POWER EQUIPMENT          20       250.00
   34    ROBIN  COMPANY             20       153.00
   56    Feenala Grund Mfg.         20     4,260.00
********   End of data   ********
```

As you can see in the result table in Figure 4-6, we have a
projected view (not all columns) and a selection view (not all
rows – just those with VNDCLS = 20). We query a set of data
and a set of data is returned to us in memory.

In the next four SQL statements, insert one record into Vendorp, update several records in Vendorp by increasing the balance owed by 20%, and then delete all the PA state records from Vendorp. As a final short exercise, delete all the remaining records from the Vendorp file.

Basic SQL Insert Statement

```
INSERT INTO SQLBOOK/VENDORP
(VNDNBR, NAME, ADDR1, CITY, STATE, ZIPCD,
VNDCLS, VNDSTS, BALOWE, SRVRTG)
VALUES (
'8020', `Phillies Phinest',
`391 Carey Avenue',
`Wilkes-Barre',  `PA', `18702',
`20', `A', `35700', 4)
```

Basic SQL Update Statement

```
UPDATE SQLBOOK/Vendorp
SET balowe =  balowe * 1.2
33 rows updated in VENDORP in SQLBOOK
```

Basic SQL Delete Statement

```
DELETE from SQLBOOK/Vendorp
WHERE STATE = 'PA'
14 rows deleted from VENDORP in SQLBOOK.
```

DELETE from SQLBOOK/Vendorp

Figure 4-7 Confirm Delete All Records

```
                          Confirm Statement

  You are about to alter (DELETE or UPDATE) all of the records in
  your file(s).

  Press Enter to confirm your statement to alter the entire file.
  Press F12=Cancel to return and cancel your statement.

  33 rows deleted from VENDORP in SQLBOOK.
```

From Figure 4-7, after we hit the enter key all the records In
Vendorp are deleted and the file is empty. So that we can run
more SQL statements against Vendorp data later in the book,
we have built a data refresh program that we call to perform
this function.

Basic SQL Data Control Language (DCL)

There are lots of ways to establish security with SQL and with
an IBM i box. Since the IBM i comes standard with capability
based addressing, security is built into the operating system at a
low level and has been a hallmark of the IBM i since it was a
System/38. For a number of years, IBM felt that it was
sufficient to use the native security commands such as Grant
Object Authority (GRTOBJAUT) and Revoke Object
Authority (RVKOBJAUT).

However, IBM is now focusing on all of its DB2s functioning in
the same way, regardless of innate capabilities or not. So,
several releases ago, IBM created the standard SQL interface
for security and delivered it in the GRANT and REVOKE SQL
commands.

In the examples below the GRANT command gives TONYS
the full authority to use the Vendorp database. Yes, TONYS
can delete Vendorp if he chooses. Rethinking TONYS' ability
to delete the Vendorp table, the next command (REVOKE)
revokes all of TONYS' authority to the Vendorp object

The Granting

```
GRANT UPDATE ON SQLBOOK/VENDORP
 TO TONYS WITH GRANT OPTION
```

GRANT of authority to VENDORP in SQLBOOK
completed.

The Revoking

```
REVOKE UPDATE ON SQLBOOK/VENDORP FROM TONYS
```

REVOKE of authority to VENDORP in SQLBOOK
completed.

All data control commands in SQL are initiated with a
GRANT or a REVOKE of authority and these commands use
the natural AS/400 security within the AS/400 objects to
protect them. The PACKAGE versions (Grant and Revoke
authority to packages) as well as the procedure versions are
very similar to the table versions of Grant and Revoke. Their
function is more for program security than data security.

The various iterations and parameters of the Grant and Revoke
commands are available in the IBM IBM i SQL Reference
Manual as well as via the ISQL prompter. We will be studying
the ISQL prompter in Chapter 9.

The intention of this book is to enable you to perform SQL
functions for application development. Therefore, we will not
devote any more time on security since that is an issue in itself
and should be attacked by the company's security officer. In
many ways, SQL security for its managed objects is no different
in concept than how security is invoked across all objects in the
native AS/400 environment.

Chapter Summary

Before we took a brief look at some of SQL's basic capabilities in this chapter we positioned SQL as a developer's tool, not an end-user query product. Sine this book is intended to get you up to speed with SQL in 17 easy chapters, we spend little time on the advanced facilities. In this chapter, we introduced referential constraints, triggers, and stored procedures as advanced tools that can take you the extra mile when needed.

To stage us for more to come, we introduced the Table facility of SQL and then using SQL's data definition language, DDL, we examined a table created with DDS and then we performed a Create Table command with SQL to show the similarities and differences in coding the two. We created a mini file and a large file with lots of records to test our skills. We used each of the four major data manipulation language statements to work with the file after it was populated with data. We saw our Select statement access data; and our Insert statement insert a record. Then we used the Update Statement and we saw how it could be used for single or multiple record updates. Finally, we used the Delete statement and we saw its utility in deleting single, multiple, or all records in a database file.

Once we had used DDL for creation, DML for manipulation, we moved to the Data Control Language facilities of SQL and we explored the Grant and Revoke commands and we demonstrated an example of each.

Key Chapter Terms

Access
Authority
CASCADE
CHAR
Data type
Client server

Create Table
CRTPF
DECIMAL
Delete
End User Tool
Grant
Insert
Marchesani, Skip
Name Game
NO ACTION
NUMERIC
Data type
Programs
Query facility
Query Language
Referential Integrity
RESTRICT
Select
SET DEFAULT
SET NULL
SQL statements
Stored procedures
Table editor
Table facility
Triggers
Update
Where Clause

Exercises

Use this chapter or look up information on the Web to answer the following:

1. Why is SQL not viewed as an End User Tool?

2. Name each of the three AS/400 ANSI SQL advanced facilities as noted in this chapter and describe each capability, its use, and its value to a business.

3. What is Declarative Referential Integrity?

4. What is a Database Trigger?

5. What is a Stored Procedure?

6. Describe SQL's Table Facility

7. Write a simple select statement to query all of the records in VENDORP and return just those records in VNDCLS 30.

8. Write an INSERT statement to add a record to Vendorp.

9. Write an Update Statement to change the status of Vendor # 40 from whatever value it may be to an "A."

10. Delete vendor 44 from the Vendorp file

Chapter 5   Introduction to RUNSQLSTM

Two Major SQL Environments

When you talk about SQL on the IBM i, there are really two
different scenarios depending on whether you have purchased
the SQL software or not.

- ✓ Ability to Run SQL Applications
- ✓ Ability to Create SQL Applications

Running SQL Applications on IBM i

To run SQL applications on the IBM i, and to Create SQL
tables and views on the IBM i (as of V5R3), or to use the IBM i
as a distributed database server for ODBC or JDBC, the only
product needed is the operating system -- IBM i/OS at version
5 release 3 or greater.. With the operating system on IBM i you
receive the integrated DB2 UDB for IBM i database package
pre-installed and ready to go.

This provides the run time query engine that you need to run
your SQL applications without having the SQL product
installed. It is the same SQL query engine as is supplied with
the SQL product. There is no difference.

Creating SQL Applications on IBM i

On the other hand, if you (1) intend to develop applications
with SQL, or (2) you would like to test the SQL component

interactively, or (3) you would like to provide super users or programmers with a cleaner interface to the database by using the SQL language in the form of a Query Manager, you must purchase the DB2 UDB for IBM i Query Manager and SQL Development Kit that IBM lists under product ID 5722-ST1. Depending on your system and software mix and your software tier, this may or may be provided in your software package and so in some cases, you may or may not have to order it to receive it. It is always best to ask your business partner about your specific needs.

When developing SQL applications using the tools provided in the IBM Query Manager and SQL Development Kit, only one IBM i machine needs to have this software installed. If you have multiple machines, you can develop on one and deploy on the others.

Any IBM i system can run the executable version of a program that includes embedded SQL even if the program is written and compiled on another IBM i – as long as the development IBM i has the toolkit. All IBM i machines come with SQL parser and run-time support. Therefore, the Query Manager and the SQL Development Kit need not be purchased for the other machines.

The Four Faces of IBM i SQL

For most of this book, we will assume that you have the SQL product on your AS/400 or IBM i and that you are at Version 5 Release 3. What we will cover, however, runs fine on earlier and later versions of the OS.

There are four basic ways that you can develop applications using SQL on your IBM i. I like to call them the Four Faces of IBM i SQL. These methods are listed below. Each of these will be explained in detail in subsequent chapters

✓ SQL Statement Processor -- (RUNSQLSTM command)
✓ Interactive SQL interface & Prompter
✓ Query Manager interactive interface
✓ Language pre-compilers used for processing and
   compiling SQL statements embedded in RPG, COBOL,
   or C programs

SQL Statement Processor RUNSQLSTM

The first of these methods is covered in this chapter. The other
methods are for subsequent chapters. Additionally, since the
RUNSQLSTM is the recommended way to execute the DDL
that is to define your SQL table, view, and other DDL-created
objects, we will follow this work in Chapter 6 with an
examination of the SQL objects that can be created by DDL as
well as the SQL statements that create those objects.
RUNSQLSTM is the recommended tool to create most SQL
objects.

The RUNSQLSTM facility does more than just DDL. In other
words, DDL is not the only SQL function that can be executed
without having the formal IBM SQL product. In fact, it seems
that just about everything other than the SQL Select statement
and some programming facilities can use this powerful batch
execution environment - RUNSQLSTM.

What is RUNSQLSTM?

The RUNSQLSTM command is a CL command that reads and
processes SQL statements stored in aIBM i source member. It
behaves as if the SQL statements that are in the member are
executed as typed on a command line. The statements in the
source member are processed immediately by RUNSQLSTM
without compiling. Both hard-coded SQL statements and SQL
statements that are dynamically generated within applications
can be run without the need for embedding them in a high-level

language such as RPG. In other words, programs can dynamically alter statements in the source file prior to your running the RUNSQLSTM command. This provides a degree of flexibility that is not intuitive.

The source file member can be loaded with more than one SQL statement giving this facility even more power and flexibility. In many ways it is like a CL program or an old S/3 or S/36 procedure in that it can handle a nice little SQL job stream. RUNSQLSTM can also be submitted to run in a batch environment. Its major drawback is that it is limited to a subset, though a reasonably large subset, of standard SQL statements. Critics suggest that the only major shortcoming in RUNSQLSTM is the lack of support for the Select statement.

Although it would be nice if IBM enhanced the RUNSQLSTM to support the Select statement, there is an alternative that I found on the Web. The RPG Developer Network at http://www.rpgiv.com/SQLLite.html offers a very inexpensive SQL Lite software package that does it all plus it has the interactive Select facility.

Is RUNSQLSTM Free?

Until V5R3, IBM i SQL users who had not purchased the SQL software could not use the SQl data definition language in any shape or form to create SQL objects on the IBM i. This did not seem to be in synch with IBM's plans for expanded use of SQL on IBM i. So with V5R3 of IBM i/OS, IBM corrected this oversight and now ships the RUNSQLSTM command along with the operating system. With RUNSQLSTM, all IBM i shops can now create most, if not all of their AS/400 database type objects with SQL as opposed to DDS – without owning the SQL product.

RUNSQLSTM is a very powerful and very worthwhile command in an SQL environment, regardless of whether you have paid for the SQL product or not. Theoretically, SQL can create the same objects as DDS can on your IBM i system so providing an SQL facility to create library and file objects with the SQL syntax clearly helps IBM give its IBM i users the tools necessary to begin a transition to SQL (if desired) without any new software product expense.

I say theoretically, because as you will learn in Chapter 8, for the typical RPG or COBOL record level access shop, the SQL Create Table, Create View, and Create Index functions do not create exactly the same type of objects that you get with DDS. Thus, to make a wholesale move to SQL DDL from DDS, if your shop is typical of RPG and COBOL shops, your applications would require a number of adjustments.

What Does RUNSQLSTM Enable?

The RUNSQLSTM command very nicely permits a number of SQL create functions, such as Create Schema, Create Table, Create View and some DML statements like Update and Insert, as well as DCL statements such as Grant and Revoke. Its greatest gift from my perspective is that now SQL can be stored and reused like DDS.

In the source file for SQL, which you may choose to call QSQLSRC or anything else that makes sense to you, you pack both SQL's data definitions along with the SQL object creations commands. This happens naturally as you type in the Create statements. So, now SQL database definitions can be stored as permanently as DDS in a source file and just like DDS, they can be executed as often as necessary.

Without this command or some work on your part, SQL object creation would have to be done interactively with the product or your SQL would have to be embedded within HLL programs. Neither of these ideas is attractive as database maintenance options. If the SQL developer chose to use interactive commands to build the SQL objects, once those commands are executed, they are gone other than in history and job logs.

SQL interactive commands are not preserved permanently. Since they disappear as opposed to being named and stored in source files, interactive SQL commands cannot be recalled at any point, or modified or rerun.

This command has been out for about five years now and before then SQL shops got by with interactive support but it was not enduring. In the former scenario there was more reliance on the database file object itself. Over time, the Alter Table command came into IBM i SQL and shops were able to perform column adds and drops without reworking the original create. However, even today, the IBM i SQL Alter Table command does not permit changing field names.

The problem that we are trying to prevent with source code storage of data definitions is the same problem solved by keeping DDS source definitions in a source file. When there is a major database change or when disaster recovery becomes a reality, it is wise to have prepared with all of the resources that you can.

Some shops solved the loss of source from interactive creates by performing all creates by embedding the SQL in an RPG or COBOL programs. However, that is akin to the olden days when file creations had to be done by a program and OCL. So, embedded SQL was not a productive step forward. It is not very productive to have to be forced to write, compile, and test an RPG or COBOL: program for each "permanent" database object to be created.

RUNSQLSTM Create Person Table

To demonstrate how RUNSQLSTM works, let's first use an AS/400 editor such as those provided by the WebSphere Development Studio Client (WDSc) or good old SEU. Let's type in the command to create this table in a IBM i source

member. In this example, I create a member with SEU called
PERSON within the QSQLSRC source file. I had previously
created a library called SQLBOOK in which to store the source
file. Our objective in the below simple exercise is merely to
create a "person" table 9database file) in the default library. To
create this with SQL, just type the source lines to create the
person table in SQL in the fashion displayed in Figure   5-1
below:

Figure 5-1 SQL Create Person Table

```
 Columns . . . :     1  71              Edit        SQLBOOK/QSQLSRC
 SEU==>                                                      PERSON
 FMT **   ...+... 1 ...+... 2 ...+... 3 ...+... 4 .... 6 ...+... 7
          *************** Beginning of data ***********************
0001.00  CREATE TABLE SQLBOOK/PERSON
0002.00                      (PERSN# CHAR(6) NOT NULL,
0003.00                      FIRSTNME CHAR(12) NOT NULL,
0004.00                      MIDINIT CHAR(1) NOT NULL,
0005.00                      LASTNAME CHAR(15) NOT NULL,
0006.00                      EDLEVEL SMALLINT NOT NULL,
0007.00                      SEX CHAR(1) ,
0008.00                      BIRTHDATE DATE ,
0009.00                      JOB CHAR(3),
0010.00                      HOME# CHAR(3) NOT NULL    )
          ***************** End of data ************************

 F3=Exit F4=Prompt F5=Refresh F9=Retrieve   F10=Cursor   F11=Toggle
 F16=Repeat find         F17=Repeat change   F24=More keys
```

Note: The SQLBOOK library can be created with the
following command

CRTLIB SQLBOOK.

However, I created the SQLBOOK library as a schema using
the CREATE SCHEMA command -- explained later in this
chapter. I created the QSQLSRC file in the schema
SQLBOOK by executing the following command:

CRTSRCPF FILE(SQLBOOK/QSQLSRC) RCDLEN(120)
TEXT('Source File for SQL Statements'))

After you create the QSQLSRC source file, use PDM and SEU or WDSc to create a new member in the file and call the member PERSON.

Executing SQL Statements with RUNSQLSTM

Once you create the objects necessary and you type in the source for the SQL DDL command, you are ready to run the command from the source file. This is where the RUNSQLSTM command comes in.

Start this process by typing in RUNSQLSTM on a IBM i command line. Then hit F4 for the system CL command prompter. Your screen will look a lot like the panel shown in Figure 5-2.

Figure 5-2 RUNSQLSTM Prompt

```
                        Run SQL Statements (RUNSQLSTM)

Type choices, press Enter.

Source file  . . . . . . . . . . > QSQLSRC        Name
  Library  . . . . . . . . . . > SQLBOOK        Name, *LIBL,
*CURLIB
Source member  . . . . . . . . > PERSON         Name
Commitment control . . . . . . .   *CHG           *CHG, *UR, *CS,
*ALL, *RS...
Naming . . . . . . . . . . . . .   *SYS           *SYS, *SQL

Bottom
F3=Exit    F4=Prompt    F5=Refresh    F10=Additional parameters
F12=Cancel
F13=How to use this display        F24=More keys
```

As you can see in Figure 5-2, you start the RUNSQLSTM command by typing the schema, source file, and member name that holds the source SQL statements that you wish to execute. That's all there is to it. Then just press the Enter key. Almost instantaneously on most IBM i machines, you will see a completion message on the bottom line that the PERSON table has been created. This creates a file called PERSON in SQLBOOK.

As noted previously in this chapter, the RUNSQLSTM command supports a rather large subset of SQL statements. The SQL statements that can be used with this RUNSQLCMD include the following:

ALTER TABLE
CALL
COMMENT ON
COMMIT
CREATE ALIAS
CREATE COLLECTION
CREATE INDEX
CREATE PROCEDURE
CREATE SCHEMA
CREATE TABLE
CREATE VIEW
DELETE
DROP
GRANT (Package Privileges)
GRANT (Procedure Privileges)
GRANT (Table Privileges)
INSERT
LABEL ON
LOCK TABLE
RENAME
REVOKE (Package Privileges)
REVOKE (Procedure Privileges)
REVOKE (Table Privileges)
ROLLBACK
SET TRANSACTION
UPDATE

RUNSQLSTM Command -- Other Details

The RUNSQL command has a number of different options that you can use when telling it to go ahead and process your SQL source file. Some of the most useful options are explained below:

Source Continuation

When you are coding your SQL commands in a source file, please note that the RUNSQLSTM doesn't use CL style continuation. Therefore, the SQL notation of the semicolon is required to end all SQL statements if there is more than one SQL statement to be executed..

Execution Printouts

RUNSQLSTM produces an output listing for your review to see how it executed on your SQL stream. It is sent to QSYSPRT file unless you specify another print output file in the PRTFILE (Print File) parameter.

Pre-Run Syntax Checking

If you are worried about getting your syntax correct before you type SQL statements into the source file, you can use Interactive SQL (ISQL), which is introduced in Chapter 9 first to get your code correct. Of course, you can only use ISQL if you have installed the fee software. Once you get your SQL correct interactively, you can cut and paste from the ISQL session on the PC "terminal" or real terminal to the source file.

There is another way to check out your source SQL if you do not own the SQL software. On the RUNSQLSTM, there is a PROCESS parameter on the command itself. This statement processing option with the PROCESS keyword permits you to specify whether SQL statements in the source file member are executed or syntax-checked only. The options are as follows

*RUN   Statements are syntax-checked and run

*SYN   Statements are syntax-checked only

The *SYN option is available so that you do not get nailed by a typo. A typo in source can burn us all. To ensure you have correctly typed SQL source statements the PROCESS(*SYN) option syntax checks your statements. To get the PROCESS option, just prompt the RUNSQLSTM command and enter your parameters. If there are errors, you'll receive a message SQL9010. You can then check the generated report which indicates the individual statement errors.


```
RUNSQLSTM SRCFILE(LIB/SOURCE)
SRCMBR(MYSQLSRC) COMMIT(*NONE) PROCESS(*SYN)
NAMING(*SQL)
```


In summary, *SYN is the option you should take so that your nice SQL source run does not bomb in the middle someplace leaving you with the cleanup task prior to being able to get it right. You get messages and a listing indicating that your stuff will bomb if you run it. So, you don't run it. Instead, since it won't execute properly, you can fix it and keep running *SYN until you get no more SQL9010 syntax messages.

Naming Parameter

The RUNSQLSTM command has a lot of other options that you should check out when you have a chance by typing the command and hitting F4 on a command line. Another option is the naming convention. With the naming parameter you choose the System or SQL option of naming. The System option separates the library and file with a slash and the SQL option uses a period as a separator. This is something of which you must be aware when you are typing in your source.

Chapter Summary

RUNSQLSTM is very necessary and the good news is that it is very available for your use. It basically provides the same facility as DDS for CREATE functions but the implementation is different. Both the create command and the data definition are stored in source. Additionally, numerous SQL Create statements as well as other SQL statements can be stacked in one source member (separated by semicolons) so that many database objects can be created in just one RUNSQLSTM execution. With DDS, the developer must create a separate CL program to accomplish a mass re-create.

If you are reading the tea leaves about what IBM would like IBM i shops to do regarding SQL, it is a big deal that this command is now included with the operating system rather then with the fee toolkit software. This demonstrates IBM's willingness to provide any shop that chooses to do so, the ability, without cost to migrate DDS physical and logical files to SQL Tables, Views, and Indexes to stage them for a potential breakaway move to SQL.

With V5R1, IBM completed its fourth tool for developing SQL applications in a IBM i environment. With V5R3, IBM stopped charging for the tool. IBM i users, equipped with the SQL toolkit can now develop SQL in four ways. These are now the four faces of SQL. .

- RUNSQLSTM
- Interactive SQL
- SQL Query Manager
- Embedded SQL in High Level Languages such as RPG

From the introduction of AS/400 SQL in the early 1990's, there have been two different SQL environments in IBM i shops because some shops have not been able to obtain the toolkit necessary to develop SQL applications on IBM i. The DB2 UDB for IBM i Query Manager and SQL Development Kit that IBM lists under product ID 5722-ST1 and in some cases, IBM i customers must purchase this product. In other cases, it is bundled. So, in some ways there are SQL development haves and SQL development have-nots today in AS/400 and IBM i shops.

IBM ships the SQL runtime environment free with the operating system so all IBM i shops can enjoy applications that have been created on other systems. In V5R3, IBM began to level the field by shipping the powerful RUNSQLSTM command to all shops with the operating system free of charge. Now, for the first time, all IBM i shops can create many of the essential SQL objects without having the SQL product installed.

This reasonably new IBM i CL command provides a means for all Series shops to package all of the create statements in a source file for permanent maintenance purpose. This is very analogous to the DDS that is kept in all IBM i shops for source changes. Just as no native IBM i database shop would part with their DDS, even though the files themselves contain the data definitions, SQL users no longer are forced to use extraordinary means to maintain Create statements for objects built in the SQL environment.

RUNSQLSTM permits the developer a *SYN option for syntax checking without execution. This is a very handy tool to assure that all of the SQL has been constructed syntactically correct before unleashing it in a source file to be executed by RUNSQLSTM.

Key Chapter Terms

5722-ST1
Alter Table,
CRTLIB
CRTSRCPF
DB2 UDB
Default library,
Execution printouts
Four faces
Naming parameter
OCL
SQL or System
PROCESS (*RUN)
PROCESS (*SYN)
QSQLSRC
RUNSQLSTM
Runtime environment
SQL Development Kit
SQL objects
SQL source file
Syntax checking
Version 5 Release 1
Version 5 Release 3

Exercises

Use this chapter or look up information on the Web to answer the following:

1. What are the four faces of SQL?

2. What do IBM i shops need in order to use all of the faces of SQL?

3. Where are the SQL statements stored prior to the RUNSQLSTM running them?

4. What is a source file?

5. What is a library?

6. List the special codes that sandwich individual DDL, DML or DCL statements so that they can be packaged for execution with the RUNSQLSTM command.

7. What are the two naming options that can be used with RUNSQLSTM and why does this matter?

8. What parameter in RUNSQLSTM determines whether your SQL statements will be run or will be examined for syntactical correctness?

9. What operation is specifically not permitted with RUNSQLSTM?

10. What operations that you have seen so far in this book are permitted and have value with the RUNSQLSTM command?

Chapter 6   Creating and Understanding the Schema and the Schema-Wide Catalog

SQL Objects

No matter what DDL command you choose to use, the place to run it is from a source file with RUNSQLSTM. That leads us to our next major topic. In this section we discuss the SQL objects created with DDL, the purpose of the objects, the DDL statements that can be run on the IBM i to create these objects, and the parameters (statement clauses) that are important to understand to assure success. Let's start by listing the unique objects that we will cover that are created with SQL DDL statements.

ALIAS
COLLECTION
INDEX
SCHEMA
TABLE
VIEW

Collection / Schema

The above list is very nicely displayed in alphabetic sequence but we will cover these objects one at a time in the sequence that they are typically used by a new SQL user.

A collection is a grouping of related SQL objects. This is the SQL name for a library in the native interface. A collection is where the tables (physical files), views (logical files), and indexes have traditionally been created. With IBM's acceptance of the word schema for the IBM i, the company is in the process of eliminating its notion of a collection from the IBM i SQL A schema and a collection are in fact synonymous. A schema or collection schema contains SQL objects such as aliases, functions, procedures, types, and packages. In this book, we will cover the original collection type objects as well as the notion of ALIAS.

If you did not know this little tidbit, you would be struggling to find the difference between a collection, a schema, and a library. The terms collection and schema as noted previously are synonymous. In prior versions of IBM's manuals, the term collection was generally used. Several years ago IBM began to use the word "schema" to mean the same as collection and the company intends to replace the term collection with schema over time since it is the standard term used by most database products. We might say that the term collection has been deprecated.

A Library is a native AS/400 object. It happens to be a directory type object and it is very handy in pointing to "collections" or "schemas" of consisting of many objects. It is a way of keeping objects together logically, though with the IBM i notion of single level store, the actual objects are stored all over the place across all of the system's disk drives.

A schema / collection is also an object created with the relational database commands. It is explicitly created using either the CREATE SCHEMA or CREATE COLLECTION statement. When you reference objects on the IBM i and other systems, a schema name (collection name) is used as the high-order part of a two-part object name. An object that is contained in a schema is assigned to the schema when the object is created. The schema to which it is assigned is determined by the name of the object if specifically qualified with a schema name or by the default schema name if not qualified.

The Syntax of the create collection statement and the Create Schema statements are identical

CREATE COLLECTION collection name IN ASP integer WITH DATA DICTIONARY

CREATE SCHEMA schema name IN ASP integer WITH DATA DICTIONARY

If you happen to be using ISQL to test this, then you can invoke the prompter for SQL collection and it gives a prompt panel similar to that shown in Figure 6-1

Figure 6-1 SQL Collection Prompt

```
                    Specify CREATE COLLECTION Statement

Type choice, press Enter.

  Library  . . . . . . . . . . .          Name

  IN ASP . . . . . . . . . . . .          1-32, ASP device name
  WITH DATA DICTIONARY . . . . .    N     Y=Yes, N=No
```

On the prompt, you type the name of the library. The name must not be the name of an existing library. Then type the Auxiliary Storage Pool (ASP) number of the system ASP (ASP number 1). If you are using other ASPs, see your system administrator for advice as to where the collection should be established.

Four completed commands follow. The first two alternate the words schema and collection and produce no data dictionary. The second two alternate the words schema and collection and produce a data dictionary.

CREATE COLLECTION TEST01 IN ASP 1
Schema TEST01 created.

CREATE SCHEMA TEST02 IN ASP 1
Schema TEST02 created.

CREATE COLLECTION TEST03 IN ASP 1 WITH DATA
DICTIONARY
Schema TEST03 created.

CREATE SCHEMA TEST04 IN ASP 1 WITH DATA
DICTIONARY
Schema TEST04 created.

Figure 6-2 Display Library TEST01 with no dictionary

Object	Type	Attr	Size	Text
QSQJRN0001	*JRNRCV		110592	COLLECTION - created
QSQJRN	*JRN		12288	COLLECTION - created
SYSCHKCST	*FILE	LF	28672	SQL catalog view
SYSCOLUMNS	*FILE	LF	94208	SQL catalog view
SYSCST	*FILE	LF	69632	SQL catalog view
SYSCSTCOL	*FILE	LF	40960	SQL catalog view
SYSCSTDEP	*FILE	LF	40960	SQL catalog view
SYSINDEXES	*FILE	LF	73728	SQL catalog view
SYSKEYCST	*FILE	LF	53248	SQL catalog view
SYSKEYS	*FILE	LF	53248	SQL catalog view
SYSPACKAGE	*FILE	LF	77824	SQL catalog view
SYSREFCST	*FILE	LF	53248	SQL catalog view
SYSTABDEP	*FILE	LF	77824	SQL catalog view
SYSTABLES	*FILE	LF	86016	SQL catalog view
SYSTRIGCOL	*FILE	LF	65536	SQL catalog view
SYSTRIGDEP	*FILE	LF	69632	SQL catalog view
SYSTRIGGER	*FILE	LF	94208	SQL catalog view
SYSTRIGUPD	*FILE	LF	45056	SQL catalog view
SYSVIEWDEP	*FILE	LF	90112	SQL catalog view
SYSVIEWS	*FILE	LF	45056	SQL catalog view

Figure 6-3 Display Library TEST04 with dictionary

Object	Type	Attr	Size	Text
QSQJRN0001	*JRNRCV		110592	COLLECTION - created
QSQJRN	*JRN		12288	COLLECTION - created
QIDCTL76	*FILE	LF	40960	Data dictionary: List
QIDCTL80	*FILE	LF	86016	Data dictionary: List
QIDCTL81	*FILE	LF	40960	Data dictionary: List
QIDCTL82	*FILE	LF	45056	Data dictionary: List
QIDCTL84	*FILE	LF	77824	Data dictionary: List
QIDCTL86	*FILE	LF	77824	Data dictionary: List
QIDCTL88	*FILE	LF	24576	Data dictionary: List
QIDCTP02	*FILE	PF	53248	Data dictionary: Long
QIDCTP10	*FILE	PF	241664	Data dictionary: Fiel
QIDCTP20	*FILE	PF	61440	Data dictionary: Form
QIDCTP21	*FILE	PF	77824	Data dictionary: Form
QIDCTP25	*FILE	PF	53248	Data dictionary: Reco
QIDCTP30	*FILE	PF	73728	Data dictionary: File
QIDCTP31	*FILE	PF	61440	Data dictionary: File
QIDCTP51	*FILE	PF	53248	Data dictionary: Reco
QIDCTP52	*FILE	PF	77824	Data dictionary: Reco
QIDCTP53	*FILE	PF	53248	Data dictionary: Reco
SYSCHKCST	*FILE	LF	28672	SQL catalog view
SYSCOLUMNS	*FILE	LF	94208	SQL catalog view
SYSCST	*FILE	LF	69632	SQL catalog view
SYSCSTCOL	*FILE	LF	40960	SQL catalog view
SYSCSTDEP	*FILE	LF	40960	SQL catalog view
SYSINDEXES	*FILE	LF	73728	SQL catalog view
SYSKEYCST	*FILE	LF	53248	SQL catalog view
SYSKEYS	*FILE	LF	53248	SQL catalog view
SYSPACKAGE	*FILE	LF	77824	SQL catalog view
SYSREFCST	*FILE	LF	53248	SQL catalog view
SYSTABDEP	*FILE	LF	77824	SQL catalog view
SYSTABLES	*FILE	LF	86016	SQL catalog view
SYSTRIGCOL	*FILE	LF	65536	SQL catalog view
SYSTRIGDEP	*FILE	LF	69632	SQL catalog view
SYSTRIGGER	*FILE	LF	94208	SQL catalog view
SYSTRIGUPD	*FILE	LF	45056	SQL catalog view
SYSVIEWDEP	*FILE	LF	90112	SQL catalog view
SYSVIEWS	*FILE	LF	45056	SQL catalog view
TEST04	*DTADCT		4096	COLLECTION - created

The SQL dictionary objects do not have much play in SQL on the IBM i and are built to support a product known as the Interactive Data Definition Utility or IDDU. IDDU is a facility that is used with System/36 environment programming.

When we view the files that are created via the two forms of the SQL CREATE SCHEMA statement, what we are looking at in SQL terms is called a schema wide catalog. When IBM needed to find a nice repository for holding SQL objects, the

IBM i already had a well equipped "container." It is the native library object. Thus, when the SQL statement processor creates schemas or collections, with and without dictionaries, the kluge of files and the schema journal and the journal receiver that it automatically builds, called a schema wide catalog, are placed in a new library. The library is also created via the Create Schema statement and it is given the same name as the schema. In addition to the schema-wide catalog, in the next chapter, after examining the library structure more closely, we introduce the notion of the system-wide catalog.

Chapter Summary

The Schema is an SQL object that is based on the IBM i object type known as a library. When a schema is created with the CREATE SCHEMA SQL statement, the first object created is the library. In the next step, the schema-wide catalog is built within the library and an indicator that this library is a schema is noted in the system-wide catalog.

If an SQL dictionary for the schema is required, then there is an option on the CREATE SCHEMA command providing the ability to have this created. The dictionary has little play in IBM i SQL and is more a compatibility throwback to the System/36 than a real dictionary.

A schema in a past iteration of the IBM i SQL implementation was not in the book. IBM chose instead to use the term "collection." Today a collection and a schema are the same thing. However, the CREATE SCHEMA command is not yet in the command prompter but it is implemented in the overall SQL packaging. Ironically, the "deprecated" term collection still thrives as of V5R3 in the SQL command prompter. When you use it to create a collection, you have indeed created a schema.

Key Chapter Terms

Alias
ASP
Auxiliary Storage Pool
Catalog
Collection
Create Schema
Dictionary
Library
Library structure
Logical files
Not qualified
Physical files
Qualified
Schema
Schema Wide Catalog
System Wide Catalog
SQL objects

Exercises

Use this chapter or look up information on the Web to answer
the following:

1. What is a library?

2. What is a schema?

3. What is the difference between a library and a schema?

4. What is an auxiliary storage pool?

5. Do all schemas have dictionaries? Explain.

6. What is a schema-wide catalog?

7. Write the SQL to create a new schema called MYSCHEMA
and include an IDDU data dictionary.

Chapter 7   Libraries and Native Objects Used for SQL Development

What is a Library?

A library is an OS/400 object that is used to find other OS/400 objects in the database. Unlike the multi-tiered directory structure of a PC file system or a Unix file system with directories and subdirectories, a library is organized as a single-level hierarchy. All OS/400 and IBM i/OS objects are located through the library structure.

Just as a PC, the IBM i has a file system with a root directory but this was not always the case. It is called the Integrated File System and it supports all types of file architectures including Unix with its symbolic directories as well as the long-time native AS/400 and IBM i File System. The IFS is a somewhat recent addition to the IBM i. Today, an IBM entry in the root directory named QSYS.LIB permits users to access the native file system when operating in PC or Unix mode.

However, as shipped by IBM, the operating system naturally begins with the QSYS.LIB file system which in essence points directly to the system library called QSYS.

To find a IBM i object within the library / file system, you need the name of the library and the name of the object. The IBM i identifies objects by their qualified name, which takes the form of LIBRARY/OBJECT. For example, to find the object BANKCASH in the library PAYROLL you would reference this as PAYROLL/BANKCASH. The system also qualifies the object name with the object type. As an object based system, there are literally tons of objects on a IBM i. Two or more objects can have the same name but they must be different types of objects. For example you could have a program named USEROBJECT and a data space named USEROBJECT, but two programs named USEROBJECT are not allowed. An object can exist in only one library. A library cannot reference other libraries except for the one library called QSYS. This is the system library and it is the only library that can access other libraries. Until the IFS were introduced, QSYS was always the genesis or starting point from which all other library file objects could be located.

System Storage Genesis

Everything starts someplace. The system library is where it starts on the IBM i. Besides containing the bulk of the operating system code, every other library type object on the system resides in (is pointed to from) QSYS. There are no sub-libraries per se, so that you cannot have a library within a library.

Libraries are objects having a directory-like structure. Library objects are located only in library QSYS. They provide some of the same facilities as directories on other system. They point to the objects in the library file system. There are many different object types on the IBM i that are stored in libraries such as:

Object Type	System Abbreviation
Programs	*PGM
Files	*FILE
Output Queues	*OUTQ
Data Communication Lines	*LIND
Data Areas	*DTAARA

All objects are located by library, much like the directories on PCs and Unix systems. No useable object in the library file system exists on the IBM i that is not "contained in a library"

Since it all starts from the QSYS Library, or the system library, you can say that QSYS is the genesis of the library file system. It is the source from which all else spawns. Though it is not the root directory, since the AS/400 has a root directory in its Integrated File System, it is the root of the library file system. As we noted above, QSYS is also the only library on the system which can contain objects of the type *LIB.

Note: The Integrated File System (IFS) is the underlying file structure of modern IBM i machines. It was built into the system in 1994 with V3R2 of the operating system. The IFS was built so that the AS/400 could be a file server for PC and Unix systems with a range of capabilities such as the NT file system as well as the Unix file system including symbolic names and all of the Unix nuances. In the Unix environment this helps the AS/400 and the IBM i run Unix applications in the Unix native directory structure rather than having to restructure applications to use the library/file system that we use in this book. SQL applications as well as DDS applications use the library/file structure instead of the IFS directory structure. However, the entire library/file system, including library QSYS is included in the root file system of the basic IBM i. Its name is QSYS.LIB and it can be seen bt running the WRKLNK command from an IBM i command line. WRKLNK is very much like a DIR command in DOS.

Create a Library

How do you create a library? For the first command in this section, in Figure 7-1, we show a picture of the IBM i command line from within the IBM i main menu, and the command to create a library called PAYROLL.

After you type "crtlib payroll" on the AS/400 command line, and you press the Enter key, the message Library PAYROLL Created appears right where the IBM copyright is displayed in Figure 7-1. A library object named PAYROLL now exists in the QSYS library. By the way, AS/400 and IBM i commands can be upper or lowercase. The system does not care.

The phrase "the object is contained in a library." is just a figure of speech. In reality, just as DOS directories on PCs point to files, libraries are directories that point to locations on the systems disk drives in which objects are stored. Of course, with a PC, the only object type is a file, so PC directory entries all point to files.

Figure 7-1 Create Payroll Library

```
MAIN                          OS/400 Main Menu
                                                          System:
HELLO
Select one of the following:

      1. User tasks
      2. Office tasks
      3. General system tasks
      4. Files, libraries, and folders
      5. Programming
      6. Communications
      7. Define or change the system
      8. Problem handling
      9. Display a menu
     10. Information Assistant options
     11. Client Access/400 tasks

     90. Sign off

Selection or command
===> crtlib payroll text('This is the payroll library')

F3=Exit    F4=Prompt   F9=Retrieve   F12=Cancel   F13=Information
Assistant
F23=Set initial menu
©) COPYRIGHT IBM CORP. 1980, 2000.
```

For this IBM i example, there would now be a directory entry in library QSYS, which contains the name PAYROLL. It points to a location in IBM i single level storage in which the

PAYROLL library object (a directory type structure) actually resides.

When objects are created "in" the PAYROLL library, for each object, a directory entry will be created in the PAYROLL library object. The entry will contain the name, object type, and the location in single level storage in which the object can be located by the system.

Thus objects "placed" in this library are merely located (pointed to) via the library entries. The objects themselves are physically located anywhere on any of the IBM i disks that the operating system chooses to put them. They are referenced by name and found through the library structure.

Since it is just a form of a directory, the amount of space, which a library occupies, is minimal. Each referenced object within a library consists of not much more than a name and a pointer. It is analogous to the index at the back of a book.

Library, Collection, Schema

So far in this chapter and the last, we have created a collection / schema with and without a dictionary and we have created a payroll library without a schema. Is a library the same as a collection/schema? The answer is yes and no. A schema is a library but a library is not necessarily a schema. For example, when we created the TEST01 schema, the system created a library named TEST01 for us and populated it with the catalog objects that SQL likes to have in a library to fully do its thing. These objects make up the essence of the schema.

For example among other things, SQL built a journal and a journal receiver object in TEST01 so that all SQL tables built in that schema (library) are automatically journaled (have all updates recorded in a log file). If we were to display the PAYROLL library before we create anything in it, we would find that it has no objects in it. Thus, a schema is a library with specific objects preloaded for work in the SQL environment. These objects are referred to as the schema-wide catalog.

The TEST04 library built from the testo4 Create Schema statement also contains an IDDU data dictionary because we asked for it. So TEST04 has seventeen more objects pre-built for it than does a schema built with no dictionary.

When the test01 and test04 schemas were created, a schema-wide catalog, journal and journal receiver were also automatically created. All of those tables collectively are called the schema-wide catalog. This catalog stores database information particular to the schema where it resides. Objects from different schemas can interact with each other; thus, tables in different schemas can be used in the same SQL query.

System-Wide Catalog

Besides the schema-wide catalog, there is another catalog consisting of libraries QSYS, QSYS2 and SYSIBM. Most of the catalog is resident in QSYS2 but to be technically correct there are parts of the system-wide catalog in other libraries. This catalog stores database information for all schemas. Under library SYSIBM, the ODBC and JDBC catalog views reside. These views are compatible with views on other DB2 systems.

While we are discussing the libraries on the system, QSYS2 is a very important library as it holds a lot of the system-wide catalog. Though similar in name to QSYS, this library cannot contain libraries. Metadata about all objects on the system is stored in a series of SQL tables. Most of these are built inside the library QSYS2, but others are built in SYSIBM, and no Virginia, there is no Q in front of SYSIBM. A snapshot of the objects in QSYS2 and SYSIBM are shown in Figures 7-2 and 7-3.

Figure 7-2 Some QSYS2 System Catalog Objects

```
                              Display Library

Library  . . . . . . :   QSYS2          Number of objects  . :   159
Type . . . . . . . . :   PROD           Library ASP number . :   1
Create authority . . :   *SYSVAL        Library ASP device . :   *SYSBAS

Type options, press Enter.
  5=Display full attributes    8=Display service attributes

Opt  Object        Type      Attribute              Size  Text
     SYSCST        *FILE     LF                    73728
     SYSCSTCOL     *FILE     LF                    40960
     SYSCSTDEP     *FILE     LF                    40960
     SYSFEATURE    *FILE     PF                   241664
     SYSFUNCS      *FILE     LF                    53248
     SYSINDEXES    *FILE     LF                    81920
     SYSJARCONT    *FILE     PF                    49152
     SYSJAROBJ     *FILE     PF                    57344
     SYSKEYCST     *FILE     LF                    61440
     SYSKEYS       *FILE     LF                    61440
     SYSLANGS      *FILE     PF                    45056
                                                                    More
F3=Exit   F12=Cancel   F17=Top   F18=Bottom
```

So, now you have evidence that when you create a schema, it places information about the schema (metadata) within the system catalog and then as objects are added to the schema, the tables in the schema as well as the system catalog get updated.

Figure 7-3 Some SYSIBM System Catalog Objects

```
                              Display Library

Library  . . . . . . :   SYSIBM         Number of objects  . :   49
Type . . . . . . . . :   PROD           Library ASP number . :   1
Create authority . . :   *SYSVAL        Library ASP device . :   *SYSBAS

Type options, press Enter.
  5=Display full attributes    8=Display service attributes

Opt  Object        Type      Attribute          Size  Text
     CPRIVS        *SRVPGM   CLE              135168  SQL FUNCTION CPRIVILE
     CPRIV00001    *SRVPGM   CLE              118784  SQL FUNCTION CPRIVILE
     CPRIV00002    *SRVPGM   CLE              126976  SQL FUNCTION CPRIVILE
     PRIVILEGES    *SRVPGM   CLE              139264  SQL FUNCTION PRIVILEG
     PRIVI00001    *SRVPGM   CLE              126976  SQL FUNCTION PRIVILEG
     SCHEMAS       *SRVPGM   CLE               98304  SQL FUNCTION SCHEMA
     SCHEM00001    *SRVPGM   CLE               94208  SQL FUNCTION SCHEMAS
     CHECK_CSTS    *FILE     LF                32768
     COLUMNS       *FILE     LF               208896
     COLUMNS_S     *FILE     LF               208896
     PARAMETERS    *FILE     LF               114688
                                                          More...
F3=Exit   F12=Cancel   F17=Top   F18=Bottom
(C) COPYRIGHT IBM CORP. 1980, 2003.
```

Create a Native Database

The native IBM i CL Command below:

CRTPF FILE(PAYROLL/MASTER) RCDLEN(136)

This will create a physical file called MASTER in a library called PAYROLL. The file called MASTER is given a single level storage address, and then it is placed on any disk on the system. A directory entry for master is added to the PAYROLL library object. Notice that there was no source file referenced in the command so there is no DDS involved in the creation of this database file object. The only definition is a 136-byte record length.

For this to work, the record length is a requirement so the database builder knows how big to make the one big field the database will contain. When MASTER is loaded with data records, the data probably will be spread across different disks since that is one way the system optimizes database performance. The applications do not care because the system keeps track of it all and it uses the directory entry in the PAYROLL library so that through the PAYROLL library, MASTER can be found by name.

MASTER is pointed to (located) by this entry in the PAYROLL Library (directory). Of course having MASTER in the library does not really give us a database. For MASTER to be a usable database file containing the structure of its data as well as its data, the structure (in DDS form stored in a source file) must be referenced on the CRTPF command (create physical file).

The system cannot guess what fields should be in the MASTER file so to use this file as in the System/36 environment, the programmer enters the field names and attributes into an RPG or COBOL source program along with the program. To create a real database that is defined within itself, however, the programmer would enter one DDS line for every field in the table and then use the CRTPF to reference these descriptors to create the structure. The Create Table command is used to do the same thing in SQL and all the attributes, such as Labels can be processed by RUNSQLSTM.

In a native environment, however, the programmer submits the DDS source for compilation using the CRTPF command for a DDS-defined file For SQL, the RUNSQLSTM command can be used with SQL source in a source file.. Both forms of database compilers read source file members as input and each creates the database physical file as its output. If it is an SQL object, the compiler adds a few more descriptive entries in the underlying physical file object description and it also updates the schema. The system-wide catalog gets updated in both cases.

Database Structures

Years ago, Ashton Tate's dBase program referred to the descriptions for databases as structures. It was another way of saying record layout. I still like to call physical database file descriptions "database structures." It makes good sense and that is how they have been referred to in the PC world since the days of Ashton Tate's groundbreaking dBase database product. Database structures are thus maintained within the file object itself on a IBM i. Yes, they also can exist in source but the real descriptors are in the physical and logical file objects themselves.

To say again, the descriptions of the file and the fields (metadata) are kept within a part of the file object on the IBM i. A physical file on the IBM i therefore contains both the structure (definition) of the data, and the data itself. When an SQL table is created, the Create Table function builds a non-keyed physical file similar to the physical file created with the CRTPF command. It dutifully places the field names from the

CREATE Table into the same structure definition area as when the file is created via CRTPF.

However, unlike dBase, an AS/400 structure can lie about the real shape of the data. As shown above, Physical files can be created without DDS, for example. Since a character field can contain binary or decimal data, this trick can work but it is certainly not a good idea for maintaining data integrity.   I

If, a database is created properly with a source definition, the structure (record format with names and definitions) will match the actual shape of the data. This is demonstrated below. However, without a source description (DDS or RUNSQLSTM source) to show the specific fields to the database as in the 136 byte record length above, the physical file would believe that it has just one big field in the file -- which happens to have a size equal to the record length.

DB With No Structure

There has actually been a lot said in the preceding paragraphs. First of all, real native IBM i databases, with fields known to the system, are created when the CRTPF command is given a source definition from which it can build the actual DB field descriptions within the database file object. The RUNSQLSTM can also be used to process a Create Table command. However, with the CRTPF native command, a database file can be created without a source definition by merely specifying a record length. In this case, the file looks and feels like the flat files you would find on other record oriented systems such as VSAM based mainframes, and System/36s. The 136-byte record creation is shown again below for closer reference:

CRTPF FILE(PAYROLL/MASTER) RCDLEN(136

This command creates a database file for sure, since there is no file on the IBM i that is not a database file. However, there are no field definitions provided to the database compiler. After this command, if you wanted to get a list of the field names in the file, you could use the display file field description command or DSPFFD. This command would show you that there was, in fact, one field defined for this file. Its name would be MASTER, it would be of type character and it would be 136 bytes long.

High Level Language (HLL) programs are not forced to use the power of the database on the IBM i. Therefore they can describe the record layout (Input in RPG and Data Division in COBOL) of a file within the program itself, just as with a non database machine. They can do the same with SQL-created tables. As long as the total size of the internally described data fields did not exceed 136, and the spots carved out in the record for numeric data actually are used for numeric data, using this method is OK on a IBM i.

It's not good. But it is OK. Of course, it does not help when you want to run system commands that demand that the database structure be contained within the DB object. Thus, without the data separated into columns, Data File Utility inquiries or Query/400 queries against the file would be worthless, since the file projects that it has just one field to show.

The ability of a IBM i database file to be " internally described" within a program has some, but few advantages. For example, this capability can come in especially handily, when you are importing data from other systems. It can also come in handy when you are running programs from another system, which does not have a database, such as an IBM System/36.
Creating and Using Source DB Files & Members

Because it gets a little hairy trying to explain that a source file which describes a database file is actually a database file itself, I will try to do this using a Q&A technique. Members are also discussed in Chapter 15. Hopefully, these are the questions you would ask.

Q & A - Data Description Specifications

Q1. How is a data description, or structure, or SQL DDL, made known to the AS/400 system?

A1. DDS - Data Description Specifications or SQL coding in a source member.

Q2. Where does DDS go?

A2. In almost all cases, DDS goes into a pre-created special source file, called QDDSSRC in one of the system's libraries. Many SQL developers have chosen the name QSQLSRC in which to place DDL statements (e.g. record definitions for RUNSQLSTM). IBM supplies a default file called QDDSSRC in the QGPL library for DDS, when an AS/400 is shipped from the plant. Most AS/400 shops continue to use this name for the source file which contains DDS specifications.

Q3. Can this QDDSSRC file or QSQLSRC file, which holds the DDS, or the SQL source be in any library besides QGPL?

A3. Yes. Multiple QDDSSRC source files can exist on the system in any library, and many libraries. As many QSQLSRC files can be built as you have libraries on the system. The libraries in which the source files exist are those specified at the time the create command is entered into the system. The command is CRTSRCPF. (Create Source Physical File). You can also use the CRTPF command but there is more work to do in order to make the file a source file if you choose this route. The recommendation is to use CRTSRCPF. With the CRTPF command, you would actually have to create DDS in order to build the source file with its record length of 92 or greater. The layout of a standard DDS type source file would be as follows:

Length	Description
6	Sequence number
6	Date
80+	DDS statement

The DDS statement "field" will be larger than 80 if the source file is created with a record length greater than 92. Since the CRTSRCPF builds the same three-field source file, without you having to define any DDS or using a Create Table with three defined fields, it does not make sense to use the CRTPF to achieve the same result since it is more work, and there is more potential for error. So, don't do the unnecessary work. Just type a command such as one of the following: (AS/400 typically does not care about case)

```
crtsrcpf payroll/qddssrc
text('Payroll File Source Descriptions')

crtsrcpf payroll/qsqlsrc
text('Payroll File SQL Descriptions')
```

Q4. How do these DDS statements get into the QDDSSRC or QSQLSRC files?

A4. By Using the Source Entry Utility (SEU) or one of the editors available in WebSphere Development Studio Client (WDSc), the intelligent Development Environment (IDE) for the IBM i..

Q5A. What stuff do I need to specify in DDS?

A5A. You need to name the file, the record formats, and the fields. Additionally, you must size the fields and describe their attributes (numeric, alphabetic etc.). There is a set format for the specifications.

Q5B. What stuff do I need to specify in SQL?
A5B. The proper syntax of the SQL statements you enter

Q6. After I type the structure for my file, say MASTER, into a member of the source file QDDSSRC or QSQLSRC, can I then put data into the File?

A6. No! After using SEU or another tool to type the DDS into the QDDSSRC source file, there is one more step required. You must take the description of the file (structure definition in source), which you typed into QDDSSRC, and make an object from it. The file object must be created with the CRTPF command or the RUNSQLSTM command, referencing the name of the DDS member containing the source description, and specifying the name which you want to give to your file object (CRTPF only). The CRTPF command would look as follows:

```
CRTPF FILE (PAYROLL/MASTER)
SRCFILE (PAYROLL/QDDSSRC)
SRCMBR (MASTER)
```

If the source member were not specified, the system would default to the name of the field to be created which, in this case, is also the name of the source member.

For the SQL source, you would run the RUNSQLSTM command against the source file to create the objects.

Q7. You mentioned the word "Member." What do you mean by a member, and do I need a QDDSSRC or QSQLSRC file to contain the DDS or SQL code for every different file I wish to create?

A7. These questions are related. Just as a library is a directory to system objects on the AS/400, a database file object contains a directory to different sets of data which are all shaped exactly the same. The sets of data are called members. The file determines the shape of the data but not the contents. In fact, files do not contain data at all. Files "contain" members. Members "contain" the data.

So, in the file QDDSSRC, there can be many different database definitions, each with its own name, and each contained in a separately named member.

For the MASTER file, for example, more than likely you would name its defining structure member in the QDDSSRC file the same as that of the file object to be created. In other words, because you want to create a database file named MASTER in HELLO, you type up your DDS specifications and store those in a member named MASTER in the source file QDDSSRC.

Sometimes a picture is worth a thousand words. Starting from QSYS, the genesis of the object MASTER, before it is created would look like Figure 7-4. The genesis of MASTER, after it is created, is shown in Figure 7-5.

Figure 7-4 QSYS Before Creating MASTER

System Library Name	User Library Names	Object Names	Object Types	Members (If file)
QSYS	Payroll	Qddssrc	*File	File1
				File2
				Master
		Menu	*Pgm	
		Prt01	*Outq	
		File1	*File	File1
	Mystuf	QRPGSRC	*File	RPG01
				RPG02
		RPG01	*Pgm	

Figure 7-4 above shows that QDDSSRC is in the PAYROLL library. It is a *file object type. Within QDDSSRC are several members, File1, File2, and Master. These are the DDS statements for the three files respectively. Notice that File2 and Master are not yet created as objects in the PAYROLL library. We know this because their object names do not exist in the PAYROLL Library.

Notice also that there is another library listed called Mystuf. This has a source file called QRPGSRC with two members, RPG01, and RPG02. These are RPG source programs. Notice also that RPG01 has been compiled and it exists as an object in the Mystuf library. Though the source for RPG02 exists, Figure 7-5 shows that it has not been compiled successfully into an object at this time.

After we compile Master, notice that in Figure 7-5, it exists as an object in the PAYROLL library. At this point, File2 and RPG02 have yet to be created, though their source has been typed.

The QSQLSRC as processed by RUNSQLSTM produces similar results.

Figure 7-5 QSYS Genesis After CRTPF PAYROLL/MASTER

System Library Name	User Library Names	Object Names	Object Types	Members (If file)
QSYS	Payroll	Qddssrc	*File	File1
				File2
				Master
		Menu	*Pgm	
		Prt01	*Outq	
		File1	*File	File1
>>>>		Master	*File	
	Mystuf	QRPGSRC	*File	RPG01
				RPG02
		RPG01	*Pgm	

Q8. If we compile source program RPG02 into the Mystuf library, will this chart (Figure 7-5) change?

A8. Yes, of course, an entry would exist in Figure 7-5 immediately after the last line RPG01 *Pgm, for RPG02 *Pgm, showing that it was compiled and had become an object in the Mystuf library.

File / Member Commands

The following is a list of native IBM i commands and descriptions which are used to create and delete database files and members:

CRTPF   **Create Physical File**
CRTLF   **Create Logical File (an index plus more)**
CRTSRCPF **Create Source Physical File**
ADDPFM   **Add Physical File Member (to a physical file)**
RMVM   **Remove Member from any type of file**
DSPLIB   **Display Library**
DSPFD   **Display File Description (File attributes)**
DSPFFD   **Display File Field Description - the database**
                        field definitions within the file itself
DSPPFM   **Display Physical File Member - displays raw**
                        data in physical files.

Other than the create commands, these other commands work on SQL-created tables also.   Let's look at some of these display commands now.

DSPLIB

The DSPLIB (display library) command examines the library object which is structured as a directory and it displays the directory contents on the default device which is typically the green screen display.   Let's execute the DSPLIB against the PAYROLL library and the Mystuf libraries that we just created as shown in Figure 7-5 above.   The commands are

```
DSPLIB Payroll
DSPLIB Mystuf
```

The results are shown in Figure 7-6 and Figure 7-7.

Figure 7-6 Payroll Library Display

```
                        Display Library

Library . . . . . . : PAYROLL    Number of objects . :   5
Type . . . . . . . . : PROD      Library ASP number . :   1
Create authority . . : *SYSVAL   Library ASP device . :   *SYSBAS


Type options, press Enter.
  5=Display full attributes    8=Display service attributes

Opt  Object    Type    Attribute     Size   Text
     FILE1     *FILE   PF           24576   Test File 1
     FILE2     *FILE   PF           24576   Test File 2
     MASTER    *FILE   PF           24576
     QDDSSRC   *FILE   PF            8192   Payroll File Source D
     QSQLSRC   *FILE   PF            8192   Payroll File SQL Desc

                                                          Bottom
F3=Exit   F12=Cancel   F17=Top   F18=Bottom
(C) COPYRIGHT IBM CORP. 1980, 2003.
```

Figure 7-7 Mystuf Library Display

```
                        Display Library

Library . . . . . . : MYSTUF     Number of objects . :   2
Type . . . . . . . . : PROD      Library ASP number . :   1
Create authority . . : *SYSVAL   Library ASP device . :   *SYSBAS


Type options, press Enter.
  5=Display full attributes    8=Display service attributes

Opt  Object    Type  Attribute       Size   Text
     RPG01     *PGM  RPG            81920   SQL Book Test Program
     QRPGSRC   *FILE PF             45056   RPG Source File in My

                                                          Bottom
F3=Exit   F12=Cancel   F17=Top   F18=Bottom
(C) COPYRIGHT IBM CORP. 1980, 2003.
```

For a look at the libraries created with the SQL Create Schema command, see Figures 6-2 and 6-3. For a look at a library display of the system libraries QSYS2 and SYSIBM, see Figures 7-2 and 7-3.

DSPFD Display File Description

Nothing brings home the point that the IBM i is an object based system as much as being able to look inside an object after it was created in order to learn about it. Metadata (data about data) is stored within each object on the IBM i. That is why the DB2 database implementation, though similar to all other DB2s cannot be the same structurally. Internally, the IBM i is the most advanced computer system ever built. The SQL catalogs in other systems typically provide the information that can be found inside of an IBM i database object. For compatibility purposes, IBM has built these catalogs into the IBM i but clearly from a functional standpoint, they are redundant with the metadata already stored within the objects themselves.

Note Physical files are like SQL tables and Logical files are like SQL views. There is one major difference between a logical file and an SQL view, a logical file is most often keyed and it provides an alternate index for the data. An SQL view has no index associated with it. An index can be created on an SQL table with the SQL Create Index statement but the index is free floating and is not associated with any view.

The DSPFD (Display File Description) is a very powerful command that tells a lot about a IBM i database file – physical or logical. Its general structure is shown in Figure 7-8.

Figure 7-8 Display File Description (DSPFD)

```
                        Display File Description (DSPFD)

Type choices, press Enter.

File . . . . . . . . . . . . . > MASTER          Name, generic*, *ALL
  Library  . . . . . . . . . . > PAYROLL         Name, *LIBL, *CURLIB...
Type of information  . . . . . .   *ALL          *ALL, *BASATR, *ATR...
                 + for more values
Output . . . . . . . . . . . . .   *             *, *PRINT, *OUTFILE
File attributes  . . . . . . . .   *ALL          *ALL, *DSPF, *PRTF, *DKTF...
                 + for more values

                        Additional Parameters

System . . . . . . . . . . . . .   *LCL          *LCL, *RMT, *ALL




        Bottom
F3=Exit    F4=Prompt   F5=Refresh   F12=Cancel   F13=How to use this display
F24=More keys
```

Notice in Figure 7-8 in the type of information parameter that
there is a long list of options over on the right showing the type
of information that can be extracted from the file object. Let's
take a closer look at this information by replacing the *all with
a question mark and pressing Enter. The information in the
table shown in Figure 7-9 gives the many choices that are
permitted for selection.

As a demonstration of the power of the DSPFD command, let's
perform an all type display of the MASTER file we created in
PAYROLL.

DSPFD PAYROLL/MASTER

The output of this command is a many-page display. The first
three pages of the output are combined into one Figure and
shown in Figure 7-10.

Figure 7-9 Type of Information to be displayed DSPFD

Type   Provides this information

Single Values

*ALL   Information about all parts of object

*BASATR   just the basic attribute information

Other Values

*ATR   Attribute information meaningful for the
                    specified file

*ACCPTH   Access paths for physical and logical files
                    are provided. For Keyed access paths, the
                    composite key description is also shown.

*MBRLIST   An alphabetical list and brief description
                    of all file members in the specified file.

*SELECT   The select/omit attribute for logical files

*SEQ   The collating sequence for physical and
                    logical files

*RCDFMT   The record format names and record
                    format level information for the specified
                    file

*MBR   Information about the file members in
                    physical and logical files

*SPOOL   The spooling attributes for the specified
                    diskette or printer file

| *JOIN | The join from-file, the join to-file, and the fields involved in the join are provided for join logical files. |

Add'l Other Values

| *TRG | For physical files only, the number of trigger programs, each trigger program name and library, and the trigger events, trigger times, and trigger update conditions for each file with a trigger.. |

| *CST | For physical files only, information about the constraint relationships associated with the file. |

| *NODGRP | For distributed physical files only, data partitioning and relational data base information copied from a node group (*NODGRP) at file creation time is provided. |

A handy attribute for a source file for those users who are not using the standard Program Development Manager (PDM) that comes with most IBM i machines is the *MBRLIST option. This option shows the list of members in a file.

Most files have just one member but a file can actually have thousands of members whose data format is the same. Files that typically have more than one member are source files. Each object requiring source, such as an RPG program or a file created with DDS or a file created with SQL and RUNSQLSTM, needs its source stored in a source file under a specific name.

The name is typically the same name as the object to be created but it does not have to be. As a convention it certainly should be, however.

Figure 7-10 PAYROLL/MASTER Object Description (3 panels)

```
                            Display Spooled File
File  . . . . . :   QPDSPFD                        Page/Line   1/1
Control . . . . .                                  Columns     1 - 78
Find  . . . . . .
*...+....1....+....2....+....3....+....4....+....5....+....6....+....7....+..
 .
   11/19/05                Display File Description
DSPFD Command Input
   File  . . . . . . . . . . . . . . . . . . : FILE        MASTER
      Library . . . . . . . . . . . . . . . . :            PAYROLL
   Type of information . . . . . . . . . . . : TYPE        *ALL
   File attributes . . . . . . . . . . . . . : FILEATR     *ALL
   System  . . . . . . . . . . . . . . . . . : SYSTEM      *LCL
File Description Header
   File  . . . . . . . . . . . . . . . . . . : FILE        MASTER
   Library . . . . . . . . . . . . . . . . . :             PAYROLL
   Type of file  . . . . . . . . . . . . . . :             Physical
   File type . . . . . . . . . . . . . . . . : FILETYPE    *DATA
   Auxiliary storage pool ID . . . . . . . . :             00001
Data Base File Attributes
   Externally described file . . . . . . . . :             No
   File level identifier . . . . . . . . . . :             1051118200959
                                                                    More...
```

```
*...+....1....+....2....+....3....+....4....+....5....+....6....+....7....+..
 .
   Creation date . . . . . . . . . . . . . . :             11/18/05
   Text 'description'  . . . . . . . . . . . : TEXT
   Distributed file  . . . . . . . . . . . . :             No
   Partitioned SQL Table . . . . . . . . . . :             No
   DBCS capable  . . . . . . . . . . . . . . :             No
   Maximum members . . . . . . . . . . . . . : MAXMBRS       1
   Number of constraints . . . . . . . . . . :               0
   Number of triggers  . . . . . . . . . . . :               0
   Number of members . . . . . . . . . . . . :               1
   Member size                                SIZE
      Initial number of records . . . . . . . :                 10000
      Increment number of records . . . . . . :             1000
      Maximum number of increments  . . . . . :             3
   Record capacity . . . . . . . . . . . . . :                   13000
   Allocate storage  . . . . . . . . . . . . : ALLOCATE    *NO
   Contiguous storage  . . . . . . . . . . . : CONTIG      *NO
                                                                    More...
```

```
*...+....1....+....2....+....3....+....4....+....5....+....6....+....7....+..
   Preferred storage unit  . . . . . . . . . : UNIT        *ANY
   Records to force a write  . . . . . . . . : FRCRATIO    *NONE
   Maximum file wait time  . . . . . . . . . : WAITFILE     30
   Maximum record wait time  . . . . . . . . : WAITRCD      60
   Max % deleted records allowed . . . . . . : DLTPCT      *NONE
   Reuse deleted records . . . . . . . . . . : REUSEDLT    *NO
   Coded character set identifier  . . . . . : CCSID       65535
   Allow read operation  . . . . . . . . . . :             Yes
   Allow write operation . . . . . . . . . . :             Yes
   Allow update operation  . . . . . . . . . : ALWUPD      *YES
   Allow delete operation  . . . . . . . . . : ALWDLT      *YES
   Record format level check . . . . . . . . : LVLCHK      *YES
   Access path . . . . . . . . . . . . . . . :             Arrival
   Maximum record length . . . . . . . . . . :             136
   File is currently journaled . . . . . . . :             No
 Access Path Description
More...
```

Note: The Program Development Manager and all the tools necessary to develop code natively on an IBM i box is well covered in another pocket guide by Brian W. Kelly and published by Lets Go Publish. The book is called The IBM i Pocket Developer's Guide. For more information on native database, see The IBM i Pocket Database Guide by Lets Go Publish.

Since a source file is also a database file, let's go inside of the QDDSSRC source file we created in the PAYROLL library and see what members there may be. The command follows and the results are shown in Figure 7-11A.

DSPFD FILE(PAYROLL/QDDSSRC) TYPE(*MBRLIST)

Figure 7-11A Member list of QDDSSRC in PAYROLL

```
                              Display Spooled File
File . . . . . :     QPDSPFD                      Page/Line   1/1
Control . . . . .                                 Columns     1 - 78
Find . . . . . .
*...+....1....+....2....+....3....+....4....+....5....+....6....+....7....+..
11/19/05                 Display File Description
  DSPFD Command Input
      File . . . . . . . . . . . . . . . . . . : FILE      QDDSSRC
        Library . . . . . . . . . . . . . . . . :          PAYROLL
      Type of information . . . . . . . . . . . : TYPE      *MBRLIST
      File attributes . . . . . . . . . . . . . : FILEATR   *ALL
      System . . . . . . . . . . . . . . . . . : SYSTEM    *LCL
  File Description Header
      File . . . . . . . . . . . . . . . . . . : FILE      QDDSSRC
      Library . . . . . . . . . . . . . . . . . :           PAYROLL
      Type of file . . . . . . . . . . . . . . :           Physical
      File type . . . . . . . . . . . . . . . . : FILETYPE  *SRC
      Auxiliary storage pool ID . . . . . . . . :           00001
  Member List
                          Source Creation   Last Change
    Member         Size   Type  Date        Date     Time        Records

  More...
  FILE1            8192 PF      11/19/05 11/19/05 17:32:09         8
      Text:  Test File 1 for SQLBook
  FILE2            8192 PF      11/19/05 11/19/05 17:32:09         9
      Text:  Test File 1 for SQLBook
  MASTER           8192 PF      11/19/05 11/19/05 17:32:09         2
      Text:  MASTER Payroll file for SQLBook
  Total number of members . . . . . . . . . :         3
  Total number of members not available  . . :         0
  Total records . . . . . . . . . . . . . . :        19
  Total deleted records . . . . . . . . . . :         0
  Total of member sizes . . . . . . . . . . :     24576
```

If you look down the display in Figure 7-11A, you will see three entries, the beginning of which look like the three entries shown in Figure 7-11B.:

Figure 7-11B Three Members in Member List

```
FILE1                    8192 PF       11/19/05
   Text:    Test File 1 for SQLBook
FILE2                    8192 PF       11/19/05
   Text:    Test File 1 for SQLBook
MASTER                   8192 PF       11/19/05
   Text:    MASTER Payroll file for SQLBook
```

You may recall that in Chapter 4 we created our first database in this book. It is called Vendorp. We defined the structure of this database with ten columns (fields). Since we created it, and subsequently removed the few records that we had added, I re-populated the file with a number of representative records so it could be used effectively as a test file. With the next two commands we are going to examine this database object in a different way than the DSPFD command.

The first command we are going to test drive is Display File Field Description (DSPFFD) and the second is Display Physical File Member (DSPPFM). The DSPFFD command does just as it says. It dips inside the database file object and pulls out the structure of the database. It does not have to go back to the source member in QDDSSRC or QSQLSRC in order to get the record layout, because it is stored inside of the object itself.

The second command bypasses all of the descriptive information and goes to the first member of the Vendorp file (unless there is an override in effect) and it grabs the data portion of the object and displays it on the screen. We first show the two commands below and then in Figures 7-12 and 7-13, we show the results of the two commands.

DSPFFD MYLIB/Vendorp
DSPPFM MYLIB/Vendorp

In Figure 7-12, notice that the first few fields have lots of
descriptive text. The next fields shown are one-liners. Actually,
they all have multiple lines of text in the commands natural
output but I trimmed the output so that you could readily see
that the database structure was included within the object itself.

Figure 7-12 Display Record Layout DSPFFD from DB Object

```
                         Display Spooled File
File . . . . . :    QPDSPFFD                  Page/Line   1/1
Control . . . .                               Columns     1 - 78
Find . . . . . .
*...+....1....+....2....+....3....+....4....+....5....+....6....+....7....+..
.
                      Display File Field Description
  Input parameters
    File . . . . . . . . . . . . . . . . . . . . . :   VENDORP
      Library . . . . . . . . . . . . . . . . . . :   SQLBOOK
  File Information
    File . . . . . . . . . . . . . . . . . . . . . :   VENDORP
      Library . . . . . . . . . . . . . . . . . . :   SQLBOOK
    File location . . . . . . . . . . . . . . . . :   *LCL
    Externally described . . . . . . . . . . . . :   Yes
    Number of record formats . . . . . . . . . :   1
    Type of file . . . . . . . . . . . . . . . . :   Physical
    SQL file type . . . . . . . . . . . . . . . . :   TABLE
    File creation date . . . . . . . . . . . . . :   11/18/05
  Record Format Information
    Record format . . . . . . . . . . . . . . . . :   VENDTMP2
    Format level identifier . . . . . . . . . . :   3F9F9E8D9EDD2
      Number of fields . . . . . . . . . . . . . :   10
      Record length . . . . . . . . . . . . . . . :   85
  Field Level Information
                    Data      Field  Buffer   Buffer          Field    Column
      Field         Type      Length Length   Position        Usage    Heading
      VNDNBR        ZONED      5  0     5         1            Both     VNDNBR
        Default value . . . . . . . . . . . . . . : None
      NAME          CHAR        25     25         6            Both     NAME
        Allows the null value
        Default value . . . . . . . . . . . . . . :
              *NULL
        Coded Character Set Identifier  . . . . . :      37
      ADDR1         CHAR        25     25        31            Both     ADDR1
        Allows the null value
        Default value . . . . . . . . . . . . . . :
              *NULL
        Coded Character Set Identifier  . . . . . :      37
      CITY          CHAR        16     16        56            Both     CITY
      STATE         CHAR         2      2        72            Both     STATE
      ZIPCD         PACKED     5  0     3        74            Both     ZIPCD
      VNDCLS        PACKED     2  0     2        77            Both     VNDCLS
      VNDSTS        CHAR         1      1        79            Both     VNDSTS
      BALOWE        PACKED     9  2     5        80            Both     BALOWE
      SRVRTG        CHAR         1      1        85            Both     SRVRTG
        Allows the null value
        Default value . . . . . . . . . . . . . . :
              *NULL
        Coded Character Set Identifier  . . . . . :      37
```

Figure 7-13 Display the data Inside VENDORP First Member

DSPPFM

```
                    Display Physical File Member
File . . . . . . :    VENDORP          Library . . . . :    SQLBOOK
Member . . . . . :    VENDTMP2         Record . . . . . :    1
Control . . . . .                      Column . . . . . :    1
Find . . . . . . .
*...+....1....+....2....+....3....+....4....+....5....+....6....+....7....+...
00038J B COMPANY            3817 N. PULASKI        SCRANTON      PA¬&¬¬¬
00040SCRANTON INC           2147 S MAIN ST         OLD FORGE     PA¬Î¬¬¬
00042PASS PAX INC           1539 OAK HILL          OLD FORGE     PA¬Ê¬¬¬
00044J B EQUIP INC          2232 FOUEST            SCRANTON      PA¬&¬¬¬
00046K D BUTTS WALLACE INC  2150 TOUGHY            SCRANTON      PA¬&¬¬¬
00048DENTON AND BALL        7934 S SCRANTON AVE    SCRANTON      PA¬&|¬¬
00049JOHN STUDIOS           2040 N BELTWAY         SCRANTON      PA¬&¬¬¬
00025A MACHINE CORP.        1345 Prill Avenue      Chicago       ILá°¬¬¬
00026B MACHINERY            45 Ginzo Lane          Wokegon       OK¬Á"¬¬
00028C ENGRAVING CO         Pedullion Avenue       Greghert      ILáo¬¬¬
00030D CONTROLS             45 Fognetta Place      Kernstin      ILá`¬¬¬
00032I POWER EQUIPMENT      56 Fineel La           Swingder      PA¬&¬¬¬
00034ROBIN  COMPANY         11 Robin Lane          Robin         PA¬ø¬¬¬
00036F STEEL CO             78 Engraved Rd.        Mattusic      PA¬ß±¬¬
07000Microsoft Corporation  One Microsoft Way      Redmond       WAq¬¬¬¬
                                                                 More...

F3=Exit    F12=Cancel    F19=Left    F20=Right    F24=More keys keys
```

In Figure 7-13, as you can see, a record view of the data is given for the first 75 characters of the record. With this display, you can window right (F20) and left (F19) and after requesting more function keys, you can hit F10 to see the bytes in hexadecimal format.

So, there you have it... the basic IBM i operating system commands to work directly with objects created with SQL or with DDS.

Now, before we discuss the artifacts necessary for a healthy development environment on your IBM i, let's look at how some of the above information could be gained using SQL and the system wide catalog and the schema wide catalog.

Exploring the SQL Catalog with SQL

On other systems, the system-wide catalog that we introduced in Chapter 6 is also known as the SQL catalog. It is a repository of all tables, column names, triggers and generally every component relevant to the database. As noted previously, on the IBM i, one can locate mostly all of the SQL Catalog tables in library QSYS2. It is worthy to note that even tables created originally as files with DDS and the CRTPF or CRTLF commands are recorded in the DB2 SQL Catalog tables. These SQL Catalog tables all start with the letters "SYS," just as the schema-wide tables as shown in Figure 6-1.

The SQL Catalog can be used to provide some of the information that you gain by performing the DSPFD and DSPFFD commands. For example, to find the SQL definition of an existing table, you can do a

```
SELECT * FROM QSYS2/SYSCOLUMNS WHERE
TABLE_NAME = 'FILE_NAME'
```

To show all the existing constraints on the system you can use

```
SELECT * FROM QSYS2/SYSCHKCST
```

Other SQL catalog files include SYSINDEXES, SYSFUNCS, SYSTRIGGER and SYSVIEWS. Since these catalog files are all SQL tables (physical files) they are query-able with SQL Query or with any other Query product including Query/400. Information about the databases on your system is always just a few queries away..

System catalog views from the SYS* files or the underlying cross-reference physical files from the QADB* files in the SQL catalog contain all of the metadata information on files in your database – SQL or otherwise built. These files do not, however, contain the real-time information such as number of records in each file. The reason this material is not maintained is that it is not technically feasible from a performance standpoint for the operating system to update a cross-reference file each time there is a record added or deleted in each file in your database. The system would not be able to tolerate all of that excess overhead. You may recall that information such as record count is kept with the file object itself in real-time. However, the SQL catalog queries do not access the internals of the DB objects.

So, if that is something that you need, then the most straightforward way to get things like the real-time count of the records in your files is with the native commands such as DSPFD, DSPDBR, WRKOBJ, DSPOBJD etc.

For those who want to be pure in their use of SQL on the IBM i and who need this information, there are non-system command ways to get this information but there is not just one command involved.

For example, you can use SQL queries on your system catalog tables to get all the metadata you need about your database (file names, column names, column data types, column keys etc.). You can then get the count of records in a physical file with a standard SQL function that we will be discussing in the coming chapters. For now, here it is:

SELECT COUNT(*) FROM Library/File

This command brings back the count of records from the library/file combination that you specify. There are always several ways to get the same thing done on the IBM i. No other system in which SQL is used is object based so no other system developers would be requesting that information from the objects be materialized via SQL interfaces. Though the SQL catalog provides as much information as it does on any other system and that is very good, if you want more because you know the IBM i has a more powerful architecture, your choice is to use the system commands or come up with your own multi-step SQL technique. When and if other SQL systems catch up to the IBM i there may be easier ways to get this stuff without a lot of work through a natural SQL interface.

Development Environment

When an IBM i system is used for application development, an implementer typically sets up a source library for the developers to use. In addition to the source library, the implementer would also create a library in which the program objects and other objects reside. If the library were going to store SQL objects such as tables and views, instead of a plain library, you would set up a schema which is in essence a fully-capable SQL library. A third library / schema would be created for the data. This is not a rule, but it is a convention that I have seen in many shops.

If, for example an Accounts Payable system is being developed from scratch, the letters AP may be used as the defining part of the library names. Three libraries would be created as follows:

```
CRTLIB APSRC TEXT('Library for AP Source')

CRTLIB APOBJ TEXT('Library for AP Objects')

CRTLIB APDTA TEXT('Library for AP Data')
```

Or with SQL

CREATE SCHEMA APDTA IN ASP 1
    (creates library with schema-wide catalog etc.)

Within the APSRC library, for an RPG and COBOL shop, you would want to create the following source files:

```
CRTSRCPF FILE(APSRC/QDDSSRC)
TEXT('Source File for DDS')

CRTSRCPF FILE(APSRC/QSQLSRC)
TEXT('Source File for SQL')

CRTSRCPF FILE(APSRC/QCLSRC)
TEXT('Source File for CL Pgms')

CRTSRCPF FILE(APSRC/QRPGLESRC)
TEXT('Source File for RPG/400')

CRTSRCPF FILE(APSRC/QCBLSRC)
TEXT('Source File for CBL/400')

CRTSRCPF FILE(APSRC/QRPGLESRC) RCDLEN(120)
TEXT('Source File for ILE RPG Source')
```

Etc.

Chapter Summary

A library is a directory object that contains entries that are used to locate system objects. Since libraries are objects, however, they must be stored someplace and they are stored in the system library called QSYS. The typical search for an object would be to find the library first in QSYS and then use that library object to locate the object in question. The SQL object type "schema" is a form of a library with special SQL objects.

Physical and logical database files are stored in libraries. If the library happens to be a schema also, they can also be stored in a schema. A source files is a special type of database file designed with three fields (Seq#, date, and text). A source file is created with its own CL command, CRTSRCPF, to avoid having to use native DDS to describe the source files. Source files may contain a virtually unlimited number of members with each member can hold different source records. Thus, in some ways, the member list in a IBM i file is a subdirectory to other file objects, all shaped the same as the original file.

SQL collections and schemas use the library object as the underlying system object. When a table is created, it is stored (pointed to) from the schema which is really a special library object. There are some nice system tools to work with library structures. For example the DSPLIB command shows all of the objects in a library, including schema specific objects. Moreover, there are lots of system commands that can be used against schema objects to provide even more information than the SQL catalog provides.

For example, the DSPFD command looks into an SQL table and can tell you at any moment how many records exist in the table. Additionally, the DSPFFD command looks into the table object and it can tell you the names, labels, types and other specifics about the columns (fields) in your SQL tables / files as stored in a schema or a library.

Finally, SQL uses its own capabilities to keep metadata about all the objects that are created in any of the four SQL faces (environments). Last chapter we discussed the schema-wide catalog that keeps information about he objects in a particular schema and in this chapter we introduced the notion of the system-wide catalog with most of it being kept in system library QSYS2.

There are a number of tables in this library that can deliver information about SQL objects as well as the native physical and logical files on the system. In many ways the IBM i catalog then is more comprehensive than those in other DB2 systems.

In these last two chapters, we outlined the considerations and the steps necessary to create the files, libraries and application development environment on your IBM i. Once you create your environment, you can use the RUNSQLSTM or the native system commands to build objects for your application.

Key Chapter Terms

*MBRLIST
ADDPFM
Catalog
Catalog- SYSCHKCST
Catalog- SYSCOLUMNS
Catalog- SYSFUNCS
Catalog- SYSINDEXES
Catalog-SYSTRIGGER
Catalog-SYSVIEWS
Create Schema
Create Table
CRTLIB
CRTPF
CRTSRCPF
Creating Source Physical File
Data File Utility
Database, internally described
DDS specifications
Dictionary
Directories
DSPDBR, Data Base Relations
DSPFD, File description
DSPFFD, File Field Description
DSPLIB, Library
DSPOBJD, Object Description
DSPPFM, Physical File Mamber
Field definitions
File architectures
File objects
File / Member Commands

Integrated File System
Journal
Journal receiver
Library file system
Library object
Library structure
Library/file notation
LIBRARY/OBJECT
Metadata
Object based system
Object type
Object-oriented
ODBC
Physical file object
Program Development Manager
PDM
QADB*
QDDSSRC source file
QSQLSRC
QSYS
QSYS.LIB
QSYS2
Qualified library
Query/400
RMVM
Root directory
RPG program
RUNSQLSTM
Schema
Select Data
Source DB files
Source description
Source development environment
Source file
SQL objects
SQL source
SQL statements
SQL tables
SYSIBM Library
System catalog

System library
System Storage Genesis
System/36
WRKOBJ, Work with Objects

Exercises

Use this chapter or look up information on the Web to answer the following:

1. What is a Library?

2. Describe the genesis of system storage on IBM i.

3. Write the command to create a library called YOURLIB. Use SQL to create s schema called YOURSQL.

4. Describe in detail the difference between a library and a schema/collection.

5. When you create a new database, where does it go?

6. Can a database have no field structure defined when it is created? Give two examples? What are the implications for the programmer, User?

7. Write the command to create a source file for SQL in YOURLIB.

8. Write the command to display YOURLIB

9. Write the command to remove a member from a source file.

10. What is DDS?

11. Write the SQL to look at the SQL catalog file containing the system columns

12. Describe the development environment on the IBM i?

13. How would you create a development environment?

Chapter 8   Creating and Dropping SQL Objects

SQL Object Review

In Chapters 6 & 7, we noted the six different object types that come into play with DDL operations for SQL databases. These are as follows:

ALIAS
COLLECTION
INDEX
SCHEMA
TABLE
VIEW

In the preceding chapters we examined the major containers of SQL objects in IBM i machines - namely the collection, schema, and the native library and file structure. Now it is time for us to study the other SQL object types that are highlighted in the above list.

Building and Working with SQL Table Objects

We have already discussed the notion of a table and the physical file object in which tables are stored on the IBM i. We know that tables are the basic structure in which data is stored in an SQL-driven database. Unless you buy a package and take what is given, in most cases, you will need to create tables in the database yourself. There are a number of database tools that allow you to create tables without writing SQL, and of course, on IBM i, there is also DDS, which is a native way of describing data and creating file objects. But given that the table is the container of all the data, it is important to understand how to naturally create a table using the proper SQL DDL syntax. As we learned in Chapter 4, the SQL DDL statement to create a table is CREATE TABLE.

What Does the SQL Create Table Statement Do?

The CREATE TABLE SQL statement provides two functions

1. It creates a physical file database object.

2. It provides a detailed data definition of the object.

Since what is in a table is actually more important than the notion of a table itself, before we delve into the full SQL syntax for CREATE TABLE, it is a good idea to understand what goes into a table. We know that tables are divided into rows and columns and are called files in file systems. We also know that each row represents one piece of data, called a record in files systems. We know that each column can be thought of as representing a component or attribute, or a fact about that piece of data, called a field in file systems.

For example, if you have a table for recording vendor information, then the columns may include information such as Name, Address, City, Zip, and so on. As a result, when you specify a table, you include the size that you expect each of these data elements to be and you specify the data types for each column. You optionally can specify column headers and other descriptive text for any particular column.

Data Types

So what are data types? Typically, data comes in a variety of forms. It could be an integer (such as 1), a real number (such as 0.55), a string (such as 'string'), a date/time expression (such as '2006-JAN-30 04:24:32'), or the data can even be stored in binary format. When we specify a table, therefore, we must specify the data type associated with each individual column (i.e., we will specify that 'Name' is of type char(40) - meaning it is a string with 40 characters). One thing to note is that different relational databases allow for different data types, so it is wise to consult the DB2 UDB for IBM i Reference Manual before beginning to use a data type that may be supported in MySQL, Oracle, SQL Server, or Ingres. Don't assume.

Syntax – Create Table

The basic SQL syntax for CREATE TABLE in all SQL implementations is as follows:

```
CREATE TABLE "table_name"
("column 1" "data_type_for_column_1",
"column 2" "data_type_for_column_2",
... )
```

There are many other keywords in SQL besides column names and data types for the Create Table statement but there is nothing more basic than defining the data. If we were to create the Vendor table noted above, it would look very much as it did in Figure 4-4 in Chapter 4. However, for this example, let's introduce a new and handy data type called date as shown in Figure 8-1..

A Close Look at SQL Data Types

In Figure 8-1, notice that the database definition uses just four different data types – numeric (zoned decimal), character, decimal (packed), and date. When you design a database, whether with DDS or with SQL, it is important to pick the correct data type for a column.

Figure 8-1 Creating a Tables/File with SQL

```
CREATE TABLE VENDORP
    (VNDNBR       NUMERIC(5,0)      NOT NULL,
    NAME          CHAR(25),
    ADDR1         CHAR(25),
    CITY          CHAR(15),
    STATE         CHAR(2),
    ZIPCD         DEC(5,0),
    VNDCLS        DEC(2,0),
    VNDSTS        CHAR(1),
    BALOWE        DEC(9,2),
    SRVRTG        CHAR(1),
    DATLAC        DATE,
Primary Key  (VNDNBR)
```

With many companies doing business in multiple countries and with supply chain management forcing companies to have compatibility with each other's IT systems, the idea of data typing has taken on a life of its own. If you are doing business in the USA or some other country for that matter, and that country is all you care about, then the basic data types supported by the native database with DDS will serve you well. However, if you will be using distributed processing techniques to access data, it is very important that data typing considerations play a large role in your DB design so that your text data conversions will occur as expected.

For more information on data typing, the IBM DB2 UDB for IBM i SQL Reference manual is available for free downloads from IBM. This book, along with the SQL Programmer's Guide is your bible for all matters regarding IBM i SQL

Table 8-2 and 8-3 show the difference between the data typing available in DDS and that available with SQL. The newer data objects are supported via SQL. However, as you will see by reading the chart in Figure 8-3, RPG has not yet caught up in its use of all data types.

Figure 8-2 Data Types for DDS

Data Type	Valid Lengths	Code
Character	1 through 32 766 characters	A or blank
Hexadecimal	1 through 32 766 bytes	H
Binary	1 through 18 digits	B
Zoned decimal	1 through 31 digits	S
Packed decimal	1 through 31 digits	P
Floating-point (single precision)	1 through 9 digits	F
Floating-point (double precision)	1 through 17 digits	F
Date	6, 8, or 10 characters	L
Time	8 characters	T
Timestamp	26 characters	Z

Figure 8-3 SQL Data Types with RPGIV Equivalence

SMALLINT	Definition specification. I in position 40, length must be 5 and 0 in position 42. OR Definition specification. B in position 40, length must be <= 4 and 0 in position 42.	
INTEGER	Definition specification. I in position 40, length must be 10 and 0 in position 42. OR Definition specification. B in position 40, length must be <= 9 and >= 5 and 0 in position 42.	
BIGINT	Definition specification. I in position 40, length must be 20 and 0 in position 42.	
DECIMAL	Definition specification. P in position 40 or blank in position 40 for a non-subfield, 0 through 30 in position 41,42. OR Defined as numeric on non-definition specification.	Maximum length of 16 (precision 30) and maximum scale of 30.
NUMERIC	Definition specification. S in position 40 or blank in position 40 for a subfield, 0 through 30 in position 41,42.	Maximum length of 30 (precision 30) and maximum scale of 30.
FLOAT (single precision)	Definition specification. F in position 40, length must be 4.	
FLOAT (double precision)	Definition specification. F in position 40, length must be 8.	
CHAR(n)	Definition specification. A or blank in positions 40 and blanks in position 41,42. OR Input field defined without decimal places. OR Calculation result field defined without decimal places.	n can be from 1 to 32766.
CHAR(n)	Data structure name with no subfields in the data structure.	n can be from 1 to 32766.
VARCHAR(n)	Definition specification. A or blank in position 40 and VARYING in positions 44-80.	n can be from 1 to 32740.
BLOB	Not supported	Use SQLTYPE

		keyword to declare a BLOB.
CLOB	Not supported	Use SQLTYPE keyword to declare a CLOB.
GRAPHIC(n)	Definition specification. G in position 40. OR Input field defined with G in position 36.	n can be 1 to 16383.
VARGRAPHIC(n)	Definition specification. G in position 40 and VARYING in positions 44-80.	n can be from 1 to 16370.
DBCLOB	Not supported	Use SQLTYPE keyword to declare a DBCLOB.
DATE	A character field OR Definition specification with a D in position 40. OR Input field defined with D in position 36.	If the format is *USA, *JIS, *EUR, or *ISO, the length must be at least 10
TIME	A character field OR Definition specification with a T in position 40. OR Input field defined with T in position 36.	Length must be at least 6; to include seconds, length must be at least 8.
TIMESTAMP	A character field OR Definition specification with a Z in position 40. OR Input field defined with Z in position 36.	Length must be at least 19; to include microseconds, length must be at least 26. If length is less than 26, truncation occurs
DATALINK	Not supported in RPG	

Date Data Types

As you would expect, the date data type is designed to store dates more intelligently than in character format and / or decimal format. For example, by storing a date as a date, high level languages and SQL procedures can recognize the data as a date and cane provide special function to derive answers to queries about different dates such as the amount of days that have lapsed between two dates etc. For the vendor file, we chose to add the date field as the last column, thereby providing a database file of 11 columns.

You can see in Figure 8-1 that the field DATLAC (date of last vendor activity) has been added as a date data type. Also note that we already had a Vendorp file in our book library (SQLBOOK,) so to use this create we would have first had to drop the table or delete it with a CL command.

The UDB for IBM i database supports a few very special data types for date, time, and timestamp. Unlike most other data types, you do not specify the length for these three data types when you define a field in DDL. The system automatically determines the length of these data types.

The database actually stores them all in a four byte internal form on disk with each record. When you run SQL statements or you compile a COBOL or RPG program that includes the date data types, you also get to specify (or take the defaults) for which external date format that you would like to use for these fields in your database. The program then uses these external definitions to translate the four byte internal values into meaningful dates, times, or timestamps. Moreover, and more importantly, these fields can be involved in special data arithmetic in SQL and in languages such as RPGIV, making it very productive to use this form of the date, rather than building your own in decimal or character format.

There are a number of tables available for the date, time, and timestamp formatting through IBM and other sources. To see up-to-date tables, rather than a table that will be quickly out of date in this book, take your favorite search engine and type in IBM i sql date data type, and you will have all the current information you need.

Field Reference File / Dictionary

Those familiar with DDS more than likely have used a notion called a Field Reference File which more or less provides the opportunity to have a passive data dictionary capability within the native database. In DDS, for example, there is a keyword called FORMAT in which the developer would place the name of the physical file (table) that would be referenced for its data definitions if the new physical file was to use all of the definitions of the file exactly as they were specified in the based on physical.

If only a partial list of field definitions were needed, then the REF keyword could be used at the file level in DDS and the developer would create a new format by specifying just the fields that were to be in the new file. The REF keyword could point to a small physical file with or without data or a big field reference file that could be serving as an application data dictionary. The column headings, text, length, decimal positions, and data type would be copied from the reference file when the new file was built. The field definitions were extracted from the referenced file merely by specifying the exact column name in the data definition of the new file.

It makes creating files with DDS lots easier than having to know all of the field definitions, text descriptions and column headings that were proper to use so it is a heavily used feature on IBM i. Because the native physical file object structure includes the names of all the columns in the database, this reference facility did not have to go back to the source file to get the definitions. It got them right out of the file object itself. Moreover, when it created the physical file object, it also stored information about the reference file so that later down the road this information could be determined and a developer would know from whence the data definitions for the file had really come.

SQL Based Field Reference Files

IBM is really trying to make SQL a viable alternative to DDS for its IBM i SQL developers. Some of the facilities announced in V5R2 such as the reference file capabilities prove that point. Of course more came with V5R3 and more again with V5R4. From V5R2 in 2002, IBM provided a tool to help in the creation of a field reference file function, similar to that provided by DDS.

To do this, OBM added some new clauses in the Create Table statement that I have seen used in other database servers. There are two new forms of the Create Table statement that provide this capability, they are as follows:

CREATE TABLE LIKE

CREATE TABLE AS   (SELECT...) WITH

We will explore both below. The facility that mimics the DDS FORMAT keyword is the Like clause of the Create Table. In the following example, we create a file called VVENDORP that gets its all of its field definitions from the VENDORP file in SQLBOOK

CREATE TABLE SQLBOOK/VVENDORP
LIKE SQLBOOK/VVENDORP

The resulting file has the entire set of field definitions from the based on VENDORP file. The next example takes the VENDORP file as the base but this time we use only five of the fields in VENDORP in the new file. Notice the two versions of the same statement below:

```
CREATE TABLE SQLBOOK/VVENDORP_FOUR
AS
(SELECT VNDNBR, NAME, ADDR1, CITY, STATE
FROM VENDORP)
WITH NO DATA
```

```
CREATE TABLE SQLBOOK/FOUR_DATA_COPY
AS
(SELECT VNDNBR, NAME, ADDR1, CITY, STATE
FROM VENDORP)
WITH DATA
```

There is just one difference in the two above examples besides the non-duplicate names of the two tables. The "With clause" in the first example says "NO DATA" so just the definition is built. The "With clause" in the second example says "DATA" so after the file is built SQL does a COPY of the data under the covers and maps the data to the fields in the copy.

No Reference in the Object

IBM's work in making this facility into an equivalent field reference file is incomplete at this point but it is a good start. .If you were to use the display file field reference command to look into the created object you would see that the reference information from VENDORP has not been captured. With DDS as noted above, the file from which the reference descriptions were gleaned is included in each of the column definitions stored in the file object. Perhaps its time that IBM proposed an extension to the SQL standard for a specific reference file capability. Even without this information, the reference capability as it stands is a great start.

System and SQL Table Names

DB2 UDB on IBM i provides long name support for SQL objects and also for column names in a table. SQL object names for Tables, Indexes and Views, for example, have a maximum length of 128 characters. SQL column names max out at 30 characters. Those of you who have used a IBM i in the past know that 30 characters are too much for many IBM i functions to handle. Many OS/400 and IBM i/OS utilities, commands, and interfaces only support a name of 10-characters in length. RPG/400 supports just six character field names. This may become an issue when using native IBM i commands to access SQL objects. However, there are ways to get around this potentially big problem.

The CREATE TABLE statement does not allow you to specify a short name for the table name. To help the IBM i user and to assure that the objects built with long names can be accessed by IBM i tools, the system does generate a short name automatically, but the short name has some natural shortcomings.

Unfortunately for the notion of ease-of-use, the generated short name is not what you might call "user-friendly." For example, when you create a table named INVENTORY_MASTER, OS/400 or IBM i/OS automatically generates a short 10-character name as INVEN00001, which is an amalgamation of the first five characters of the table name and a unique 5-digit number. Any other object built with the first five characters INVEN will get sequence 00002 and the next sequence # 00003 and so forth. After awhile, it will be hard to tell just what each file is at the system level, merely by knowing its name.

In some ways this is like the old DOS naming issues on PCs in which you had to shorten the DOS name in order to get at the

Windows created files. As long as you know the rules, however, this method can work for you. For example the command to look at the file description using a system command for INVENTORY_MASTER would be as follows:

DSPFD SQLBOOK/INVEN00001

Of course, that's as long as the file was the first one built. If not, you'd have to query the amalgamated name suffix by incrementing it and performing the DSPFD again. The good news is that there is a way to use the RENAME statement to make this situation lots better. The format of the RENAME TABLE statement is as follows:

RENAME TABLE   schema/original table name   to SYSTEM NAME   new table name

Let's rename the INVENTORY_MASTER short name of INVEN0001 to a more meaningful short name of INVNMASTER. Here is the statement that does that followed by the system response:

RENAME TABLE SQLBOOK/INVENTORY_MASTER TO SYSTEM NAME INVNMASTER

RENAME for INVEN00001 in SQLBOOK completed.

So now for system commands, such as the DSPFD command, the new name can be used as follows:

DSPFD SQLBOOK/INVNMASTER

With the RENAME command, we could have also have changed the long name of the INVENTORY_MASTER file but we did not. So, the file is now known by two names. The short name is how it can be addressed through the operating system and the long name can be used with SQL as shown in the example below:

```
select * from SQLBOOK/INVENTORY_MASTER
```

The RENAME TABLE works with both TABLES and VIEWS. If you ever need to rename an index, then you would use the second form of the RENAME command. RENAME INDEX.

Creating an Alias

You can create an alternative name, called an ALIAS for any table or view built with SQL. When you assign an alias, you are assigning a name (long name) to the short name, so for some this might suffice rather than using the RENAME since the name you create as an alias as in the second example below can in essence alias a short name with another short name.

```
CREATE ALIAS SQLBOOK/INVENTORY_MASTER  for
SQLBOOK/INVNMASTER ( NEW )

CREATE ALIAS SQLBOOK/INVEN2  for
SQLBOOK/INVNMASTER  ( NEW )
```

Why would you use the Create Alias statement? There are a number of reasons why you might want to use an alias. However, one thing the experts agree on is do not overwork the use of alias because it can get "hairy." Here are some of the valid reasons:

1. You may want to rename an object and still have existing applications that refer to the old object name

2. You may want to create a different SQL long name for users who might relate better to a different name

3. You may want to use SQL to access an existing database file object that has multiple members (as explained in Chapter 7).

In the two examples above, if you include the (NEW) parameter, you will be working with a specific member.

Alias for Selecting Specific Members

Suppose we have a multiple member table called Invoices and each week we segregate the daily invoices by the name of the day. In other words, the Invoice file has members for Sunday, Monday, Tuesday, Wednesday, Thursday, Friday, and Saturday. Since all of these members are less than ten characters these work out fine as member names.

Suppose it is now Friday and we need to perform some special analysis on the Wednesday data member of the Invoice file. Without an alias, there is no way (other than an override database in a CL program) that we can access a file member other than the first member of a file (the natural member that would be selected by default).   The SQL code to provide an alias for Wednesday is as follows:

```
CREATE ALIAS SQLBOOK/WedInvoice   for
SQLBOOK/INVOICE   ( Wednesday )
```

From this point on, WedInvoice can be used in all SQL operations to refer to the Wednesday member of the INVOICE table. The following SQL Select shows how this new "Alias" can be used:

Column Names

Using IBM i SQL, column names can be created initially with long names up to 30 characters.

The first tool that we will examine is another clause of the CREATE TABLE statement. The name of this clause within the CREATE TABLE statement is:

FOR COLUMN

The FOR COLUMN clause of the CREATE TABLE command allows you to specify a short name for your long column names. This short name can be used with all of the IBM i functions that must use the short field names. For those familiar with DDS, it is exactly the opposite. In DDS, you specify the short column and alias the long column. With SQL, you specify the long column and use the FOR COLUMN clause to provide the short alias for the column (field).

To add column names, you can use the following clause when creating the table:

FOR COLUMN Clause

A sample statement to create a two-field inventory master file and then create the equivalent of a large alias field name for each of the two columns, would be the following:

```
CREATE TABLE SQLBOOK/INVENTORY_MASTER4

INVENTORY_NUMBER FOR COLUMN INVNBR
INT NOT NULL WITH DEFAULT,

INVENTORY_ITEM_NAME FOR COLUMN
ITEMNAME VARCHAR ( 50) NOT NULL WITH
DEFAULT)
```

This gives you one column name for each of the two fields in this table.

Adding Column Headings and Field Text

The SQL CREATE TABLE command has no clause to enable text or column headings to be applied to the columns in an SQL table. If you work with native database, then you might expect that the CREATE TABLE, just as the CRTPF command in native with DDS should, with just the same one command be able to place the headings on columns as well as place the text that best describes the column.. However, this cannot be done with one command in SQL.

Those familiar with DDS or who use data warehousing / query products to work against flat files already know that any database worth its salt permits a nice amount of text as well as descriptive column headings within each database table to describe fields. SQL can do this. However, it is not a clause of the CREATE TABLE statement. The SQL tool to use is called:

LABEL ON

For this example, we will create an earnings file with some of the fields well described with text and column headings. We will also provide an alias field definition (EMPLOYEE_NAME) so that you can get a full picture of what you need to do to dress up the insides of your tables. The better dressed, of course, the more ready they are for inquiry and query programs.

Here is the CREATE TABLE statement for a Payroll Earnings file:

```
SQLEARN File
CREATE TABLE SQLBOOK/SQLEARN
(EMPLOYEE_NAME FOR COLUMN EMPNAM  CHAR(35)
          CCSID 37 NOT NULL DEFAULT '' ,

EMPFNAME  CHAR(15)         CCSID 37 NOT NULL DEFAULT '' ,
EMPLNAME  CHAR(20)         CCSID 37 NOT NULL DEFAULT '' ,
EMPINL    CHAR(1)          CCSID 37 NOT NULL DEFAULT '' ,
ACCT#     NUMERIC(6, 0)             NOT NULL DEFAULT 0 ,
EMPAD1    CHAR(35)         CCSID 37 NOT NULL DEFAULT '' ,
EMPAD2    CHAR(40)         CCSID 37 NOT NULL DEFAULT '' ,
CITY      CHAR(20)         CCSID 37 NOT NULL DEFAULT
'WILKES-BARREE',
PAYCOD    CHAR(1)          CCSID 37 DEFAULT NULL ,
RATE      NUMERIC(5, 2) NOT NULL DEFAULT 0 ,
STATUS    CHAR(1)          CCSID 37 NOT NULL DEFAULT '' ,
MGRNO     NUMERIC(6, 0) NOT NULL DEFAULT 0 ,
EMPNO     DECIMAL(6, 0) NOT NULL DEFAULT 0 ,
SALARY    NUMERIC(9, 2) NOT NULL DEFAULT 0 ,
TXTINF    VARCHAR(50)      CCSID 37 NOT NULL DEFAULT '',

Primary Key (EMPNO)  )  ; (semicolon for RUNSQLSTM
use)
```

Before we move on to other topics, let's create one more table that we will be using later in the book. It is called the EMP or Employee table

```
EMP File
CREATE TABLE SQLBOOK/EMP (    EMPNO      CHAR(6)
CCSID 37 NOT NULL ,      FIRSTNME   CHAR(12)       CCSID
37 NOT NULL ,     MIDINIT    CHAR(1)         CCSID 37
NOT NULL ,        LASTNAME   CHAR(15)        CCSID 37
NOT NULL ,        WORKDEPT   CHAR(3)         CCSID 37
DEFAULT NULL ,    PHONENO    CHAR(4)         CCSID 37
DEFAULT NULL ,    HIREDATE   CHAR(8)         CCSID 37
DEFAULT NULL ,    JOB        CHAR(8)         CCSID 37
DEFAULT NULL ,    EDLEVEL    SMALLINT
NOT NULL ,        SEX        CHAR(1)         CCSID 37
DEFAULT NULL ,    BIRTHDATE  DATE
DEFAULT NULL ,    SALARY     DECIMAL(9, 2)
DEFAULT NULL ,    BONUS      DECIMAL(9, 2)
DEFAULT NULL ,    COMM       DECIMAL(9, 2)
DEFAULT NULL ) ;
```

Column Headers

If we were running with the RUNSQLSTM command, we would end the statement with a semicolon as above and we could place the LABEL ON statement immediately following this if we chose.

However, the fact is that you can create a table one day and weeks later you can add the descriptive text with LABEL ON. However, this is not a good method for a database designer to use. An SQL DDL - LABEL ON statement that touches many of these fields and adds column headers to the SQLEARN table is shown below:

```
LABEL ON COLUMN SQLBOOK/SQLEARN

(EMPLOYEE_NAME IS
        'COMPANY              EMPL                  NAME' ,
EMPFNAME IS
        'EMP                  FIRST                 NAME' ,
EMPINL IS
        'EMP                  INIT' ,
ACCT# IS
        'EMP GL               ACCT                  NBR' ,
EMPAD2 IS
        'EMPAD1' ,
PAYCOD IS
        'PAY                  CODE' ,
RATE IS
        'PAY                  RATE' ,
 STATUS IS
        'AC                   REC                   CD' ,
 MGRNO IS
        'MGR                  NBR' ) ;
```

The operative word for each column is the word "IS" This
word means that the text that follows is for the column heading
and it is not to be construed as plain old descriptive text.

If the column headings that you see above are put in as if they
are three 20-character segments of a 60-character string, it is
because that is exactly how this is implemented. For years,
SQL permitted just on column header line but DDS permitted
the headers (used for column headings in reports) to be defined
with three parts – each part being printed on a different line of
the heading of a report. For example The
EMPLOYEE_NAME and EMPFNAME fields would appear
as below as report columns:

COMPANY   **EMP**
EMPL   **FIRST**
NAME   **NAME**

This is in contrast to taking lots of column width on a report by stringing out the text a follows:

COMPANY EMPL NAME   EMP FIRST NAME

Column Text

In addition to being able to dress up the column headings in a table, another form of the LABEL On clause as shown below permits us to add descriptive text to fields in the database to provide documentation as to what each field is all about. The theory here is that the column header is a public notion and may not reflect what the database designer wants to say about any particular element.

```
LABEL ON COLUMN RUNSQLLIB.SQLEARN
( EMPLOYEE_NAME TEXT IS 'COMPANY EMPL NAME' ,
  EMPFNAME       TEXT IS 'EMPLOYEE FIRST NAME' ,
  EMPLNAME       TEXT IS 'EMP LAST NAME' ,
  EMPINL         TEXT IS 'EMPLOYEE INITIAL' ,
  ACCT#          TEXT IS 'GL # FOR EMPLOYEE' ,
  RATE           TEXT IS 'PAY RATE' ,
  STATUS         TEXT IS 'ACTIVE RECORD CODE' ,
  MGRNO          TEXT IS 'MGR NBR' ,
  SALARY         TEXT IS 'EMPLOYEE SALARY' ) ;
```

The operative phrase for each column is in the words "TEXT IS." This phrase differentiates the text message from the heading method. It means that the text that follows is for a description of the field and it is not to be construed as a column heading.

Creating an Index

Indexes are created on existing tables. Unlike DDS, they are not assigned to logical files or views. They are used by the SQL optimizer to locate rows more quickly and efficiently. SQL has an intelligent 'Query Engine" of its own on the IBM i and the engine optimizes its performance by intelligently mapping out the path that it will take to find the data in an SQL request. In many systems, this optimizations scheme, stored with the database, is called an access plan.

Just as the term indicates, it is a plan of attack for SQL queries. When any of the underlying objects that had been a part of any access plan are deleted, a plan may be invalidated by the optimizer. The next time the plan is needed; it invalidates itself and creates a new plan. While creating access plans, the database engine (optimizer) looks for the best indexes to use to optimize the access request.

> Note: A native IBM i logical file is a mechanism that permits "views" of data to be built using DDS. The views are database objects and, just as an SQL view, they provide physical data in a different form from the underlying table.

An SQL index can be built on one or more columns of a table. Each index gets its own name in much the same way as a native logical file. Unlike logical files, however, SQL users do not get to see indexes via SQL. They are just there for the optimizer to speed up SQL queries. Other than for system use, for SQL use, they are "invisible." They are typically created by an IT person serving in the role of a database administrator since all indexes affect performance in one way or another – positively or negatively. A knowing source should always be involved in SQL index creation.

For example, all things being equal, the process of updating a sorted table containing indexes takes more time than updating a sorted table without an index. This is because the indexes also need to be updated. So, it is a good idea to create indexes only on columns that are often used for searches.

Let's say we wanted to create a unique index over our illustrious Vendorp file on the name field. A unique index means that two rows cannot have the same index key contents (value). The syntax of the command would be as follows:

```
CREATE UNIQUE INDEX index_name
ON table_name (column_name)
```

A quick example follows:

```
CREATE UNIQUE INDEX vendori ON VENDORP
(ADDR1 ASC)
```

Result:

Index VENDORI created in SQLBOOK on table VENDORP in SQLBOOK.

Let's continue by creating an index over the SQLEARN table that we built with the CREATE TABLE statement earlier in this chapter. The statement to perform this SQL function and its completion message is as follows:

```
CREATE INDEX SQLBOOK/EARNIDX ON
SQLBOOK/SQLEARN (EMPNO)
```

Index EARNIDX created in SQLBOOK on table SQLEARN in SQLBOOK.

IBM i data management creates a "native" keyed logical file as the home object for the SQL index. In this example, EMPNO is the key with which data will be sorted when using the EARNIDX SQL index. However, if you try to look inside the index itself with either the DSPFD or DSPFFD native commands, you may be surprised that the file EARNIDX looks almost exactly the same as a logical file would that was created with DDS.

There is an indicator in the database file object that it was created as an SQL type Index so, without even going to the schema-wide or system-wide catalog, SQL can tell that this guy is not really a logical file that may be an SQL View. It is in fact, an index. For example, if we were to execute the following command:

```
select * from SQLBOOK/EARNIDX
```

IBM i SQL data management would very quickly notify us that we were trying an illegal operation on the index as you can see in the message I received below:

EARNIDX in SQLBOOK not table, view, or physical file.

It definitely knows!

SQL Table Indexes are Structurally Native Logical Files

Though access as a View via SQL is taboo as shown above, the index file object is available for your use as a native logical file when you use native OS/400 commands. In other words, you can make use of this logical file called EARNIDX as stored in

SQLBOOK with DFU, Query/400, or HLL languages such as RPG and COBOL. When SQL data management creates the index object it takes the fields that exist in the table object and it makes them all part of the internal logical file and it gives the logical the keyed access path as specified for the SQL index. All the fields that exist in the based on physical table are thus included in the nave form of the index, a logical file /view. Though they are not usable to SQL, they are however, very usable to native methods and this can mean a lot.

IBM is moving the IBM i database to an SQL orientation though admittedly it will take a long time. That is a given. So, why would IBM give the Index object more power for native than for SQL? By permitting the SQL index object to actually be used as a bona fide logical file in native mode, IBM gives the native programmer (most IBM i shops) the opportunity to use the same key-based record at a time program operations against the Index object as could be done with a logical file with all fields projected.

Therefore, it helps IBM to make it easier for IBM i shops to change their data definition language to SQL's DDL from DDS. If all the tables were SQL instead of DDS today, the job for IBM would be half over. That's where Big Blue is heading.

The SQL View and the Create View Statement

Now, it's time to take a look at the last SQL object that we will be covering in this chapter – the SQL View. Check out the code to create a view on the IBM i using the longer notation:

```
CREATE VIEW SQLBOOK/EARN_PROJECTION
(EMPFNAME, EMPLNAME, EMPINL, EMPAD1,
EMPAD2, CITY)
AS SELECT
   EMPFNAME,
   EMPLNAME ,
   EMPINL,
   EMPAD1,
   EMPAD2,
   CITY
FROM SQLBOOK/SQLEARN
```

This view will be created in the SQLBOOK schema. Of course
if you would prefer not to be long-winded as in the definition of
the SQL View above, you can eliminate the first projection with
a shorter statement that does the same thing. You can then use
the results of the select as needed:

```
CREATE VIEW SQLBOOK/EARN_PROJECTION
AS SELECT
EMPFNAME,
EMPLNAME,
EMPINL,
EMPAD1,
EMPAD2,
CITY
FROM SQLBOOK/SQLEARN

View EARN_PROJECTION created in
SQLBOOK.
```

An SQL View is a virtual table. It is based on the result-set of a
SELECT statement. It is like a native logical file and in fact, a
logical file is created whenever you create a view. Unlike a

native logical file, however, an SQL View cannot be built with a key. It contains rows and columns, just like a real table. In fact it contains fields from one or more real tables in the database. A View can span multiple tables – up to 32.

You can add SQL functions to a view by using the WHERE, and JOIN clause which we will be examining more in Chapter 14. The View presents data to the user or to a program through the view as if the data were coming from a single table – regardless of how many tables make up the view.

The database design and structure of the underlying physical data is not affected by the functions, where, or join statements in a View.
As you can see from the introductory CREATE VIEW functional statement above, the Create View has its own unmistakable syntax as follows:

Create a View – Syntax

```
CREATE VIEW view_name AS
   SELECT column_name(s)
   FROM table_name
   WHERE condition
```

A simple example view follows:

```
CREATE VIEW SQLBOOK/vendorv
   AS SELECT *
   FROM vendorp
   WHERE balowe > 500
```

View vendorv created in SQLBOOK

You may recall in Chapter 5 that we created this view as an early example. Once you create a view, you can treat it as if it were a table itself and get additional query power from the SELECT statement as follows:

```
Select * from vendorv where SRVRTG = 'R'
```

Figure 8-4 SQL Query Against a View

```
                        Display Data
                                Data width . . . . . . :       134
Position to line  . . . . .        Shift to column  . . . . . .
....+....1....+....2....+....3....+....4....+....5....+....6....+....7....+..
..
VNDNBR   NAME                      ADDR1                    CITY
    48   Denton and Ball           7934 S SCRANTON AVE      SCRANTON
    26   Lockhart Machinaws        45 Ginzo Lane            Wokegon
    30   Detweiller Controls       45 Fognetta Place        Kernstin
********   End of data   ********



                                                           Bottom
F3=Exit       F12=Cancel      F19=Left      F20=Right      F21=Split
```

The table shown in Figure 8-4 is the result of the simple select against the view Vendorv. The view is the object that actually provides the selection of records with SRVRTG of 'R' even though the SRVRTG field is not shown in the panel. You would have to hit F20 to shift the data to see it.

Now, let's review the simple view of the Vendorp file from above that we first created in Chapter 5. To make it more convenient, we repeat the coding for the view below:

```
CREATE VIEW vendorv
   AS SELECT *
   FROM vendorp
   WHERE balowe > 500
```

The Essence of a View

The creation of a view in essence is the same as running an SQL Select query and then saying that is a great query, then memorializing the SELECT statement by packaging it in the operative form of an permanent SQL object   Since we have not spent much time discussing the SELECT statement at this time it is still obvious in this simple language that this select uses the WHERE clause. The Where clause is SQL's way of limiting the rows returned in an SQL query. As you would expect from the code, only a subset of the rows in the Vendor table will be returned by the Select statement in this View.

Once we create the view, as shown above, operations on it are similar if not mostly identical to operations performed on SQL tables. If we choose to perform a Select on this view later in the month, or later next year, by having saved the View, we can later treat it as if the View is a table by itself:. In the example below, we execute the view from a more populated version of Vendorp.

SELECT * from SQLBOOK/VENDORV

Figure 8-4 Returned Data from a Select upon a View

```
                                 Display Data
                                          Data width . . . . . . :
  Position to line  . . . . .              Shift to column  . . . . . .
  ....+....1....+....2....+....3 |  .9....+...10....+...11....+...12....+.
  VNDNBR    NAME                 |   ZIPCD  VNDCLS  VNDSTS       BALOWE
      48    DENTON AND BALL      | 18,504     20      A         3,500.00
      25    A MACHINE CORP.      | 45,903     10      A         7,500.00
      26    B MACHINERY          | 23,657     20      A         1,495.55
      30    D CONTROLS           | 45,793     20      A           900.25
   7,020    Sun MicroSystems     | 95,054     10      A         8,000.00
   8,030    Phillies Phinest     | 18,702     20      A        35,700.00
   8,020    Bings Music          | 58,702     20      A        79,700.00
  ********    End of data    ********
```

One of the first things that you may notice in Figure 8-4, is that this select has returned only those records (rows, tuples) in which the balance owed is in fact greater than $500.00. [Note: We used a split screen technique in SQL to show the right side while freezing the number and name columns.] If you look further, you will notice that the data is in no particular sequence. That is another feature of SQL. Unless you say to order (sequence) the data by something, it comes back the way SQL wants, not necessarily the way you may want it. We examine the ORDER BY clause with select in the next section below.

SQL Views cannot be built with keys (indexes) on the IBM i or any other SQL machine that conforms to the SQL standard. With SQL you create your Views and then you create indexes as separate objects, as we did at the beginning of this chapter. The indexes are created over the base tables, however. There is no relationship between the view and the index other than that the view may reference a table that uses an index as a performance helper.

When you make an SQL request to access the SQL View, it is the SQL query optimizer's job to find an index to use to access your data through the specified SQL View. If the optimizer finds an appropriate index, your query runs faster. If it doesn't find one, it doesn't run any faster; regardless of whether you use the ORDER BY or not. You can do nothing to make the query use an index. That is the nature of SQL.

"Order By" Clause -- Projection / Selection of a View

The Order By clause is used to retrieve data in a specified sequence. For example, we could use an order by clause in the example in Figure 8-4, and we could sort the data on vendor name. For our purposes, let's go back to the Vendorv view and let's provide a simple select statement with a subset of fields and let's add the Order By on it.

Type in this statement as follows:

```
SELECT name, balowe, vndcls
 FROM sqlbook/vendorv
 WHERE vndcls = 20
 ORDER BY balowe DESC

SELECT statement run complete.
```

This statement projects three fields from the Vendorv View, further selects records for VNDCLS of 20 [Note: the Vendorv view selected balowe > 500.00] and the statement then uses the Order By to sort the balance owed column in descending sequence. Ascending is the default. The results of this Order By SQL is shown in Figure 8-5.

Figure 8-5 Order By Clause Descending on BALOWE

```
                          Display Data
                     Data width . . . . . . :        48
Position to line   . . . . .     Shift to column  . . . . . .
....+....1....+....2....+....3....+....4....+...
NAME                             BALOWE    VNDCLS
Bings Music                   79,700.00      20
Phillies Phinest              35,700.00      20
Denton and Ball                3,500.00      20
Lockhart Machinaws             1,495.55      20
Detweiller Controls              900.25      20
********   End of data   ********



Bottom
F3=Exit        F12=Cancel       F19=Left       F20=Right
F21=Split
```

Dropping (Deleting) SQL objects

In this chapter, we have proven that SQL can create lots of good stuff. In IT whenever there is a facility that can create stuff that resides on a disk drive and therefore takes space, you can count on there also being a way to free up that space with a statement designed to get rid of created things. The statement name to do that in SQL is not the DELETE; it is the word highlighted immediately below:

DROP

So, what are the things we can drop / remove with the drop statement and how do we use the various commands. Rather than list the objects and then show you how to delete them using DROP, the DROP commands are so short that I can list both the statement and the object below and intuitively you will know how to delete all of the SQL object types that we studied in this chapter. In fact, to make it more real, let's use object names that we have created this chapter.

```
DROP  COLLECTION  SQLBOOK
DROP  SCHEMA  SQLBOOK
DROP  TABLE  SQLBOOK/Vendorp
DROP  INDEX   SQLBOOK/EARNIDX
DROP  ALIAS  SQLBOOK/WEDINVOICE
DROP  VIEW  SQLBOOK/VENDORV
DROP  DISTINCT  TYPE  TYPENAME
```

OK, we did not yet cover the DISTINCT Type so when we do, you now know how to delete it.

Collection / Schema Considerations

Before you drop a schema, exercise due caution. When a schema is deleted, all objects in the collection are also deleted. Moreover, when you drop the Schema, all dependent objects – views, indexes, foreign key constraints, etc. that reference a table being dropped --- are also dropped. The only way to get them back is with a backup tape.

There is a technique that can be used with a DROP SCHEMA that minimizes your exposure to an inadvertent delete. The drop schema has a keyword called RESTRICT that can assure that the Schema and its associate objects are not deleted unless all objects have first been removed from the schema. If you use this option, you are forcing yourself to examine all of the objects before you eliminate them all. When data is critical and its reconstruction would be problematic, the RESTRICT option is a very good idea.

The keyword gets added to the end of the statement as in the following:

DROP SCHEMA SQLBOOK Restrict

SQL Object Naming Guidelines

In Chapter 16 we delve head-on into the notion of entities and entity relationships. We know that tables represent the instances of an entity. Take vendor information as an example. You store all your vendor information in a table, perhaps even several tables. Here, 'vendor' is an entity and all the rows in the vendor table represent the instances of the entity 'vendor'. So, why not name your table using the entity it represents, 'VENDOR'.

There are those who would argue that such a table is storing 'multiple instances' of vendors, so you should make your table name a plural word, such as Vendors, not Vendor. The most prevailing notion in this regard, however is that the database represents a set of data by definition and there is just one "set," and thus the name should be singular. With that in mind, consider

- ✓ Naming your vendor table as "Vendor"
- ✓ Naming your order table as "Order"
- ✓ Naming your item table as "Item"

If your database deals with different logical functions and you want to group your tables according to the logical group they belong to, consider prefixing your table name with a two or three character prefix that can identify the group of tables as being related in some way.

For example, your database has tables which store information about your Sales department, you could name all your tables related to Sales department as shown below:

- ✓ SLS_Leads
- ✓ SLS_Regions
- ✓ SLS_RegionsManagers

For transaction files in which you build "junction tables" that are used to provide a physical transaction record for each instance of a many-to-many relationship within base tables, you might consider a multi-part name. An Example of this would be a "Student_Class' file in which many students take one particular class and many classes can be taken by one student. When a student enrolls in a class, a transaction occurs and the naming for that transaction table should reflect its purpose.

Since Views are often a combination of two tables based on a join condition, representing two or more entities, consider combining the names of both the base tables. For example, if there is a view combining two tables "Vendor" and "Addresses," name the view as 'Vendror_Addresses."

For field names, many experts like the idea of adding about a three character prefix or suffix to each column in a table to help differentiate the data names when they are used in a program or procedures.

Here are ten additional thoughts for establishing SQL table and index naming conventions.

1. Avoid using the object type as part of the object name. For example, do not use the words FILE, TABLE, or INDEX as part of the name.

2. Use the table name and a suffix for SQL indexes. With SQL, you do not need to be concerned about the length of the name, as indexes cannot be specified in an SQL statement. SQLEARNIDX in this scenario would easily be recognized as an SQL index over SQLEARN. Obviously, it is not a good idea in practice to include the name SQL in your names unless you are differentiating such objects from native objects.

3. Avoid overly complicated, long names for tables or other database objects.

4. Be careful using 'Mixed case' names instead of using underscores to separate two words of a name so that you can assure that all developers are consistent with case through out their code. Though this does not really matter on IBM i, there are case sensitive SQL Servers. Having to guess the case of a character in a name is an extra burden for developers.

5. Use underscores only between the prefix/suffix and the actual object name.

6. Do not break the name of an object with underscores

7. Do not use spaces within the name of database objects. IBM i uses spaces as delimiters.

8. Do not use reserved words for naming my database objects. You will either get poor or unpredictable results

9. If you plan to implement over multiple databases, find out the lowest common denominator names and attributes that will work. In most databases and file systems, the first character of a name must be a letter, while subsequent characters may be letters, digits, or _ (underscore). There are DBMS packages out there that allow $, #, @ -- but so far, no DBMS has been inclined to allows all three. Even when special characters allowed, they are not allowed in all instances. For example, Microsoft attaches special meaning to names that begin with @ or # and Oracle discourages special characters in the names of certain objects.

10. If you plan to implement over multiple databases, also be aware of the differences in data typing and length. All SQLs are not equal and the IBM i has grown up substantially in data typing over the last few years. Length is very inconsistent, For example, for columns, constraints, and tables, Microsoft permits 128 across the board, whereas Oracle has traditionally been 30 across the board and IBM is 30, 18, and 128 respectively. For field names, a nice oracle convention is to prefix the fieldname with a 2 or 3 character contraction of the table name

Qualifying SQL Object Names

You have the option of qualifying SQL objects with the Schema name or choosing to use defaults. If you use defaults when you create a new SQL object (do not use qualified library name with the object name) what happens when you create the object? Which schema does it go in? It actually goes into the schema that is in your current library.

Current Library

What is a current library? When each user on the IBM i signs on, they are assigned a current library for the work that they are about to commence. If that library name were SQLTEST, then that is the default library in which the SQL object, say the

VENDORX Table will be created. See Figure 8-6 for a look at the notion of a library list.

Let's run this command in interactive SQL or with RUNSQLSTM and see what we get:

CREATE Table   SQLTEST/VENDORX ….

Table VENDORX in SQLTEST created but could not be journaled.

As you can see, the file is created in the current library, SQLTEST is the library in this case.

All Libraries Are Not Schemas

All libraries are not schemas. This says a few things. First of all, it says that the VENDORX table was created in a "schema" called SQLTEST. However, it also says that the schema was not a real SQL-built schema; it was a plain old library. Since it was not really a schema, SQL could not update the schema-wide catalog since it did not exist and SQL could not cause journaling to begin on the new database object because the proper artifacts of a schema did not exist in the SQLTEST library.

When an SQL Table Is Created

By now, you have been well introduced to the notion of a physical file and the idea that an SQL table when created becomes a IBM i physical file. This is all true, but there is a lot more that happens when the file object is created through SQL. These things include the following:

1. The schema- wide catalog is updated if it exists along with the system-wide catalog.

2. The file is marked specially as an SQL table to differentiate it from those created with DDS or other means.

3. The file is built with just one member, the name of which is the same as the table. As with all physical files, the default member that is used, unless an override is in effect, is always the first member.

4. The record format name is the same as the file name. This is a major departure from DDS and in some languages such as RPG/400, this can cause some issues during compilation.

5. The table has no maximum size.

6. The file is automatically journaled, providing there is a schema. Both before and after journal images are performed.

7. The database management system automatically reuses deleted records or holes in the database without the user having to perform reorganize functions.

The Primary Key Constraint

IBM i SQL has grown up quite a bit and will continue to grow up over the next several years until it has all of the function of all of the other SQLs in the industry including all of the DB2 versions. Many enhancements have been made to the product in recent years including the primary key clause of the CREATE TABLE command.

Its format is as follows:

```
Primary Key (field1, field2...)
```

Figure 8-1 shows the primary key constraint within the SQL DDL used to create the Vendorp table. This constraint does two things. First of all, it enforces the relational database primary key rule. Secondly, it builds a unique index over the primary key that can be used in a high level program. Ted Codd's primary key rule applied to the Vendorp file says basically that no two rows will have the same vendor number. This identifier will serve as a unique identifier for each row.

The Primary key clause for the vendor file is repeated below:

Primary Key (VNDNBR)

As a free format language, SQL does not care if you use multiple lines for a statement as well as multiple blanks between words. Most examples that you see, however, show a style that appears to be very rigid and very same, not very flexible. Although the rigid style, especially in DDL is very evident in training examples end in most implementations, it is not required. It does, however, make statements much easier to read than an unaligned stream of text. Thus, I suggest you continue with the style as shown in Figure 8-1.

You may have noticed already that SQL is not case sensitive. You can type create table or Create Table and it means the same. The AS/400 operating system likes upper shift; yet it too permits lower shift to be entered. But, when it stores the characters that are typed, unless they are quoted strings, it stores them in upper case. When it displays them, it displays in upper case even though you can reference the VENDORP file as the vendorp file and still get a hit.

The Notion of "Null"

In the description of the vendor file shown in Figure 8-1, you may have noticed the word null. It follows the word "NOT" as in the line below:

```
VNDNBR        NUMERIC(5,0)        NOT NULL,
```

The VNDNBR field has also been selected as the primary key, which is by definition, is not allowed to be null. When a field is defined to be able to accept null values, it means that there will be times that the column has no value for that particular record. An example would be a student record in a class test grade list in which the student was absent for the test and did not receive a zero. If the student received a zero, it would be averaged into the class average.

However if the student has yet to take the exam or was excused entirely from the exam, that student's record would not be included in the class average. Thus a null has more implications than a blank or a zero and because there could be numerous nulls in a primary key field if they were permitted, it would violate the primary key rule and therefore, they are not permitted.

The Library Search List

The library search list is a phenomenon unique to the IBM i. It has some of the capabilities of a path statement in DOS. Basically, it is a mechanism for avoiding searching the whole system for unqualified objects (objects not specified with a library name). It is a job phenomenon, not a fixed object on the IBM i. In other words, when you sign on to he IBM i a job starts on your behalf. Every job has a library list supplied by an object called a job description. When you submit a batch job or a procedure on the IBM i, the submit function supplies a job description with a library list that cane be overridden by the

Submit command itself or it can be changed within the job stream with a change job CL command (CHGJOB).

Figure 8-6 The Library Search List

```
                    Display Library List
                                        System:    SYSTEM3
Type options, press Enter.
 5=Display objects in library

                        ASP
Opt Library     Type    Device    Text
    QSYS        SYS               System Library
    QSYS2       SYS               System Library for CPI's
    QHLPSYS     SYS
    QUSRSYS     SYS               System Library for Users
    SQLTEST     CUR
    QGPL        USR               General Purpose Library
    QTEMP       USR
                                                    Bottom
3=Exit    F12=Cancel    F17=Top    F18=Bottom
C) COPYRIGHT IBM CORP. 1980, 2003.
```

Display Library List

The panel shown in Figure 8-6 is the result of a command that is executed interactively on a IBM i most often from the command line but it could be embedded in a program. The command is DSPLIBL. That's it. The IBM i verb to display anything is DSP, the IBM i adjective or noun for library is LIB, and the IBM i shortcut for list is L. Once the command is processed, it returns the current library list.

Three Parts to a Library List

As you can see in the display shown in Figure 8-6, there are three parts to a library list. There is the system library list, the current library and the user library list. There can be 250 objects listed in all of the parts of a library list but normally there are less than 25. When you ask for an object by name, the IBM i dutifully searches every library from those specified in the system library list to the current library to the user library list. When the name is not located, the system returns a message saying object not found.

For SQL Select commands, for example, the system will search the entire list for the tables or views that are requested. However, for SQL create commands, the system checks the current library to be sure that the object does not exist and then it creates it in the current library. Each user on the system can have a different current library but often the current library is set up as the same for all users of a major group.

Current Library

It is fun to learn about all of the advanced notions of the IBM i but there is enough material to write a huge book so I am trying to simplify the notion of IBM i work management without burdening you to understand it all. However, I could not skip the topic. When you run the RUNSQLSTM command or the interactive SQL facility, the library list that exists in your job is the list of libraries where the SQL functions will look for SQL objects if you do not qualify the object name.

When you create a new object and you do not specify the library name as a qualifier, it will be built in your current library. That is important if you are trying to find these objects after a successful RUNSQLSTM run or a successful ISQL session in which you created SQL objects.

The Library Qualifier

When you choose to use the library qualifier, as we discussed regarding the RUNSQLSTM CL command, you must be careful within in the source file to use the proper naming convention for library qualifier. To qualify an object such as Vendorp as living in the SQLBOOK library, it would be qualified as follows using System naming and SQL naming.

SQLBOOK/VENDORP   **System naming**
SQLBOOK.VENDORP   **SQL Naming**

Proper Naming SYS or SQL?

Both the RUNSQLSTM command, as well as the STRSQL command used to invoke interactive SQL (ISQL), have lots of other options that you should check out when you have a chance by typing the command and hitting F4 on a command line.

Another option worth noting for both is the naming convention. With the naming parameter you choose the System (SYS) or SQL (SQL) option of naming. When you choose the SQL style for naming references, you specify your source SQL for library and file with a period (.).

The System option, like all IBM i commands that reference a library uses a slash (/) as a separator. This is something of which you must be aware when you are typing in your source or it will be interpreted improperly by the SQL statement analyzer.

The CL Override Command

One of the most powerful facilities in the command language that drives the IBM i at the command level is the override with database file command. OVRDBF. This command has lots of facility. Just as the system job structure has the notion of a library list, it also has a list of overrides to named objects. So, let's say for example that the Vendorp file and another file, say the VENDORX file are exactly the same.

Let's say that one has new vendor data and one has old vendor data. If the RPG or COBOL program is written to use the Vendorp file but at execution time, you may want to use the VENDORX file instead, you can issue an override database file command that looks like the one below from the command line.

The override stays in effect until it is deleted or the job ends. It can be issued within the CL program that processes the RUNSQLSTM command, or the CL program that drives the HLL programs that contains the embedded SQL.

The command would look like this:

```
OVRDBF FILE(VENDORP)
TOFILE(SQLBOOK/VENDORX)
```

Multiple Member Files and SQL

When the command processor is getting ready to open the file in the program it checks the override list and finds that VENDORP should not be used, VENDORX should be used and it goes ahead and uses it dynamically. For SQL and multi-member files, this command also comes in handy. If you have a member called OLDVEND in the VENDORX file that you want to use, rather than the first member called VENDOR, the override can specify which member you wish to use. This command would look like the following:

```
OVRDBF FILE(VENDORP)
TOFILE(SQLBOOK/VENDORX) MBR(OLDVEND)
```

In V5R2, IBM added a member name clause to the CREATE ALIAS command so now; you can actually create an alias for each member that you want to use without the OVRDBF command. The ALIAS is a permanent object and whenever it is used the member selected is not variable.

Chapter Summary

Placing the SQL Create or the DROP verb in front of any of the following SQL object types will be your entrée into creating that object in the schema or creating the schema itself. It is also your entrée into deleting the schema or deleting any of the SQL objects within a schema.

* ALIAS
* COLLECTION
* INDEX
* SCHEMA
* TABLE
* VIEW

SQL gives long names to all of the objects that it creates and it uses the first five characters of the long name plus a five digit suffix to build a short name for IBM i internal use. There are examples shown in this chapter to help you be able to change the short names or the long names of these objects.

One of the most time consuming job in using SQL databases is creating them. Care must be taken for every entity that is created as a table. All of the attributes (fields) need to be defined exactly on the Create Table command with the proper name, length and data type. If the name is a long name, internally the name is shortened for native use. You can also change this name with a RENAME command. When you select a length, depending on the data type, the column may actually take less or more space than you expect.

Therefore it helps to understand the data types that can be selected for the columns you define. If you need math to be performed on a column value, for example, choose one of the numeric data types. If you need decimal places, choose the numeric type, the decimal type or one of the floating point (real) types depending on your intended use. If the field is to contain a date, time, or timestamp value, code its data type accordingly.

IBM has enhanced SQL in V5R2 with a capability that permits alias names to be assigned to members. This may be a better option for you than using the OVRDBF command in CL prior to using the member at execution time.

Table indexes are for performance only with SQL. However, if you use the primary key clause in creating a table, SQL will build an index on the primary key and the physical file underneath will behave as a keyed physical file just as if it were created with DDS. If you are switching to DDL from DDS, this is good to know.

The For Column clause enables you to rename your short column names to make them more meaningful for native DB operations. The Label On Column statement is very handy in getting both column heading and text information into the table object to betted describe a column.

When you have Select operations that you want to permanently capture so they can be used by anybody in the organization, it is good to create a View. Once you create a View, which is structured as a logical file with no key, you can use that View in further SQL queries or you may embed the View into a program just as if it were an SQL table.

The default sequence for any SQL operation without an explicit Order By clause is indeterminate. Thus the Order By clause is very valuable in providing data to your views, queries, or programs in the proper sequence.

Though, you can name any of your objects anything that you want to the length limits, it is good to think about your naming convention so that it is easier to work with your SQL objects and their attributes. When you qualify object names with the schema (library) name, you must use the format of the STRSQL, STRQM, RUNSQLSTM or the HLL precompiler you are using. You can either use the System option (/) or the SQL option (.) of naming. If you pick the wrong option, it will give you a bad day.

The Library Search List is a structure that is job oriented on the IBM i but it can have an effect on your SQL in any of the four faces. If you do not qualify your SQL objects, then you are at the mercy of the library list as to where SQL finds your objects and where it creates them.

Key Chapter Terms

Alias
Batch job
Bigint
Binary
Blob
Case sensitivity
Char
Character
CHGJOB
CL program
Clob
Column headings
Column names
Column text
Compile
Create alias
Create Table
Create View
Creating Index
CRTPF
Current library
Data types
Datalink
Date
DB design
DBClob

Views
Virtual table
Zoned decimal

Exercises

Use this chapter or look up information on the Web to answer the following:

1. Name the SQL object types that can be created or dropped?

2. Is there a difference in the default naming for objects with long names from the native to the SQL environment? If so, What Is the difference?

3. Name seven data types that you can see using in SQL and give a description of the data type and your reasons for choosing each of the seven types.

4. What does the SQL Create Table statement do?

5. Write the SQL to Create a table named Customer_Static_Information with about eight data columns. Be sure to use the For Column clause with some of the fields. Explain what the For Column clause does. Assign a primary key. Create the table in the YOURSQL schema you created in the Chapter 7 exercises.

6. Write the SQL to change the short column names that were produced for some of e long column names. Why is this a good idea?

7. Write the SQL to add column headers and text to the fields you defined in your customer file.

8. What are the Date, Time, and Timestamp data types and why would you use them.

9. Write the SQL to create an Alias for a table on your system called "THIS_IS_A_LONG_TABLE_NAME"

10. Write the SQL for Creating an Index on your customer file

11. Write the SQL to create a view over the customer file that includes just five fields and includes a Where clause.

12. Write down the full system commands to display the customer file information, the field information, the member list, and the data from the file.

13. When you execute a DSPPFM command against this new customer file will any data appear on the report?

14. Write the SQL to perform a select against the customer view you created. Project and select the data even further and order it by customer name.

15. What do you have to be concerned about when you are dropping a schema?

16. Why are some SQL objects not journaled when they are created?

17. Explain the notion of the primary key constraint.

18. Explain the notion of "Null"

19. What is a library search list and what bearing does it have on an SQL environment.

20. Write the full command to display a library list? The command to intelligently modify a library list is EDTLIBL. Type in this command on your AS/400 and create a printout of the first panel for submission Add YOURSQL library to the list.

21. Write the full command to display a library list? Is there an extra library in the list? If so, what is its name?

22. What are the three parts to a library list?

23. What function does the CL command to "override a database with" provide? Why would you use it?

24. Write the command that would enable you to use an add physical file member command to add a member called Member2 to the customer table you created in step X

25. Write the CL to override the customer file so that you will be using the Member2 set of data rather than the default member.

26. Write the SQL command that creates an alias for the Member 2 file so that the override in Exercise 25 does not have to be executed.

Chapter 9   Interactive SQL (ISQL)

Interactive v. Batch

An interactive SQL facility is associated with every database manager. Essentially, every interactive SQL facility is an SQL application program that reads statements from a terminal, prepares and executes them dynamically, and displays the results to the user. Such SQL statements are said to be issued interactively.

The interactive facilities for DB2 UDB for IBM i are invoked by any of the following commands / interfaces:

STRSQL   **Start Interactive SQL**
STRQM   **Start Query Manager**
SQL Script **IBM i Navigator**

Unlike the RUNSQLSTM command facility that depends on SQL statements being first entered in a source file, the Interactive SQL facility (ISQL) is fully interactive. There is no batch process as in RUNSQLSTM. You can do what you want, when you want it "on the fly" – as long as it's SQL that you are using.

It is by far the greatest testing tool for SQL on the IBM i. It comes with the SQL product, DB2/400 Query Manager and SQL Development Kit LICPGM (5722-ST1) and once it is installed, it is like the Energizer Bunny. It keeps going and going and going...

Like just about all aspects of SQL, as a powerful development language it is intended for programmers & database administrators. It is used mostly for testing SQL DML statements before they are deployed. When you get it right with ISQL, you can copy / paste your ISQL session results into a source file for safe keeping.

Unless your work is ad hoc, most of the time, you will be placing the SQL statements from your SQL interactive session inside an RPG, COBOL, or C program for implementation.

Interactive SQL has been used by many for DDL though this is not recommended. It works but the information about the object activity is deleted when the interactive workspace is cleared. So, even though the temptation is there to "just do it," take the time with DDL and use the RUNSQLSTM for all your SQL creates to avoid having to say you're sorry.

Static SQL vs. Dynamic SQL

No discussion of SQL is complete without covering the notion of static and dynamic SQL. Basically the difference is in the name. Static SQL is fixed and mostly unchangeable whereas dynamic SQL is provided or can be provided on the fly during execution.

Static SQL

The source form of a static SQL statement is embedded within an application program written in a host language such as COBOL. It does not change during execution or after. The statement is prepared before the program is executed and the operational form of the statement persists beyond the execution of the program.

The key point is that a source program containing static SQL statements must be processed by an SQL precompiler before it is compiled. The precompiler performs a lot of functions long before the program is executed. For example, it checks the syntax of the SQL statements to assure they are correct. Then it takes the source statements and changes them into host language comments. Finally, it generates host language statements to call the database manager.

When we cover program development in Chapter 13, you will see the steps in running programs with embedded static SQL. Again the first step is the preparation of the program with the static SQL statements. The second step is pre-compilation, and the final setup before execution is the full compilation of the modified source program.

Dynamic SQL

A dynamic SQL statement is prepared during the execution of an SQL application. The operational form of the statement persists until the last SQL program leaves the call stack. When the call stack is empty, that SQL is gone.

The source form of the statement is a character string that is passed to the database manager by the program using the static SQL statement PREPARE or EXECUTE IMMEDIATE. These are examined in Chapter 13.

SQL statements that are submitted to the interactive SQL facility that we are now exploring are also dynamic SQL statements as are those executed by the RUNSQLSTM command and Query Manager.

Extended Dynamic SQL

There is a notion called extended dynamic SQL statement that is neither fully static nor fully dynamic. On the IBM i, there is an API called QSQPRCED that provides users with extended dynamic SQL capability. Like dynamic SQL, statements can be prepared, described, and executed using this API. Unlike dynamic SQL, however, SQL statements prepared into a package by this API persist until the package or statement is explicitly dropped.

DML and ISQL

The major DML statements that ere used with Interactive SQL are as follows:

SELECT
INSERT
UPDATE
DELETE

There is no question that Select is the most popular of the DML statements. Therefore, the bulk of this chapter is devoted to helping you get a very good feel for this most powerful operator. So, what we are going to do in the next few panels is start ISQL and get ourselves ready to run some interactive Select statements followed by other DML statements. Then in Chapter 13, we will demonstrate how to put some of those select and update statements into some RPG and COBOL code to see how IBM i high level languages work with embedded SQL.

Start Interactive SQL ISQL

Technically the command to start an SQL interactive session is called Start Structured Query Language. However, most users say that they are using Interactive SQL (ISQL). This command starts the interactive SQL program with default parameters unless they are changed. The program starts the statement entry of the interactive SQL program which immediately shows the Enter SQL Statements display. This display allows you to build, edit, enter, and run a SQL statement in an interactive environment. Any messages during the running of the program are shown immediately on this display.

The IBM i command that kicks off an ISQL session on the IBM i is as follows:

STRSQL

As in all IBM i commands, including the RUNSQLSTM command, there are a number of options of which you should be aware prior to using the command. Several of the most important parameters of the SQL command are shown below in Figure 9-1, along with an explanation as to what function or facility the parameter provides.

When you type the STRSQL command, and you press F4 from the command line, prior to the session starting, you will see all of the options for the STRSQL command. These are shown in Figure 9-1. You can change any of these options prior to starting your session.

Figure 9-1 Prompted STRSQL – The Option Parameters

```
                    Start SQL Interactive Session (STRSQL)

Type choices, press Enter.

Commitment control . . . . . . .   *NONE        *NONE, *CHG, *CS, *ALL...
Naming convention  . . . . . . .   *SYS         *SYS, *SQL
Statement processing . . . . . .   *RUN         *RUN, *VLD, *SYN
Library option . . . . . . . . .   *LIBL        Name, *LIBL, *USRLIB...
List type  . . . . . . . . . . .   *ALL         *ALL, *SQL
Data refresh . . . . . . . . . .   *ALWAYS      *ALWAYS, *FORWARD
Allow copy data  . . . . . . . .   *YES         *YES, *OPTIMIZE, *NO
Date format  . . . . . . . . . .   *JOB         *JOB, *USA, *ISO, *EUR...
Date separator character . . . .   *JOB         *JOB, /, ., ,, -, ' ',
  *BLANK
Time format  . . . . . . . . . .   *HMS         *HMS, *USA, *ISO, *EUR, *JIS
Time separator character . . . .   *JOB         *JOB, :, ., ,, ' ', *BLANK
Decimal point  . . . . . . . . .   *JOB         *JOB, *PERIOD, *COMMA...
Sort sequence  . . . . . . . . .   *JOB         Name, *HEX, *JOB, *JOBRUN...
  Library  . . . . . . . . . . .                Name, *LIBL, *CURLIB
Language identifier  . . . . . .   *JOB         *JOB, *JOBRUN...


                                                                   Bottom
F3=Exit    F4=Prompt    F5=Refresh    F12=Cancel    F13=How to use this display
F24=More keys
```

Commitment Control

This STRSQL parameter specifies whether SQL statements are run under commitment control in this ISQL session.

Naming Convention

This parameter specifies the naming convention used for SQL objects for this ISQL session. The options are the same as RUNSQLSTM:

*SYS -- The system naming convention (library-name/file-name) is used.
*SQL -- The SQL naming convention (schema-name.table-name) is used.

Statement Processing

This STRSQL parameter specifies what values are used to process the statements. Should the SQL be run, or just checked?

*RUN -- The statements are syntax checked, data checked, and then run.
*VLD -- The statements are syntax checked and data checked but not run.
*SYN -- The statements are syntax checked only.

The ISQL Main Panel

When you hit Enter, you are taken to a panel that looks similar to the command processing menu (QCMD) for CL commands on the IBM i. This panel is shown in Figure 9-2.

Figure 9-2 The ISQL Main Panel

```
                         Enter SQL Statements

Type SQL statement, press Enter.
  > CREATE VIEW SQLBOOK/VENDORV AS SELECT *  FROM SQLBOOK/VENDORP
    WHERE BALOWE> 500
    VENDORV in SQLBOOK type *FILE already exists.
    Session was saved and started again.
    Current connection is to relational database S999777K.
===>  _____
      _____
      _____
      _____
      _____
      _____
      _____
      _____
      _____
      _____
                                                      Bottom
F3=Exit    F4=Prompt   F6=Insert line   F9=Retrieve   F10=Copy line
F12=Cancel             F13=Services     F24=More keys
```

The first thing that you should notice in Figure 9-2 is that there is already stuff on the display. Where did that come from? It came from "my" last ISQL session. There are a number of ways to exit ISQL.

I always exit with the Save session option so that all of the good work I did in a prior session is there when I come back. Of course, sometimes I blindly pick another option and the command manager very nicely wipes out my whole workspace.

If you have worked with CL command panels in the past, you are already familiar with how SQL works. It is not completely the same but it is very similar. For example, you can hit F9 and bring down the last command that you ran, change it or leave it alone and run it again.

You can also go way back using the roll up key to work you did several months ago and you can press F9 next to a complicated SQL statement that you were able to make work then and the system will bring it back for you so you can change it or run it again, or at any stage, you can copy and paste it into a program.

From the SQL command line you can type in any SQL statement and press ENTER. It will execute immediately and provide feedback on the results. Sometimes it may even bring back a report depending on what you are doing. If you are just learning the syntax of SQL, you will find the Prompter most helpful.

Let's try it now. Position your cursor on the first line of the portion of the ISQL panel that is available for entry (by the --> arrow). Then, hit Command Key 4 (PF4). You will get page 1 of the main prompter panel as shown n Figure 9-3

Since most of our work in ISQL will be DML and mostly we will be using the SELECT statement, pick option 30 from the SQL prompt panel and you will be taken to a panel similar to the one shown in Figure 9-4.

When you hit the Enter key from the panel shown in Figure 9-4, you will see the results of the query displayed on your "terminal" screen as shown in Figure 9-5. Then, when you return to your SQL interactive screen, you will see the SQL statement as built by the ISQL prompter as shown in Figure 9-6. If all goes well, it will look as if you had typed it in yourself.

Figure 9-3 SQL Main Prompter Panel

```
                        Select SQL Statement

Select one of the following:

     1. ALTER TABLE
     2. CALL
     3. COMMENT ON
     4. COMMIT
     5. CONNECT
     6. CREATE ALIAS
     7. CREATE COLLECTION
     8. CREATE INDEX
     9. CREATE PROCEDURE
    10. CREATE TABLE
    11. CREATE VIEW
    12. DELETE
    13. DISCONNECT
    14. DROP ALIAS
    15. DROP COLLECTION
    16. DROP INDEX
    17. DROP PACKAGE
    18. DROP TABLE
    19. DROP VIEW
    20. GRANT PACKAGE
    21. GRANT TABLE
    22. INSERT
    23. LABEL ON
    24. LOCK TABLE
    25. RENAME
    26. RELEASE
    27. REVOKE PACKAGE
    28. REVOKE TABLE
    29. ROLLBACK
    30. SELECT
    31. SET CONNECTION
    32. SET TRANSACTION
    33. UPDATE
Selection   30 ___
F3=Exit    F12=Cancel
```

Figure 9-4 Specify Select Statement Parameters

```
                        Specify SELECT Statement

Type SELECT statement information.  Press F4 for a list.

   FROM files . . . . . . . .    VENDORP
   SELECT fields . . . . . .     NAME, CITY, STATE, VNDCLS, BALOWE
   WHERE conditions . . . . . .  BALOWE > 95.00
   GROUP BY fields . . . . . .
   HAVING conditions . . . . .
   ORDER BY fields . . . . . .
   FOR UPDATE OF fields . . . .                          Bottom

Type choices, press Enter.

   DISTINCT records in result file . . . . . . . .   Y    Y=Yes, N=No
   UNION with another SELECT . . . . . . . . . . .   N    Y=Yes, N=No
   Specify additional options . . . . . . . . . .    N    Y=Yes, N=No

F3=Exit        F4=Prompt    F5=Refresh   F6=Insert line   F9=Specify subquery
F10=Copy line  F12=Cancel   F14=Delete line   F15=Split line   F24=More keys
```

Figure 9-5 Display Results of Prompted Query

```
                            Display Data
                                     Data width . . . . . . :       73
Position to line  . . . . .          Shift to column  . . . . . .
....+....1....+....2....+....3....+....4....+....5....+....6....+....7...
NAME                        CITY            STATE  VNDCLS       BALOWE
J B COMPANY                 SCRANTON        PA     10           100.00
SCRANTON INC                OLD FORGE       PA     20           250.00
PASS PAX INC                OLD FORGE       PA     10           300.00
K D BUTTS WALLACE INC       SCRANTON        PA     30           500.00
DENTON AND BALL             SCRANTON        PA     20         3,500.00
JOHN STUDIOS                SCRANTON        PA     10           325.00
A MACHINE CORP.             Chicago         IL     10         7,500.00
B MACHINERY                 Wokegon         OK     20         1,495.55
C ENGRAVING CO              Greghert        IL     20           100.00
D CONTROLS                  Kernstin        IL     20           900.25
I POWER EQUIPMENT           Swingder        PA     20           250.00
ROBIN  COMPANY              Robin           PA     20           153.00
F STEEL CO                  Mattusic        PA     30           290.00
Sun MicroSystems            Santa Clara     CA     10         8,000.00
ATG Dynamo                  Cambridge       MA     20           352.56
McFadyen Consulting         Indianapolis    IN     10           250.00
                                                              More...
F3=Exit      F12=Cancel     F19=Left     F20=Right     F21=Split
```

Figure 9-6 Prompter-Built SQL Statement

```
                         Enter SQL Statements

Type SQL statement, press Enter.
  > CREATE VIEW SQLBOOK/VENDORV AS SELECT *  FROM SQLBOOK/VENDORP
    WHERE BALOWE> 500
    VENDORV in SQLBOOK type *FILE already exists.
    Session was saved and started again.
    Current connection is to relational database S102F52E.
  > SELECT DISTINCT NAME, CITY, STATE, VNDCLS, BALOWE FROM VENDORP
    WHERE BALOWE > 95.00
    VENDORP in *LIBL type *FILE not found.
  > SELECT DISTINCT NAME, CITY, STATE, VNDCLS, BALOWE FROM
    SQLBooK/VENDORP WHERE BALOWE > 95.00
    SELECT statement run complete.
===> _____
     _____
     _____
     _____
     _____
     _____
                                                              Bottom
F3=Exit    F4=Prompt    F6=Insert line   F9=Retrieve    F10=Copy line
F12=Cancel              F13=Services     F24=More keys
```

Select Distinct

You may notice by looking at the panel in Figure 9-6 that we invoked the distinct clause of the SELECT statement without explaining it. This clause has implications regarding what records are actually returned

Preventing Duplicate Rows (Distinct)

When SQL analyzes a select-statement, several rows might qualify to be in the result table, depending on the number of rows that satisfy the select-statement's search condition. Some of the rows in the result table might be duplicates. You can specify that you do not want any duplicates by using the DISTINCT keyword as we did above, followed by the list of column names that you want to see in the table. This is exactly what we did in Figure 9-6. However, the nature of the VENDORP data is such that there are not duplicate vendors in the vendor file so the result would be the same with or without the distinct clause.

However, if we switch to an Employee file now similar to the one we called EMP and created in Chapter 8, you will see that the notion of distinct and the prevention of duplicates means lots more Again, the DISTINCT clause means you want to select only the unique rows. If a selected row duplicates another row in the result table, the duplicate row is ignored (it is not put into the result table). For example, suppose you want a list of employee job codes. You do not need to know which employee has what job code. Because it is probable that several people in a department have the same job code, you can use DISTINCT to ensure that the result table has only unique values.

The following example shows how you would to do this:

```
SELECT DISTINCT JOB
    FROM SQLBOOK/EMP
    WHERE WORKDEPT = 'F11'
```

From IBM's sample data referenced in the DB2 Reference Manual this would result in two rows:

Job
Designer
Manager

Though there may be two or more designers and managers in department F11, only one entry is returned for each distinct job name. If you choose not to include DISTINCT in a SELECT clause, you might find duplicate rows in your result, because SQL returns the JOB column's value for each row that satisfies the search condition. Null values are treated as duplicate rows for DISTINCT.

When you include DISTINCT in a SELECT clause and you also include a shared-weight sort sequence, even fewer values are returned. The sort sequence causes values that contain the same characters to be weighted the same regardless of upper or lower case. If 'MGR', 'Mgr', and 'mgr' were all in the same table, for example, only one of these values would be returned.

The sort sequence is specified as a parameter at the time you invoke an SQL create program (CRTSQLXXX) function or when you begin an ISQL session (STRSQL) or you use RUNSQLSTM to process an existing SQL source file.

Now that we have fired up ISQL and we have worked in a few SELECT statements interactively, we can close out the ISQL session now by pressing F3 from the main SQL command panel as shown in Figure 9-6. When you hit the F3 key, you will see a panel similar to the one shown in Figure 9-7.

Figure 9-7 Exit Interactive SQL

```
                            Exit Interactive SQL

Type choice, press Enter.

   Option . . . . . . .    1=Save and exit session
                           2=Exit without saving session
                           3=Resume session
                           4=Save session in source file

F12=Cancel
```

As you can see there are four options on the Exit SQL panel shown in Figure 9-7. With option 1, you can either save your current session and SQL will dutifully keep your entire work area with all the commands and results messages until you issue the STRSQL command again. When you come back in to ISQL, the system automatically puts you in the same work area and other than the reconnected message you get, it is like you never left.

You can also choose # 2 to get out of SQL and save nothing. This is a bad idea unless you have done absolutely nothing in SQL and you want to start with a clean work area. The third option is the 'I was only kidding" option in that it returns you back to the session without exiting.

The last option on the list is very valuable. Instead of your having to cut and paste the triumphs that you have had in your ISQL session, you can copy it to a source file at the session close and then you can tweak it and perhaps later use the RUNSQLSTM command against the file to perform these functions as needed.

Save Session Caveat

If you saved only one interactive SQL session by using option 1 (Save and exit session) on the Exit Interactive SQL display, you may resume that session at any workstation. However, if you use option 1 to save two or more sessions on different workstations, interactive SQL will first attempt to resume a session that matches your work station. If no matching sessions are available, then interactive SQL will increase the scope of the search to include all sessions that belong to your user ID. If no sessions for your user ID are available, the system will create a new session for your user ID and current workstation. In this case, of course, you start with a blank slate.

Chapter Summary

Interactive SQL also known as ISQL is one of the most powerful features of the SQL toolkit. It is not just a testing environment; it can perform any of its operations on any live schema or any live database. Thus, it is also dangerous and should not be easily granted to an end user.

ISQL permits the developer to fashion any and all SQL statements (most with a prompt assist) and have those statements syntactically verified or actually validated prior to running the command. Additionally, there is a full run option that treats every SQL statement that you type and Enter as a statement that gets immediately executed. Most SQL developer use ISQL to prove their work before embedding it in an HLL program or creating a View of data to save the result of the ISQL query and run it as often as need be.

The STRSQL command gets you into the environment. F9 brings down the last command and every SELECT entry that is satisfied returns its unformatted results to the design screen for your review.   Rather than use RUNSQLSTM for functions that are supported, if you use ISQL, there is less work in determining the fate of your submissions. As in all of the four faces, you have to be careful about picking the proper naming conventions – SQL or System when you enter the session.

At the end of your session when you press F3, you get a number of options giving you great flexibility to wipe out your workspace and exit; or saving to a source file and exiting, returning to the work session without exiting or my favorite, exiting and saving the workspace which will automatically reconnect when you sign on again.

Key Chapter Terms

*RUN
*SYN
*VLD
Distinct clause
DML
Duplicate rows
Dynamic SQL
Execute immediately
Exit Interactive SQL options
Extended dynamic SQL
IBM i Navigator,
Naming convention,
QSQPRCED API,
Save session caveat

ISQL Select
ISQL Select Distinct
SQL Development Kit
SQL script
SQL statements
Statement processing
Static SQL
STRQM

Exercises

Use this chapter or look up information on the Web to answer the following:

1. Describe the interactive SQL environment (ISQL) on IBM i.

2. What purpose does IBM i ISQL serve?

3. What does the term Interactive SQL mean?

4. Is there a batch SQL?

5. Compare the benefits of interactive SQL to batch SQL if there is a batch SQL facility?

6. What command is used to START interactive SQL? What are the major options of the command and how should they be filled out?

7. What does it mean to prevent duplicate rows?

8. When saving your SQL session after and exit, under what circumstances might your session be wiped out?

9. How would you take your SQL statements that you have proven with ISQL and make them work in your chosen environment?

Chapter 10   Relational Database Operations

Integrated Relational Database

You have learned that AS/400 has an integrated relational database. You also know that a relational database consists of tables that are perceived to be stored in flat files, consisting of rows and columns, regardless of their true underlying structure. Unlike the complicated structures of the 1970's, records are linked by data, not by imbedded pointers.

The database is conceptually easy to understand, thus making it usable by folks like us, who prefer to let the rocket science to the rocket scientists. With a relational database, for example, if you have a set of data in physical structures, you can create new relationships simply by making a new table (View) and relating it to existing structures. The database supports all of the powerful cardinality data relationships: one to one, one to many, and many to many.

A relational file, or table, called a physical file on the AS/400, is composed of rows, which are made up of columns. In relational database terminology, rows are called tuples; columns are called attributes; and tables are called relations. Tuples (records or rows) are logically linked together by the data in the attributes (fields or columns.) Each record in a relation (file, table) has a unique key which is called the primary key. A key within the record that is used to link the file with another file in a join operation is called a foreign key.

Renaming simple notions in IT for special purposes is not unique to the database realms. Long before database terminology, for example, there was file system terminology. In file system terminology, rows are called records, columns are called fields, and relations are called files. Now you know the big dark secrets of database and file terminology. However, it still may be a safe bet that you won't use the term "tuple" again in your AS/400 or IBM i or IBM i career ever again – even if you use SQL..

Database Operators

When Ted Codd devised his theory for a database structure founded in mathematical principles, his research was not intended for only the math inclined. In fact, Codd's wish was to hide the internal complexity from users while assuring logical simplicity and correctness within the database itself. He hoped to have a management facility and a language, based on proven mathematical principals.

In fact, Codd's wish was that users could access information from the tables he envisioned, using simple, English-like commands, as opposed to writing code. He found the following matrix algebraic operations quite helpful in building the data language which became SQL:

```
UNION
INTERSECTION
DIFFERENCE
DIVISION
PRODUCT
SELECT
PROJECT
JOIN
```

We find the most commonly used operations to be Union, Projection, Selection, and Join. These are supported on the AS/400 in SQL (DB language invented by Chamberlin and Boyce of IBM) and DDS (DB Language invented by IBM originally for the System/38.)

The other four operators are functions that are (1) somewhat more difficult to understand, (2) not as valuable, and (3) not necessarily fully supported by the AS/400 and IBM i but more are being introduced with each release.

We will not cover these operators in any level of detail in this chapter but we will show what they are all about, and if implemented, we will show how they are implemented. If you would like a better appreciation of these algebraic relational operators, you may enjoy this Web article at: http://www.w3schools.com/sql/default.asp

Information on the Internet

There are many SQL lessons to be found on the Internet besides the above reference. Just go to your favorite search engine and type in SQL and the SQL command DIFFERENCE or INTERSECTION or any of the above operators, and you will be greeted by a host of references and facilities to fill many days of learning. You certainly will have plenty of references to get you well past the challenge.

There is another relational operator which is very useful, but it is not listed as algebraic. The Order by operation is most helpful in arranging data in sequences.

The name Chamberlin and Boyce gave to their database language was Structured Query Language (SQL). It consisted of three parts: Data Definition Language (DDL), Data Manipulation Language (DML), and Data Control Language (DCL). Codd defined the operators, the structure, the syntax, and all the rules for manipulating a relational database. Originally, when IBM came out with its language, it was actually called SEQUEL for Structured English Query Language, and it quickly received the nickname "sequel." However, there was already a company called Advanced System Concepts, who named their SQL-like SEQUEL product long before IBM coined the term. Additionally, the acronym SEQUEL was found to be a trademark held by a company in the UK IBM later dropped the name in favor of SQL.

Looking Closer at Relational Operators

A more complete explanation of each of the five commonly used operators is as follows:

ORDER

As you can see in Figure 10-1, ORDER sequences rows of a table, without making a second copy

Figure 10-1 Ordered and Unordered Records

```
      Ordered                              Unordered

 |                         |           |                  |
 |   Smith     |           |           |   Adams          |
 |             |           |           |                  |
 |   Jones     |    ==     |           |   Brown          |
 |             |           ==          |                  |
 |   Brown     |  ===========          |   Jones          |
 |             |           ==          |                  |
 |   Adams     |    ==     |           |   Smith          |
 |             |           |           |                  |
 |   Thompson  |           |           |   Thompson       |
 |             |           |           |                  |
 *                         |           *                  |
```

Union

As you can see from Figure 10-2, Union takes two similarly shaped files and creates one complete file from the two.

Projection

Projection allows you to logically rearrange the columns in a table and also create subsets of the columns, or fields, in a table. As an example, in Figure 10-3, you have a new view of the Payroll Master file, which does not include the salary. This view of the real data can be given to employees through relational projection. It is a projected image of a file, which limits and/or rearranges the columns which are included in the view.

Figure 10-2 Relational Union Operation

```
ORDER   MASTER1                              ORDER MASTER2
|          |          |         |         |          |          |          |
|Order No  |Part No   |Date     |         |Order No  |Part No   |Date      |
|          |          |         |         |          |          |          |
|159244    |55511     |7/1/94   |         |187654    |34567     |4/21/94|
|          |          |         |         |          |          |          |
|263255    |29999     |7/7/94   |         |322456    |23456     |4/24/94|
|          |          |         |         |          |          |          |
|978121    |64444     |6/9/94   |         |457676    |44567     |4/30/94|
|          |          |         |         |          |          |          |
|. . .     |. . .     |. . . |         |. . .     |. . .     |. . . |
*          !          !                  *          !          !
                      V                             V
                    V                             V
                  V                             V
                         UNIONED  FILE
              |          |          |                      |
              |Order No  |Part No   |Date                  |
              |          ¬          ¬                      |
              |159244    |55511     |7/1/94                |
              |187654    |34567     |4/21/94               |
              |263255    |29999     |7/7/94                |
              |322456    |23456     |4/24/94               |
              |978121    |64444     |6/9/94                |
              |457676    |44567     |4/30/94               |
              |. . .     |. . .     |. . .                 |
              *          !          !
```

Figure 10-3, Relational Projection Operation

```
   NAME      EXT       SALARY                    EXT       NAME
|        |        |        |               |        |        |
|        |        |        |               |        |        |
| Jones  | 3677   | 16000  |               | 3677   | Jones  |
|        |        |        |               |        |        |
| Smith  | 3605   | 14000  |      ==       | 3605   | Smith  |
|        |        |        |         ==    |        |        |
| Adams  | 3939   | 17000  | ============  | 3939   | Adams  |
|        |        |        |         ==    |        |        |
| Brown  | 4200   | 35000  |      ==       | 4200   | Brown  |
|        |        |        |               |        |        |
| ...    | ...    | ...    |               |        |        |
|        |        |        |               |        |        |
```

Selection

Just as projection provides a subset of the columns in a table, selection provides a subset of the rows. If, for example, you wanted a view of all salaried employees who made more than $100,000 per year, more than likely, you would receive a subset of the payroll records . . . those which met that selection criterion. In the selection example in Figure 10-4, (Just those customers from Michigan), you can see that the image after selection does not include A B Distributors.

Figure 10-4 Relational Selection Operation

```
|                         |    |              |                         |
| ABC Inc     Detroit  MI |    |              | ABC Inc     Detroit  MI |
|                         |  ==           |              |                         |
| A B Distrib Lima     OH |  ==  | 123 Trucking Alma     MI |
|                         | ======== |              |                         |
| 123 Trucking Alma    MI |  ==  | Allied Ent  Detroit  MI |
|                         |  ==           |              |                         |
| Jones Inc   Akron    OH |    *          |
|                         |
| Allied Ent  Detroit  MI |
|                         |
| Sun Ind     Tucson   AZ |
|                         |
*
```

In this process, the database does the record selection. A program would receive records that have already been selected by the database. Since the database can fetch and test records substantially faster than a program, in addition to saving both coding and the associated programmer time, using the database operators for selection also enhances performance.

Both projection and selection can be used for many purposes, including security. For example, a user could be authorized to a secure view of desired payroll data, instead of the entire file.

JOIN

With the Join operator, data in primary records (first file defined) gets joined with data from secondary records creating new "virtual" records with both sets of fields. Of course, more than two files can be joined. In fact, up to 32 files can be joined using the DB2/400 database.

To continue a Join to a third file, and to subsequent files, you would join the data in the 1st secondary file, to that in the 2nd secondary (tertiary – third) file. You would continue joining from file n to file n + 1 (where n = the sequence # of the last file joined, and n + 1 = the sequence # of the next file to be joined.)

You would be able to repeat this until you had no more joins to specify, or you had reached thirty-one joins using thirty-two physical files.

There is no reason to include a particular file in a Join logical view unless one or more fields from that file were going to be in the view provided by the file. We've coined the term "virtual record" to describe the resulting record format after all of the files are joined and the fields from those files are picked and placed in the new record format of the new logical file.

Thus, if a Join view consists of thirty-two files, it is safe to say that the record layout for that view contains at least thirty-two fields - a minimum of one from each of the Join files.

The Join operator plays upon the relationships of related fields - equal, greater than, or less than. In the example in Figure 10-5, you can see that the Order Master file is joined (equal) with the Parts Master file so that the parts within an order can logically contain the part's description, which exists only in the Parts Master file.

Figure 10-5 Relational Join Operation

ORDER MASTER

Order No	Part No	Date
159244	55511	7/1/88
263255	29999	7/7/88
978121	64444	6/9/88
. . .	. . .	. . .

PARTS MASTER

Part No	Description	Loc
66342	Size 7 Seal	Whs 1
18818	No 12 ring	Whs 3
97676	Brass plate	Whs 1
. . .	. . .	. . .

JOINED FILE

Order No	Part No	Description
159244	55511	CKK Valve
263255	29999	Left bracket
978121	64444	No 8 washer
. . .	. . .	. . .

As shown in Figure F-5, one or more data files can be joined together to create a view, or "virtual image." The view is very powerful and presents a record image to a program or query as if all the data fields were gathered from one file. With such work being performed by the database itself, application programs can become much simpler to design and code.

Overall, it is much easier for a programmer, or for a Query user, to work with a single, joined file, than deal with the complexity of multiple files. As previously noted, the AS/400 supports up to 32 physical files for a JOIN and the result is the formation of one new "joined" view of the data.

DIFFERENCE

The four operations coming up now include the Difference relational operation as derived from relational algebra is not used that often compared to those set operations described above. Its purpose is gives a result that includes all rows in one table that do not appear in another similarly defined table. See the diagram of difference in Figure 10-6.

As you progress in this book, you will learn that the difference operation is similar to a left/right outer join since it returns the non-hits. The shorthand symbol for the difference operation is a minus sign "-" It is implemented on the AS/400 database in V5R3 SQL as the Except operation.

On the AS/400 and IBM i as of V5R3, the Difference operation is supported in SQL. The example below "joins or unions" two almost identical files in terms of record content. Assume there are, say, five records missing from one of the files. The Difference select format is shown immediately below and the diagram of the format of a difference selection is shown in Figure 10-6.

Select *
  From vndp
Except distinct
Select *
  From vndp2

Figure 10-6 Difference Operation

```
PARTS MASTER 1                                     PARTS   MASTER2
|       |            -----|        |        |       |            |       |
|Part No |Description |Loc  |       |       |Part No |Description |Loc   |
|       |            -----|        |        |       |     ¬      |      ¬|
|66342  |Size 7 Seal |Whs 1|       |       |66342  |Size 7 Seal |Whs 1|
|       |            |      |       |       |       |            |      |
|97676  |Brass plate |Whs 1|       |       |18818  |No 12 ring  |Whs 3|
|       |            |      |       |       |       |            |      |
|98121  |Ropey Dope  |Whs 3|       |       |97676  |Brass plate |Whs 1|
|       |            |      |   |   |       |       |            |      |
|. . .  |. . .  |. . . |. . .       |. . .  |. . .       |. . .|
   *        !            v              *        !             !
                         v                       v
                         v                       v
                         v                       v
                   Result of Minus (Except) Operation
                |        |              |-----|
                |Part No |Description   |Loc  |
                ¬        ¬              |-----|
                |98121   |Ropey Dope    |Whs 3|
                |        |              |     |
                |        |              |     |
                |        |              |     |
                |        |              |     |
                |. . .   |. . .         |     |
                   *        !   -------   !   |
```

With a 17 record file VNDP (a subset of the vendor and vendorp files used throughout this book) sample data for this book, we would receive as a result the following table noting the 5 differences. In the sample tables, there are no duplicate records so the distinct operation was unnecessary.

Figure 10-7 Table Results W/ Difference using IBM i

```
                             Display Data
                                        Data width . . .
Position to line  . . . . .            Shift to column  . .
....+....1....+....2....+....3....+....4....+....5....+....6.
VENDOR    NAME                     ADDRESS LINE 1
NUMBER
  7,030    ATG Dynamo               25 First Street
  7,060    WRQ Reflections          1556 Emulation Avenue
  7,090    Fat Brain                65 Books Online
  7,130    McFadyen Consulting      521 Wedoitall Avenue
  7,150    Texas Instruments        45 Jones Rd.
********  End of data   ********
```

INTERSECTION

The Intersection relational operation, also derived from relational algebra, is as obscure to most SQL advocates as the Difference operation. When invoked, it returns a list of rows where the exact same row appears in two similarly defined tables. The shorthand symbol for this operation is an upside-down "U"

Figure 10-8 Intersection Operation

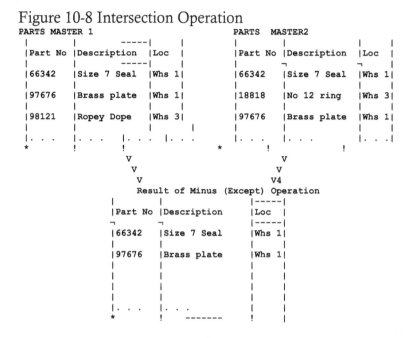

Using the same files as above in which five records are different, the Intersection operation will show us the twelve records in Figure 10-9 that are exactly the same.

```
Select *
  From vndp
Intersect distinct
Select *
  From vndp2
```

In the sample tables, there are no duplicate records so the distinct operation was unnecessary.

Figure 10-9 Display Data from IBM i Intersection

```
                             Display Data
                                           Data width
Position to line  . . . . .               Shift to column
....+....1....+....2....+....3....+....4....+....5....+.
VENDOR    NAME                      ADDRESS LINE 1
NUMBER
 7,000    Microsoft Corporation     One Microsoft Way
 7,010    Oracle Corporation        1234 Relational Stre
 7,020    Sun MicroSystems          4150 Network Circle
 7,040    Education Direct          925 Oak Street
 7,050    Merant                    125 Micro Focus
 7,070    Red Hat                   985 Linus Street
 7,080    Thomson Corporation       5664 Publisher Road
 7,100    Office Max                584 Office Supplies
 7,110    Home Depot                5697 Fix It Street
 7,120    American Vending Corp.    5687 Eating Drive
 7,140    Kensington                78 Clean Street
77,777    Left Outer Join           1234 Address Avenue
********  End of data  ********
```

PRODUCT (Cartesian Product)

The final set operator is the Cartesian Product. Just as in traditional set theory in mathematics, the Cartesian Product of two record sets (matrices) combines every record in one set with every record in the other.

The Cartesian product, or just "product," as noted in the list of relational functions of two record sets, is returned by a multi-file SELECT statement with no JOIN clause. This will make more sense when we cover the Join statement in Chapter 14.

The statement below for example, will return every vendor with every open voucher.

SELECT VENDORP.VENDNR, NAME, VCHNBR
from VENDORP, VOUCHRP

Cartesian products are occasionally useful for analysis purposes. However, I must admit I never needed one. They often serve as interim results for further manipulation as in a

Join. The Join, for example, always produces a Cartesian product of all combinations and then without burdening the user, selects the tuples that apply and displays only those. .

DIVISION

The final relational operation is Division. The relational divide operator (so called to distinguish it from mathematical division) returns the records in one record set that have values that match all the corresponding values in the second record set. For example, given a record set that shows the categories of products purchased from each supplier, a relational division will produce a list of the suppliers that provide products in all categories.

This is not an uncommon situation, but the solution is not straightforward since the SQL SELECT statement does not directly support relational division. There are numerous ways to achieve the same results as a relational division, however.

The easiest method is to rephrase the request.

Instead of "list the suppliers who provide all product categories," which is difficult to process; try "list all suppliers where the count of their product categories is equal to the count of all product categories."

This is an example of the extension operation that we'll discuss later in this chapter. It won't always work, and in situations where it doesn't, you can implement division using correlated queries. Correlated queries are, however, outside the scope of this book. Please refer to one of the references listed in the bibliography.

To SQL or Not to SQL?

Despite its availability, and its acceptance as the industry standard, IBM chose not to use SQL as its native database language when the company introduced the AS/400 in 1988, and again when it introduced the IBM i in 2000 and again, when it introduced the IBM i in 2006. Instead, the company used the same, and only database model native to the System/38 – DDS.

The DDS Factor!

That model was specifically built to help make it easier for IBM's small business computer customers to migrate to the System/38 platform. It helped IBM achieve a major objective of migrating its current users to a database platform without burdening them by even a modicum of large system complexity. Because of IBM's unique design, many who migrated to the system, never even had to learn about the database.

Changing compilers to use SQL and eliminating native "read and write" operations in favor of SQL were not in IBM's interests with either the AS/400 or IBM i announcements. Without SQL as the default language for the database, IBM had a number of issues when trying to port AS/400 applications to other database systems that were based on the SQL language.

DDS is very powerful and intuitive that it enables non-database professionals to quickly get acquainted with the integrated database. Thus, it would not have been a good idea then, nor would it be a good idea now for IBM to eliminate DDS. However, with more and more companies running multiple system types, SQL has gotten new life in AS/400 shops and IBM has responded by making the new IBM i SQL more powerful than ever.

Shortly after the AS/400 was announced in 1988, IBM made SQL available as an optional database language for a charge. By making it optional and charging for the package, eventually there were SQL "haves" and "have nots." Over the years , however, as IBM software marketing packages began to include SQL as a feature, more and more users were able to use its facility in their daily work. Though DDS is still the preferred language for AS/400 database shops, SQL is becoming more and more popular.

With all IBM AS/400 systems including the newest IBM i, IBM ships an SQL runtime environment with the operating system. Thus, software vendors do not have to depend on SQL being purchased for their SQL-based products to run.

Chapter Summary

All relational database DML operations are founded in mathematical theory. The integrated relational database called DB2 UDB on the IBM i is no exception, with or without SQL. In defining the types of things users may like to do with data, and proving that they will work in mathematics, Ted Codd came up with eight operators that are implemented to one degree or another in all RDBMS systems, including the IBM i.

In this chapter, we examined the look and feel of all of these operations by providing a pictorial representation of data when it was reasonably easy to accomplish and by providing the new SQL for some of the more esoteric of Codd's operations that are just now coming into the SQL operations set of the IBM i.

Key Chapter Terms

Cardinality
Commonly used operations
Difference

Division
Foreign key
Integrated RDBMS
Internet
Intersection
Join
Matrix algebraic operations
Order
Primary key,
Product (Cartesioan)
Project
RDBMS operations,
Relational operators,
SEQUEL
Set theory
Tuples
Union
Unique key

Exercises

Use this chapter or look up information on the Web to answer the following:

1. Ted Codd's relational database operations were all proven before implementation because of his reliance on what discipline?

2. Is the Order operation one that Codd would say is founded in mathematical theory?

3. Describe the Union operation.

4. How is a projection operation implemented in practice?

5. What is Selection and which clause of which SQL statement would you use to provide it.

6. What is a Join operation?

7. Describe the Difference operation?

8. What is the Intersection operation?

9. What is the Cartesian product operation and how is it developed? What value may it serve in practice? Give an example of how you can get the Cartesian product using just two files

10. What is the Division relational DB operation and how is it implemented on the IBM i?

11. Are any of these operations implemented in DDS? Which ones if any?

Chapter 11   The Basic Select Statement

Function of SELECT Statement

The SELECT statement is SQL's data access statement. In a programming language, the READ, CHAIN, and READ for UPDATE operations are how record at a time operations are performed. There is no such thing as record at a time access and therefore there is no such thing as a "READ" operation per se in SQL. So, if you plan to read anything for any purpose using SQL, you will find yourself using the SELECT statement.

The SQL SELECT starts by you specifying a file or files from which to access data and in the rest of the statement you tell this powerful data access statement just what data it is that you want to retrieve. It all starts by your specifying the columns that you want to see as a result of a database query.

The columns you select may be column names that exist already in one of the data bases that you are accessing or they may be arithmetic expressions in which you create new virtual columns (fields) from other values in a row (record). Regardless of what you request, if SQL returns anything to satisfy your query, it is always in the form of a new "table."

Where Does SQL Put the New Table?

So far, we have studied the RUNSQLSTM and the ISQL methods of working with SQL. We have yet to study the Query Manager and embedding SQL in programs. Select works in three out of these four environments. IBM did not build the RUNSQLSTM command to process a Select statement so don't even bother trying.

In all three cases in which a Select statement is supported, the table result is returned in "memory." The result that comes back to memory is known as a result set. Sometimes this result set (memory table) is further analyzed with additional Select statements in the form of a query within a query a.k.a. sub-query in order to get the final results. In other cases, further selections and groupings are performed with the Group By and Having clauses of the Select statement. In a nutshell, at the end of Select statement processing in any environment, one of three things is returned to a new area of memory representing the results of the query. These three possible results are as follows:

✓ No rows returned
✓ One row returned
✓ Multiple rows returned

Once the lack of data, data, or set of data is built in memory in column and row format as the result set, it can be used in a variety of ways. For now, let's concentrate on the basics. In ISQL, if there are no results, you will get a panel that looks just like the panel you would get if there were results except there would be no data included in the panel. At the bottom of the panel, you would see the following message:

No data selected for output

If there is one row returned or many rows returned, the panel looks the same and the rows and columns of the memory table are displayed on the screen. Since most often the number of columns does not fit on the screen, there are left and right function keys and roll functions for the top to bottom windows so that you can toggle through the various rows and columns in the result set of data. There is also a split screen facility using F21 that is like the freeze spreadsheet function. It permits you to keep an identifying part of the record visible on the left side while you look at the rest of the columns on the right side of the window.

If you are using the Query Manager (QM) product Chapter 13), the result set of your Select run is turned over to the QM function where it can be better formatted. From here the information included in the resultant data set is formatted and then either displayed or printed.

If you are using the Select statement for data access in a high level language program such as RPG and COBOL, or even low level languages such as C Language, the result of the query is stored in memory that is accessible only via your program. If there are no records or just one record returned to the program, the data or lack of data can be processed very similarly to how the language would process any other record at a time data access function.

However, if the program is to receive a table set of data in memory from a SELECT query, the programmer must code specific statements within the program, in much the same way as a subfile, or an OPNQRYF query to be able to "cursor" through the returned records in memory to process them one at a time.

In its basic form, the Select Statement specifies to the SQL data manager:

1. What data to retrieve
2. The columns to be returned as result of the Select
3. The Table(s) or View(s) from which data is to be retrieved
4. Optionally – a condition which must be satisfied in order to retrieve the data record(s).

The Basic Nits and the Grits

The most basic form of the select is as follows

1. SELECT - the verb or action word for the statement
2. Column Names -- the data you want
3. FROM. -- some source (table or view name(s))
4. WHERE -- conditions which are to be met (if any)

The Where clause in the basic SELECT operation is where lots of work occurs. This is where logical operators are defined to limit the set of data returned. The Where clause can also contain another SELECT clause to further refine the returned data set. This is called a sub-query request.

The best way to take a look at the basic components of the SELECT statement is to go back to a section of the panel we first showed in Interactive SQL back in Figure 9-4. The germane parts of this panel are repeated below as Figure 11-1 to serve as a convenient reference:

Figure 11-1 Specify Select Statement Parameters

```
   FROM files . . . . . .   VENDORP
   SELECT fields  . . . .   NAME, CITY, STATE, VNDCLS, BALOWE
   WHERE conditions . . .   BALOWE > 95.00
   GROUP BY fields  . . .
   HAVING conditions  . .
   ORDER BY fields  . . .
   FOR UPDATE OF fields .                        Bottom

Type choices, press Enter.

   DISTINCT records in result file  . .   Y    Y=Yes, N=No
   UNION with another SELECT  . . . . .   N    Y=Yes, N=No
   Specify additional options . . . . .   N    Y=Yes, N=No
```

In Figure 11-1 we get the basics of the SELECT statement and we also get a method of achieving the advanced capabilities of the SQL language. Let's begin our examination of this statement by taking it apart, one clause at a time. We'll start by taking a closer look at the three clauses that we have been using as examples throughout the book, namely the From, Select Fields, and Where clauses.

The From Clause of the Select Statement

In the FROM Clause, you merely type in the name of the table (physical file) or tables or the view (logical file) or views from which you want the result table to be derived.. The files that you call out in the FROM clause form the full population of data records to be queried. Unless you use an asterisk in the Select Fields clause, the resulting table that is obtained from the query in most cases will be smaller (projection) than the combination of columns and rows in the based-on tables.

The "Select Fields" Clause of the Select Statement

In this clause, you type the names of the columns (fields) to be used in the result table (file). The columns (fields) must be separated by commas. You may also use expressions, such as (balowe * 1.1) to perform math functions on data and return the results. In this case it can be that we are adding a 10% late charge or something else that is derived form the data. Expressions also are separated by commas.

It is actually the result of the expression, not the expression itself that will be returned in the resultant memory table set of data. It is the Select clause via the selection of fields that the relational database operation of projection is performed. Thus, fewer columns are typically returned in the result set than are in the queried tables.

The Where Clause of the Select Statement

In this clause, you type the search condition for each row (record) resulting from the From clause. The result table contains the rows (records) where the search condition is true. This is where the SQL operation of selection is performed. Thus, less rows are typically returned than are in the queried tables.

The Group By Clause - Select Statement

When you use the GROUP BY clause of the SELECT statement, you are signaling that there is more processing that must be done against the original returned memory table from the memory result set of the projections and selection operations. The GROUP BY operates on the returned result set (intermediate) of the initial Select. It then groups this set of returned rows (records) according to certain specified columns (fields). The columns (fields) must be separated by commas. The GROUP BY is typically followed by the HAVING clause.

The Having Clause -- Select Statement

As the Group By examines the initial table and groups and it prepares the grouping, the Having provides an opportunity to apply additional selection criteria against the returned and grouped data so far in the query. It is like "having" another Where clause available to use against the result of the functions applied earlier in the query that were not available in the original table. So the Having clause uses the grouped intermediate result table (file) and produces a final result set by applying a search condition to each group of the previous clause.

The Order By Clause -- Select Statement

Unless you specifically choose to tell the Select statement that the resulting table should be sorted in some sequence, the sequence of the returned table is indeterminate. One time the query may deliver records in one sequence and the next time the query may deliver the same data in a different sequence.

The clause in the Select statement that gives you control of the sequence of the rows returned to your result table is the Order By clause. This clause orders the rows (records) of the result table (file) according to the column (field) names you identify. If you identify more than one column (field), the rows (records) are initially ordered by the column (field) names you identified first, then by the column (field) names you identified second within the sequencing of the first column (field), and so on.

The For Update Of Clause-- Select Statement

The For Update Of clause is an optional part of a SELECT statement. When used in high level language programs, it specifies whether the result set of a simple SELECT statement that meets the requirements for a cursor (result table row / record access) is updatable or not. Only simple, single-table SELECT cursors and FORWARD_ONLY result sets of date can be updatable

Forward-only Cursors

As many things in SQL, there is a chicken or egg problem in describing the utility of a function by having to use something that has not been described yet as a descriptor. In above explanation of For Update Of, we used the term Forward_Only result sets. Though we are not yet prepared to learn cursors and embedded SQL, it would help now and then to define this term since it is a restriction on the For Update Of clause.

In essence, all of this has to do with the returned data set. A forward-only cursor does not support scrolling. It supports only the fetching of the returned rows serially, one at a time from the start of the memory table to the end of the memory table. It basically means that when processing the returned memory table, the cursor cannot be scrolled backward. You will see in embedded SQL that you define a way to access the returned data via a notion called a cursor. Unlike a cursor on a screen that can be moved backward and forward, this cursor can only be advanced forward.

To satisfy the For Update Of conditions, you type the names of the columns that can be updated through the cursor. The columns named must belong to the table (physical file) or view (logical file) named in the From clause of the Select statement and the columns must be separated by commas.

Union with Another Select

At the bottom of the Specify Select Statement there are three more options for SELECT processing. They are as follows:

- ✓ DISTINCT records in result file
- ✓ UNION with another SELECT
- ✓ Specify additional options

In Chapter 9, we covered the notion of the distinct option to prevent duplicates in the result set so we have just two more aspects of the SELECT statement to cover in this chapter. The first of these two is the Union with another Select.

This feature gives you the option of performing a Union function to combine two result tables (files) into one result table (file). If you answer yes to this prompt, you get another prompt so that you can indicate whether you want duplicate rows (records).

Specify Additional Options

When you pick this line on the prompter, you are given three more items to specify:

1. Number of records to optimize
2. For Read Only
3. With isolation level

Let's look at these individually:

Number of Records to Optimize

The OPTIMIZE for ROWS clause is used to give the perception of better performance. This is the same facility used with the native OPNQRYF command that enables the first page of displayed output to display while a query, expected to be long running, is working on getting the rest of the result set prepared. You select the number of rows (records) that you want to show on the first and subsequent panels with the OPTIMIZE FOR ROWS clause. If this clause is not specified, the database manager assumes all rows (records) of the result table will be retrieved before any are displayed.

For Read Only

The For Read Only clause specifies that the result table (file) is read-only. If the clause is provided, since there is no concern for locking records, it should significantly improve the performance of FETCH operations.

With Isolation Level   :

The With Isolation Level clause of the SELECT statement permits the developer to specify the level of sharing for updates.

Derived Fields

The SELECT statement can create new virtual fields using the following operations:

Add
Subtract
Multiply
Divide
Concatenate
Substring

Look at the following example:

SELECT VENDNR, BALOWE- 200,
SUBSTR(name, 1,15) as ShortName FROM
vendorp

The Results as stored in the memory table or what is commonly called the result set is as follows:

Figure 11-2 Results of Derived Field Query

```
                           Display Data
                                         Data width
Position to line  . . . . . ___       Shift to column  ___
   ...+....1....+....2....+....3....+....4
VNDNBR     BALOWE - 200    SHORTNAME
    38          100.00-    John B Stetz Cl
    40           50.00     Scranton Fabric
    42          100.00     Pass Pax Inc
    44          150.00-    Cliffy Equipmen
    46          300.00     Butts & Wallace
    48        3,300.00     Denton and Ball
    49          125.00     John Studios
    25        7,300.00     Macone Corp Of
    26        1,295.55     Lockhart Machin
    28          100.00-    Charley Engravi
    30          700.25     Detweiller Cont
    32           50.00     Irfing Power Ma
    34           47.00-    Blind Robin Cop
    36           90.00     Facile Steel Co
 7,000          190.46-    Microsoft Corpo
 7,010          105.00-    Oracle Corporat

3=Exit       F12=Cancel       F19=Left      F20=Right
```

Closer Look at Where Clause

I keep reminding you that there is no order in the results unless we use an ORDER BY clause. We'll get to some examples shortly. Let's first take a look at some examples using the Where clause to select rows.

The Where clause, in a nutshell, does row selection. Logical operations and keywords help the user construct the selection criteria. The typical phrases used in the Where clause are as follows:

Greater than	>
Less than	<
Equal	=
Greater than or equal	>=
Less than or equal	<=
Not Equal	<>
AND, OR, NOT	
RANGE	**inclusive constant range**
BETWEEN	**high and low values**
VALUES	**list of constant values (IN)**
Wild Card	**Constant pattern matching**
Like	
Etc.	

And Conjunction

The term "And" is used to combine more than one Where clause condition. When "And" is used, the conditions on both sides of the And need to be true in order for the statement to be true.

Example: **AND Fieldname = 56**

Or Conjunction

The term "Or" is also used to combine more than one Where clause conditions to be tested. When "Or" is used, the conditions on either side of the "Or" need to be true in order for the statement to be evaluated true. If both are true, the statement is true; if both are false, the statement is evaluated as false. If one side is false and one side is true, the statement is evaluated as true.

Example: `OR Fieldname = 56`

Between Test

The between function is used to select rows that are between values. When the conditions are met, the row is selected into the result set..

Example: Select within range of values

```
Where Fieldname BETWEEN 56 AND 70
Where Fieldname BETWEEN 'AC' AND 'DF'
```

For numeric values, no quotes are required. For alphabetic vales, quotes are required.

The NOT Modifier

Not is used to negate a true statement. If we are looking for he negative of a condition and it is true, the record is selected into the result set.

Let's take an example in which we want to select if the tested column in the record is not within a range or list of values.

Example: Select when not in range or list:

Where Fieldname NOT BETWEEN 56 AND 70

List of Values – IN

The IN test gives us a tool to see if the record being processed has a column value that fits with a list of specified values.

Example: Select if the value is in a list of values

Where Fieldname IN (56, 64, 70)
Where Fieldname IN ('AC' 'AD' 'DF')

Now let's wrap up this chapter with some fairly simple, sample Selects:

Exercise 1

SELECT *   FROM PERSON

This statement retrieves all data from PERSON table as shown in Figure 11-3.

Figure 11-4 Person Data

EMP NO NME n i t NAME lvl E X DATE JOB	FIRST I			LAST ED S		BIRTH HM#			
999900	John	F		Jones	12	M	07/26/89 STA		121

```
999901   Emily      A   Smith     11        F   01/01/85 STA   122
999902   Caroline   M   Bayer     12        F   07/05/75 AQS   123
12345    Joseph     H   Smith     12        m   02/07/80 STA   124
23456    Anny       H   Jones     14        F   02/01/70 MGR   125
3456     Daniel     J   Grindick  16        M   03/01/70 MGR   126
001      Kevin      F   Fiedler   3         M   06/23/79 AQS   127
26913    Ronnie     B   Beezer    19        F   03/21/82 STA   332
70017    James      T   Torregard 1         M   08/30/84 AQS   333
12654    Finster    Q   Fadillo   10        F   12/08/56 STA   334
43298    Nongo      D   Connie    16        M   08/23/61 RET   335
31856    Gaus       V   Herndon   10        M   11/16/83 STA   491
83523    Fonnsworth     KNoommin  12        M   01/30/77 MGR   492
39245    Maryanne   X   Toole     19        F   05/22/72 MGR   493
41717    Catherine  D   Damsforth 12        F   02/12/81 STA   622
41578    Paul       A   Gollera   11        M   04/11/78 STA   731
34466    Benia      A   Arflatts  12        F   08/05/87 STA   820
```

Exercise 2

SELECT * FROM VENDORP

This statement retrieves all data from the VENDORP file in no apparent sequence. Since the columns of this book are narrow and I wanted you to see the contents of the file, I split the results into two parts as shown in Figures 11-4 and 11-5. To relate rows properly, I duplicated the VNDNBR column in both halves of the output.

Figure 11-4 Left Half of Vendorp File from Select *

VNDN	NAME	ADDR1	CITY
38	John B Stetz Clothier	3817 N. Pulaski	Scranton
40	Scranton Fabrics	2147 S Main St.	Old Forge
42	Pass Pax Inc	1539 Oak Hill	Old Forge
44	Cliffy Equipment Co.	2232 Fouest	Scranton
46	Butts & Wallace Inc	2150 Toughy	Scranton
48	Denton and Ball	7934 S Scranton Ave	Scranton
49	John Studios	2040 N BELTWAY	Scranton
25	Macone Corp Of Chicago	1345 Prill Avenue	Chicago
26	Lockhart Machinaws	45 Ginzo Lane	Wokegon
28	Charley Engraving Co	Pedulllion Avenue	Greghert
30	Detweiller Controls	45 Fognetta Place	Kernstin
32	Irfing Power Machinery	56 Fineel La	Swingder
34	Blind Robin Copany	11 Robin Lane	Robin
36	Facile Steel Co	78 Engraved Rd.	Mattusic
7000	Microsoft Corporation	One Microsoft Way	Redmond
7010	Oracle Corporation	123 Relational St	Redwood Shre
7020	Sun MicroSystems	4150 Network Circle	Santa Clara
7030	ATG Dynamo	25 First Street	Cambridge
7040	Education Direct	925 Oak Street	Scranton
7050	Merant Glass Works	125 Micro Focus	Phoenix
7060	WRQ Reflections	1556 Emulation Ave	Tampa Bay
7070	Red Hat Club	985 Linus Street	Albany
7080	Thompson Corporation	5664 Publisher Road	Austin
7090	Fat Brain	65 Books Online	Cleveland
7100	Office Max	584 Office Supplies	Detroit

```
7110    Home Depot              5697 Fix It Street    Jackson
7120    American Vending Corp. 5687 Eating Drive     Portland
7130    McFadyen Consulting     521 Wedoitall Ave     Indianapolis
7140    Kensington Mines        78 Clean Street       Lancaster
7150    Texas Instruments       45 Jones Rd.   San Antonio
7777    Left Outer Join         1234 Smirth Ave       Scranton
8020    Phillies Phinest        391 Carey Avenue      Wilkes-Barre
8020    Bings Music             91 Peeliere Ave       Oanoke
```

Figure 11-5 Right Half of Vendorp File from Select *

VNDN	STATE	ZIPCD	CLS	STS	BALOWE	SRVRTG
38	PA	18503	10	A	100	R
40	PA	18762	20	A	250	R
42	PA	19722	10	A	300	R
44	PA	18503	20	A	50	X
46	PA	18503	30	A	500	R
48	PA	18504	20	A	3500	R
49	PA	18505	10	A	325	X
25	IL	45903	10	A	7500	X
26	OK	23657	20	A	1495.55	R
28	IL	45963	20	A	100	X
30	IL	45793	20	A	900.25	R
32	PA	18503	20	A	250	R
34	PA	18702	20	A	153	A
36	PA	18598	30	A	290	X
7000	WA	98052	10	A	9.54	P
7010	CA	92626	10	A	95	G
7020	CA	95054	10	A	8000	G
7030	MA	2141	20	A	352.56	A
7040	PA	18515	20	A	0.25	A
7050	AZ	19954	30	A	0.56	G
7060	FL	12374	20	A	4.99	G
7070	NY	85743	10	A	7.85	A
7080	TX	98735	20	A	9.65	G
7090	OH	47895	10	A	2.56	G
7100	MI	85742	10	A	19	G
7110	MS	65412	30	S	6.54	B
7120	OR	65478	20	D	0	P
7130	IN	98523	10	A	250	A
7140	PA	65471	20	A	0.25	G
7150	TX	87459	10	A	0.15	G
77777	PA	18515	10	A	5	A
8020	PA	18702	20	A	35700	4
8020	VA	58702	20	A	79700	3

Exercise 3

```
SELECT    FIRSTNME, LASTNAME FROM        PERSON
WHERE     EDLEVEL = 12
```

Retrieves the names of those who are seniors

Figure 11-6 Display the Seniors

```
                              Display Data
                                        D
Position to line  . . . . .             Shift
....+....1....+....2....+....
FIRSTNME      LASTNAME
John          Jones
Caroline      Bayer
Joseph        Smith
Fonnsworth    Nortstommin
Catherine     Damsforth
Benia         Arflatts
********  End of data  ********
```

Exercise 4

```
Select name, balowe, vndcls
from vendorp
where vndcls = 10
```

This query retrieves selected fields from Vendorp in class 10.

Figure 11-7 Display Vendors of Class 10

```
                              Display Data
Position to line  . . . . .             Shift to
....+....1....+....2....+....3....+....4....+...
NAME                          BALOWE    VNDCLS
John B Stetz Clothier         100.00    10
Pass Pax Inc                  300.00    10
John Studios                  325.00    10
Macone Corp Of Chicago      7,500.00    10
Microsoft Corporation           9.54    10
Oracle Corporation             95.00    10
Sun MicroSystems            8,000.00    10
Red Hat Club                    7.85    10
Fat Brain                       2.56    10
Office Max                     19.00    10
McFadyen Consulting           250.00    10
Texas Instruments                .15    10
Left Outer Join                 5.00    10
********   End of data   ********
```

Chapter Summary

In this chapter we completed the examination of the Basic Select statement that began lightly in the early chapters of this book. When you build a table with SQL if you qualify the name on the Create Table statement then it goes into the qualified library. If not, it goes into your current library. Once you create your tables and have them populated with test data, you are ready to roll in your SQL learning endeavors. When you do your first select and a table is retuned, where does that table go? You might want to check your current library.

For this chapter, the examples continue with the Vendorp file and the Person file which have been two of our mainstays throughout this book. Both are located in the SQLBOOK library. Yet, when you do a Select operation on either of these tables, the resulting table (result set) is not stored back on disk in SQLBOOK under a different name. It may be held in memory and then displayed. Sometimes the Select may be complex. The initial results of a big Select statement may provide results in an intermediate state, waiting for the second half of an SQL statement to do its thing, which eventually results in a completed result set – also in memory.

Since SQL fosters set processing, its result also comes back in a set. Unlike the original set, however, the result set is always in memory. Sometimes there is an intermediate result set and sometimes there is not, depending on the nature of the query. At the end of an interactive SQL statement if data is retuned it is displayed.

One you get past the Where clause in SQL, a consensus of first time SQL users would say that SQL gets more sticky. We won't get there until Chapter 14. There was actually enough in this Chapter to keep us busy in the Where clause for the whole chapter. There are many predicates that can be used in the

Where clause to select data and we already examined most of them in this chapter including the following:

- **Greater than**   >
- **Less than**   <
- **Equal**   =
- **Greater than or equal**   >=
- **Less than or equal**   <=
- **Not Equal**   <>
- **AND, OR, NOT**
- **RANGE**   inclusive constant range
- **BETWEEN**   high and low values
- **VALUES**   list of constant values (IN)

In Chapter 14 we will pick up with the Wild Card facilities of the Like predicate and we will move on to multi-file queries with lots of exercises.

Key Chapter Terms

And conjunction
Between
C language
Chain
Column names
Cursor
Equal
Expressions
For Read Only
For Update Of clause
Forward_only
From clause
Greater than
Group By
HAVING clause
In
Less than
Like
List of values

Memory table
New table
Not
OPNQRYF
Optimize
Or conjunction
Order By
Range
Read
Result set
RUNSQLSTM,
SELECT statement
SELECT cursor
Split screen
Subfile
Union
Values
Where clause
Wild card

Exercises

Use this chapter or look up information on the Web to answer the following:

1. What are all the four parts of a basic SELECT statement and explain each part.

2. What is the purpose for having, group by, and order by?.

3. What are the six operators that can be used in expressions to derive new columns for output in an SQL query?

4. Write the SQL query to select all the records and all the fields from the Vendorp table if the BALOWE is less than $1000.00

5. Write the SQL to select the records from Vendorp in which the VNDNBR is in an inclusive range from 30 to 40.

6. Write the SQL to select all of the records from VENDORP whose SRVRTG is R, P, or G.

7. Write the SQL to select all of the records From Vendorp whose VNDNR is greater than 1000, and whose VNDCLS is 20 or 30.

8. Write the SQL to select the records from the Persons file who have yet to achieve a high school education?

9. What purpose does the FOR UPDATE clause of the select clause provide? Can this be used in ISQL?

Chapter 12   Query Manager

What is Query Manager for IBM i?

The IBM official name for Query Manager is the DB2 UDB for IBM i Query Manager. It is shipped as part of the IBM DB2 Query Manager and SQL Development Kit for IBM i licensed program. It consists of a collection of software tools that you can use to obtain information from DB2 Universal Database™ for IBM i (DB2 UDB for IBM i) databases.

Just as ISQL, you can use Query Manager to select and analyze information stored in one or more database tables. In addition to these functions, you can also arrange the information to produce reports or new permanent SQL tables. After you go through the effort of building a query, you can create and run your query definitions, or you can run queries from stored definitions that you did not create.

The major differentiating factor between ISQL and Query Manager is that you can format the way that retrieved query data is presented by creating a report form, and applying the form to the SQL statements when you run a query. If you would prefer to let Query Manager format the query information for you, you can do that also, using a simple default report form.

All of these functions are called from the DB2/400 Query Manager Menu. From here, you can define, maintain, and run queries, and you can produce reports or tables from data gathered from database files. You can also define, maintain, and run report forms, and create and maintain database tables.

The tool for inserting data is a major plus for the Query Manager over the Insert statement in SQL. In some ways, the Table Manager function makes entering data into SQL tables almost as easy as IBM's popular Data File Utility (DFU.)

For those comfortable with the SQL language, the data retrieval part of a Query Manager Query can be created using SQL. But, for those who have little or no experience using SQL language, they can create their queries using Query Manager's (QM) prompted query creation mode. A series of displays prompts the user to enter all of the information that Query Manager (QM) needs to create a query.

QM queries can retrieve data from a single table or from as many as 32 tables. You can select all table columns, or only a few columns, and organize them for the type of output you desire. You can have all table rows in the output, or you can select only a few to be included, using row selection tests. You can also use report breaks and arithmetic summary functions to include additional information in your report, to make it easier to read.

Just as with SQL, you determine what data the query is to retrieve, but with QM Query you also decide the format of the report, and whether the output should be displayed, printed, or sent to another database table.

By sending query output to a database table, you can create a new populated SQL table. As noted previously, you can also create and maintain database tables using Query Manager's prompt-guided table entry option.

Another way of creating tables is through Query Manager's command window. Using the command window, you can enter Query Manager statements and system commands to perform tasks such as:

- ✓ Creating and saving queries
- ✓ Running queries
- ✓ Connecting to other databases

✓ Importing and exporting objects
✓ Running procedures that were created outside Query
    Manager

Queries & SQL Language in Query Manager

In general terms, a query is a question asked of the database.
For example, you use a query to get information from database
tables to produce a report. All queries created in QM are
eventually written in the DB2 UDB for IBM i SQL language.
Most of the queries you write or run will be SQL SELECT
statements used to generate reports on existing database
information. Just as ISQL, QM queries can contain all
interactive SQL statements except for the CONNECT,
DISCONNECT, RELEASE, and SET CONNECTION
statements used for DRDA access.

Prompted Queries in Query Manager

Users with little or no experience in using the SQL language
can create and change SELECT statement queries using Query
Manager's prompted query creation mode.

Report Forms in Query Manager

While a query is a question asked of the database, a report form
specifies the format of the answer. The report itself is the result
of applying a report form to the data generated by running a
query. If you run a query without specifying a report form, QM
generates a default report form and produces a simple report.
This default report form is referred to as *SYSDFT, the system
default form.

Making Reports Easier to Read in Query Manager

You can improve the presentation of the report by creating a report form and applying it to the query data. The report form could specify a page heading and footing, and column headings that are more descriptive,

Using Level Breaks in Report in Query Mgr.

You can further improve the presentation of the report by including level breaks in the report form. You use level breaks (also known as report breaks and control breaks) to separate the report information into meaningful groups. For each break group, you can specify descriptive text and calculate totals, averages, and other summary values. For example, you can improve on any report using the following type of formatting options:

- ✓ Cause a break to occur when a control field such as the department number changes

- ✓ Print a break heading and footing for each control field (department)

- ✓ Total the several values such as salaries and commissions for each department

- ✓ Cause additional control breaks such as a second break to occur when a job value changes

- ✓ Print a break footing for each job

- ✓ Total values for each control total such as the total of the salaries and commissions for each job

- ✓ Print final text and grand totals at the end of the report

Figure 12-1 is included below to demonstrate in pictorial form the type of output that can be produced by QM. This report is courtesy of the IBM Corporation from the Redbook titled IBM i DB2 Universal Database for IBM i Query Manager Use.. For those who would like to learn more and more about Query Manager, this Redbook is free on the Internet for the downloading. Just go to www.redbooks.ibm.com and search for Query Manager.

Figure 12-1 QM Query Report Form Demonstrating Level Breaks

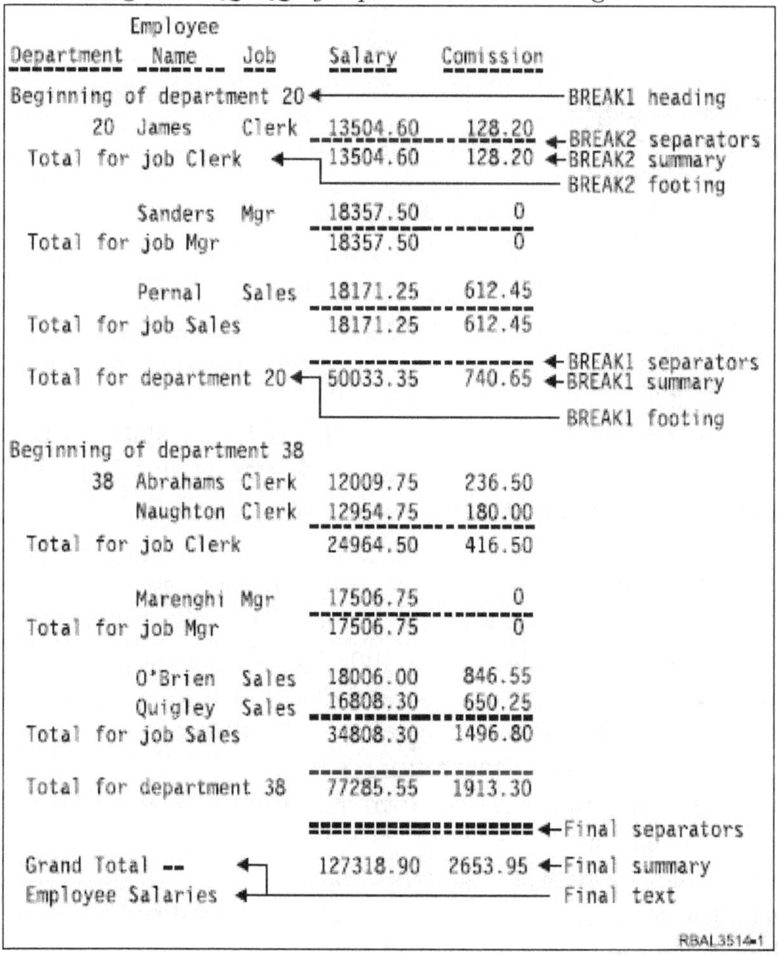

In Figure 12-1, you can see many of the things described in the points noted above. A high-level break, BREAK1, for example is specified for the DEPT column. The break is defined so that whenever the department number changes, the summary details are displayed (in this case, the total salaries and commissions for the department).

A second-level break, BREAK2, is specified for the JOB column. The second break is defined so that whenever the job type changes, the summary details are displayed (the total salaries and commissions for employees of that job type within that department).

In summarizing this report in the Redbook, IBM cautions that when using break levels, you must sort the row data into an order that is logical for the breaks. For example, if you want the report to break when the value in the DEPT column changes, you need to sort the row data by DEPT. That means that all departments will be grouped together (as you specify in either ascending or descending order of the sorting sequence).

If you are creating or changing an SQL query, you sort row data using the ORDER BY clause of the SELECT statement. If you are creating or changing a prompted query, you sort row data using the Select Sort Columns display.

You need also be concerned about columns for which you specify break levels since they are not automatically shown on the left of the report, and the columns for which you specify summaries are not automatically shown on the right. There are steps that you must perform to make this happen properly. For example, to make your report more readable, you can specify a column sequence in the report form definition so that break columns appear on the left of the report, and columns with summary data appear on the right. Figure 12-1 shows two break levels. However, many additional levels can be defined as long as they make the report more, and not less, readable.

How Does QM Query work?

The best was to get acquainted with QM Query is to use it. It is very intuitive. Having written a whole book on AS/400 Query, I can assure you that there is more than ample material within QM Query to write an even larger book. Rather than do that however, within this book, (this chapter), I have broken Query Manager into five manageable parts that we will cover in a tutorial fashion. From this tutorial, the intuitive nature of the QM facility and the HELP text will guide you through other QM adventures.

The five parts that the tutorial covers are as follows:

- A. Producing a default query with SQL
- B. Creating a report form for a query report with SQL
- C. Modifying an in process report form for a query report with SQL
- D. Producing a default query with the query prompter.
- E. Using the QM Edit facility to create and maintain databases

A. Producing a Default Query with SQL

The ten steps to get a QM Query Menu launched and get a default report created are as follows:

1. Start Query Manager by typing STRQM on a IBM i command line and hit the Enter key. You will then see the QM main menu in Figure 12-2.

Figure 12-2 Query Manager Main Menu

```
                       DB2 UDB for IBM i Query Manager
                                      System:   SYSTEM3
Select one of the following:

     1. Work with Query Manager queries
     2. Work with Query Manager report forms
     3. Work with Query Manager tables

    10. Work with Query Manager profiles

Selection
      _1__
F3=Exit   F12=Cancel    F22=QM Statement
```

2. Select menu option 1, Work with Query Manager queries
and press Enter

Figure 12-3 Prompt or SQL? Pick SQL

```
              Work with Query Manager Queries

Library . . . . . . _____    Name, F4 for list
Query creation mode. PROMPT
```

3. Look for PROMPT or SQL as shown in Figure 12-3.
PROMPT will take you through the QM prompter, which is
similar, but better than the ISQL prompter. It will guide you
through the construction of your SQL statement. Change the
mode here from PROMPT to SQL as shown in Step 4 below.

4. If the mode is listed as PROMPT, as in Figure 12-3, Press
F19 to toggle the display back to SQL.

Figure 12-4 Prompt or SQL? Is SQL

```
              Work with Query Manager Queries

Library . . . . . . _____    Name, F4 for list
Query creation mode. SQL

Type options, press Enter.
1=Crt 2=Chg 3=Copy 4=Dlt 5=Dsply 6=Print 7=Rename
9=Run 10=Convert to SQL

 Opt  Query       Type       Description
 1    QM02E
```

5. The display changes to SQL, as in the top of Figure 12-4

6. Take Option 1 as shown at the bottom of Figure 12-4.

7. Type in a name for your new query from bottom of Figure 12-4 (QM02E) and then press Enter.

Figure 12-5 Type SQL Statement

```
                        Edit Query
Columns . . . :   1 70                        Query  . . . : QM02E
QM . .  _____

Type SQL Statement
    ********************* Beginning of Data *******************
''''''' Select * from vendorp_____
'''''''

    *********************** End of Data ***********************
2=Alternate keys F3=Exit F4=Prompt  F5=Run report   F6=Run sample
9=Retrieve       F15=Check syntax    F24=More keys
```

8. Type in a simple SQL Statement as in Figure 12-5 with QM.

9. Take Option F5 to get the Run Query Prompt as in Figure 12-6

10. Leave all defaults on Figure 12-6 to produce default report Figure 12-7.

Figure 12-6 Run Query Prompt

```
                        Run Query

Query . . . . . . . . . :   *
  Library . . . . . . . :

Type choices, press Enter.
  Run query mode  . . . .   1          1=Interactive
                                       2=Batch
  Run sample only . . . .   N          Y=Yes, N=No
  Form  . . . . . . . . .   *SYSDFT    Name, *SYSDFT, F4 for list
    Library . . . . . . .              Name, *CURLIB, *LIBL
  Output  . . . . . . . .   1          1=Display, 2=Printer
                                       3=File

                                                       Bottom
F3=Exit   F4=Prompt   F12=Cancel
```

Figure 12-7 QM Query Default Report

```
                              Display Report
Query . . . . .:    SQLBOOK/QM02E              Width . . .:        142
Form . . . . .:     *SYSDFT                    Column . .:         1
Control   . . . .
Line
....+....1....+....2....+....3....+....4....+....5....+....6....+....7.
           VNDNBR  NAME                         ADDR1                      CITY
           ------- ------------------------     ------------------------   -----
  -
000001        38   John B Stetz Clothier        3817 N. PULASKI            SCRANT
000002        40   Scranton Fabrics             2147 S MAIN ST             OLD FO
000003        42   Pass Pax Inc                 1539 OAK HILL              OLD FO
000004        44   Cliffy Equipment Co.         2232 FOUEST                SCRANT
000005        46   Butts & Wallace Inc          2150 TOUGHY                SCRANT
000006        48   Denton and Ball              7934 S SCRANTON AVE        SCRANT
000007        49   John Studios                 2040 N BELTWAY             SCRANT
000008        25   Macone Corp Of Chicago       1345 Prill Avenue          Chicag
000009        26   Lockhart Machinaws           45 Ginzo Lane              Wokego
000010        28   Charley Engraving Co         Pedulllion Avenue          Greghe
000011        30   Detweiller Controls          45 Fognetta Place          Kernst
000012        32   Irfing Power Machinery       56 Fineel La               Swingd
000013        34   Blind Robin Copany           11 Robin Lane              Robin
000014        36   Facile Steel Co              78 Engraved Rd.            Mattus
                                                                           More...
```

B. Creating a Report Form for a Query Report w/ SQL

Now that we have seen how the default report is created with QM Query, let's try to create a specially formatted report to get a sense of how QM Query permits us to dress up our report output.

Hit the Enter key from the panel in Figure 12-7 and then you will see the Exit panel. For our purposes take option 1 to save the results of the query so it does not have to be redone for the formatting part. Now, you are back to a panel that looks like the one shown in Figure 12-5 with your SQL on it.

From here, there are actually two ways to create a formatted report. You can (1) continue to exit until you hit the main menu as shown in Figure 12-2. We'll call this option "Starting Over." Option (2) is that you can choose to enter the report formatting facility directly from the panel shown in Figure 12-5 without getting out. We'll call this option, "Enter from Query." In both of these scenarios, as long as we have already built one query and saved the work space with option 1, the QM form designer believes that it is working with the simple select all from the Vendorp file that we built earlier in this chapter.

Starting Over

When starting over to get to formatting, let's assume that we have already entered the STRQM command and we are sitting at the Query Manager Main Menu as in Figure 12-2. From the menu shown in Figure 12-2, you would select Option 2 to Work with Query Manager report forms. Once you select that option, you will see a panel as in Figure 12-8 below:

In this scenario, name the first form that you build, FirstForm. Take the option 1 to create it as in Figure 12-8, and press the Enter key. You will then be taken to the panel shown in Figure 12-9 to "Select Report Format."

Figure 12-8 First Panel Work With QM Forms -- Name Form

```
                   Work with Query Manager Report Forms

Library  . . . . . . . . . .    SQLBOOK      Name, F4 for list

Type options, press Enter.
  1=Create 2=Change 3=Copy 4=Delete 5=Display  6=Print   7=Rename
  9=Run report

Opt   Form        Description
  1   FirstForm

  (Cannot find object to match specified name.)


Bottom
F3=Exit   F4=Prompt  F5=Refresh F11=Display form only   F12=Cancel
F16=Repeat position to   F17=Position to   F22=QM Statement
```

Enter From Query F13

When you have already run a query as we did with a default form at the beginning of this chapter, and you have hit the Enter key after examining your report output on the display, and you are sitting on a panel that looks a lot like the one shown in Figure 12-5, you can move directly into forms creation.

The one trick is that you will not see the Edit Output Form option (F13) on your panel, but it is available for your use. Check out Figure 12-5 and you will not see it anywhere. It is not displayed on the bottom of the screen.

If you want to see the option, just hit F24 and it will appear. However, you do not have to see it, to use it. Hit F13 and you can immediately begin to dress up this sample report. You will see a panel similar to that shown in Figure 12-9 to select your report format.

So, both options, "starting over" and F13 from the Edit Query panel take you to the same report formatting panel in Figure 12-9. The one big difference is that your report form will have the same name as your query when you come in form F13, whereas when you start the forms definition process from Option 2 on the main menu. You get to name your form differently from the query as we did with the name "FirstForm." in Figure 12-8.

Figure 12-9 Formatting the Query Report

```
                        Select Report Format

Form . . . . . . . :    *

Type options, press Enter.  Press F21 to select all.
  1=Select


  Opt      Report Format
  1        Edit column formatting
           Edit page heading
           Edit page footing
           Edit final text
           Edit break text
           Specify formatting options
  _____
                                                          Bottom
F3=Exit    F5=Display report    F12=Cancel    F13=Edit query    F18=Display SQL
F21=Select all    F22=QM Statement
```

Figure 12-10 Unmodified Edit Column Panel

```
                        Edit Column Formatting
```

```
Type information, press Enter.
For Usage and Edit, press F4 for list.
For Heading, press F4 for prompt.

Column          Heading                    Usage   Edit  Seq  Indent  Width
VNDNBR          VNDNBR                                     1     2        7
NAME            NAME                                       2     2       25
ADDR1           ADDR1                                      3     2       25
CITY            CITY                                       4     2       16
STATE           STATE                                      5     2        5
ZIPCD           ZIPCD                                      6     2        7
VNDCLS          VNDCLS                                     7     2        6
VNDSTS          VNDSTS                                     8     2        6
BALOWE          BALOWE                                     9     2       13
SRVRTG          SRVRTG                                    10     2        6
                                                                     Bottom
F2=Alternate keys    F3=Exit   F4=Prompt    F5=Display report   F6=Insert line
F10=Copy line        F11=Edit heading       F12=Cancel          F24=More keys
```

When you type in the 1 in the panel shown in Figure 12-9 for Edit column formatting, you will be taken to an Unmodified Edit Panel as shown in Figure 12-10 above.

Figure 12-11 Modified Edit Column Panel

```
                              Edit Column Formatting

Type information, press Enter.
For Usage and Edit, press F4 for list.
For Heading, press F4 for prompt.

Column          Heading                    Usage   Edit  Seq  Indent  Width
VNDNBR          VNDNBR                                     1     2        7
NAME            NAME                                       2     2       25
ADDR1           ADDR1                                      3     2       25
CITY            CITY                                       4     2       15
STATE           STATE                      BREAK1          5     2        5
ZIPCD           ZIPCD                                      6     2        8
VNDCLS          VNDCLS                                     7     2        6
VNDSTS          VNDSTS                                     8     2        6
BALOWE          BALOWE                                     9     2       13
SRVRTG          SRVRTG                                    10     2        6
                                                                     Bottom
F2=Alternate keys    F3=Exit   F4=Prompt    F5=Display report   F6=Insert line
F10=Copy line        F11=Edit heading       F12=Cancel          F24=More keys
```

Type in the keyword "BREAK1" in the usage column, which appears next to the state field. Your panel will look like the modified Edit Panel shown in Figure 12-11. To see a report formatted with this break on the state column, press F5 and you will be taken to the panel shown in Figure 12-12

Figure 12-12 Formatted Report wth State Break

```
                              Display Report
Query . . . . . :   *                      Width . . . :       142
```

```
Form  . . . . . :     *                        Column  . . :        1
Control  . . . .
Line
....+....1....+....2....+....3....+....4....+....5....+....6....+....7.
          VNDNBR  NAME                          ADDR1                    CITY
          -------  ------------------------     -------------------------  -----
-
000001       38   John B Stetz Clothier        3817 N. PULASKI          SCRANT
000002       40   Scranton Fabrics             2147 S MAIN ST           OLD FO
000003       42   Pass Pax Inc                 1539 OAK HILL            OLD FO
000004       44   Cliffy Equipment Co.         2232 FOUEST              SCRANT
000005       46   Butts & Wallace Inc          2150 TOUGHY              SCRANT
000006       48   Denton and Ball              7934 S SCRANTON AVE      SCRANT
000007       49   John Studios                 2040 N BELTWAY           SCRANT
000008
000009
000010
000011       25   Macone Corp Of Chicago       1345 Prill Avenue        Chicag
000012
000013
000014
                                                                        More...

   F3=Exit      F12=Cancel      F19=Left     F20=Right      F21=Split
```

Of course, State is over more to the right on the panel but you can see the level break on line # 11.

C. Modifying an in Process Report Form for a Query Report with SQL

Press Enter from the displayed report panel shown in Figure 12-12. We have a few more report formatting options to examine starting with Figure 12-13 below. Our next step is to return to column editing and make further formatting revisions to the FirstForm form.

Figure 12-13 More Edit Column Formatting

```
                        Select Report Format

Form . . . . . . . :     FIRSTFORM

Type options, press Enter.  Press F21 to select all.
  1=Select

  Opt     Report Format
  1       Edit column formatting
  __      Edit page heading
  __      Edit page footing
  __      Edit final text
  __      Edit break text
  __      Specify formatting options


                                                        Bottom
F3=Exit           F5=Display report   F13=Edit query   F18=Display SQL
F21=Select all    F22=QM Statement
```

Take option 1 as the Edit column formatting option in Figure 12-13 just as you did before as shown in the panel in Figure 12-9 to start the formatting process. This will bring you back to the modified panel shown in Figure 12-14.

From the modified panel shown in Figure 12-14A, you can perform a number of additional tricks to help your output look even better. For example, by hitting F4 on the usage column, you can change or add usage to a particular column. When you hit F4, you will see the types of usage changes that you can make to a given field. These are shown in Figure 12-14-B as possible entries for the usage field:

Figure 12-14A Modified Edit Column Panel

```
                    Edit Column Formatting

Type information, press Enter.
For Usage and Edit, press F4 for list.
For Heading, press F4 for prompt.

Column          Heading            Usage    Edit   Seq  Indent  Width
VNDNBR          VNDNBR                              1     2        7
NAME            NAME                               2     2       25
ADDR1           ADDR1                              3     2       25
CITY            CITY                               4     2       15
STATE           STATE              BREAK1          5     2        5
ZIPCD           ZIPCD                              6     2        8
VNDCLS          VNDCLS                             7     2        6
VNDSTS          VNDSTS                             8     2        6
BALOWE          BALOWE                             9     2       13
SRVRTG          SRVRTG                            10     2        7
                                                               Bottom
F2=Alternate keys    F3=Exit   F4=Prompt   F5=Display report   F6=Insert line
F10=Copy line        F11=Edit heading      F12=Cancel          F24=More keys
```

Figure 12-14B Description of the Usage Column Values

Usage Column

Value	Description
Break1	Highest level break
Break2	Second level break
Break3	Third level break
Break4	Fourth level break
Break5	Fifth level break
Break6	Cowest level break
Omit	Omit column from report
Average	Average of the column values
Count	Number of column values
First	First value in column
Last	Last value in column
Maximum	Maximum value in column
Minimum	Minimum value in column
Sum	Sum of values in column

Edit Column

By hitting F4 on the Edit column, you can also change the data type of the field accordingly. Your choices for data type for output formatting are as follows:

Data Type
✓ Character data
✓ Numeric data
✓ Date and time data
✓ Graphic data

Edit Heading

If you take another look at the bottom of Figure 12-14A, you will see that there is an Edit Heading Function key (F11). If you look at the heading column, you will also notice that it is not underlined, which means it is not changeable in its current state.

By hitting F11 with the cursor on the Usage Column, the panel will toggle the input fields to the column heading area and make the rest of the panel unmodifiable as shown in Figure 12-15. This enables you to edit the column headings, making them bigger or smaller for your report. You can also just go ahead and change the names to suit your style. When you press F11, you see a panel similar to that shown in Figure 12-15. Then you can make the changes as you see for the column headings.

Figure 12-15 Edit Column Headings

```
                    Edit Column Formatting

Type information, press Enter.
For Usage and Edit, press F4 for list.
For Heading, press F4 for prompt.

Column              Heading
VNDNBR              Vendor No._____
NAME                Vnd Name_____
ADDR1               Address Line 1_____
CITY                City_____
STATE               State_____
ZIPCD               Zip Code_____
VNDCLS              Vendor Class_____
VNDSTS              Vendor Status_____
BALOWE              Balance Owed_____
SRVRTG              Service Rating_____

                                                    Bottom
F2=Alt keys F3=Exit F4=Prompt F5=Display report  F6=Insert line
F10=Copy F11=Edit usage F12=Cancel F13=Edit query F24=More keys
```

The reason the panel was merely similar and not the same is because I took the opportunity to pre-change the prompts for the report. The panel would have had the column headings as in Figure 12-14A if I had not pre-keyed them prior to showing you Figure 12-15.

Hit the Enter key and you will be back to the Select Report Format panel as shown last in Figure 12-9. From here, you can pick a few more formatting options such as the Break level heading and the Report Heading which you can see in Figures 12-16 and 12-17 respectively.

Figure 12-16 Edit the Break Heading

```
                    Edit Break Heading

Break level  . . . . . . . . . :    1

Type choices, press Enter.
    Put on new page  . . . . . . . . . . . . .  N        Y=Yes, N=No
    Repeat column heading  . . . . . . . . . .  N        Y=Yes, N=No
    Blank lines before . . . . . . . . . . . .  0        0-999
    Blank lines after  . . . . . . . . . . . .  0        0-999

Break text:  Use &col to cause variable insertion.

Line  Align         Break Heading Text
  1   LEFT              This is the Break Level 1 Text by Brian Kelly
                                                            Bottom
F2=Alternate keys    F3=Exit    F4=Prompt      F5=Run report  F6=Insert line
F10=Copy line    F12=Cancel   F13=Edit query   F14=Delete line   F24=More keys
```

From the panel in Figure 12-13, I took the option to Edit the Break Text and was presented with the panel in Figure 12-16. I then created a heading for the break field STATE. I put my name on the break heading so that it would be easily identifiable when it is displayed or printed in this tutorial.

Figure 12-17 Edit the Page Heading – Line 1

```
                         Edit Page Heading

Type choices, press Enter.
  Blank lines before . . . . . . . . . . . .   0          0-999
  Blank lines after  . . . . . . . . . . . .   2          0-999

Page text:  Use &col, &DATE, &TIME, and &PAGE to cause variable insertion.

Line  Align              Page Heading Text
  1   CENTER             Line 1 Page Heading Brian Kelly

                                                          Bottom
F2=Alternate keys    F3=Exit    F4=Prompt      F5=Run report   F6=Insert line
F10=Copy line    F12=Cancel    F13=Edit query    F14=Delete line    F24=More keys
```

From the panel in Figure 12-13, I took the option to Edit page heading. In Figure 12-17, you can see that I created a one line page heading that would be easily identifiable in a display or a report. The other edit options from the panel in Figure 12-13 are also very intuitive so as you are doing this little QM tutorial, feel free to include these also.

If you were to hit F5 to see your report on the display at this time, if you were building the form independent of the QM Query, you would see the following prompt as in Figure 12-18 before the report would display as in Figure 12-19. Note the QM01E query name in Figure 12-18. That is because a form is not a query. The Query must be done and have its output brought into memory or saved under a name in order for that particular query to be used to get the data into the QM form that you are designing.

Figure 12-18 Run Query Prompt – Give Query name if New

```
                              Run Query

Form  . . . . . . . . . :       *
  Library . . . . . . . :

Type choices, press Enter.
  Run query mode  . . . .     1            1=Interactive
                                           2=Batch
  Run sample only . . . .     N            Y=Yes, N=No
  Query . . . . . . . . .     QM01E        Name, F4 for list *** (to be entered)
    Library . . . . . . .     SQLBOOK      Name, *CURLIB, *LIBL
  Output  . . . . . . . .     1            1=Display, 2=Printer
                                           3=File
                                                                  Bottom

F3=Exit    F4=Prompt    F12=Cancel
```

When you hit the Enter key in Figure 12-18, the QM01E Query
will run and the output will display using the definitions for
FirstForm that you have been working on in this tutorial. You
will see the report displayed as shown in Figure 12-19.

Figure 12-19 Formatted Rpt w State Brk & Modified Headings

```
                          Display Report
Query . . . . .:   SQLBOOK/QM01E          Width . . .:       142
Form  . . . . .:   SQLBOOK/FIRSTFORM      Column  . .:         1
Control . . . .
Line
....+....1....+....2....+....3....+....4....+....5....+....6....+....7.
        VNDNBR  NAME                      ADDR1                    CITY
        -------  ------------------------  ------------------------  -----
-
000001 This is the Break Level 1 Text by Brian Kelly
000002     38   John B Stetz Clothier     3817 N. PULASKI          SCRANT
000003     40   Scranton Fabrics          2147 S MAIN ST           OLD FO
000004     42   Pass Pax Inc              1539 OAK HILL            OLD FO
000005     44   Cliffy Equipment Co.      2232 FOUEST              SCRANT
000006     46   Butts & Wallace Inc       2150 TOUGHY              SCRANT
000007     48   Denton and Ball           7934 S SCRANTON AVE      SCRANT
000008     49   John Studios              2040 N BELTWAY           SCRANT
000009
000010
000011
000012 This is the Break Level 1 Text by Brian Kelly
000013     25   Macone Corp Of Chicago    1345 Prill Avenue        Chicag
000014
                                                              More...

  F3=Exit    F12=Cancel    F19=Left    F20=Right    F21=Split
```

When you hit the Enter key, you will get the pop-up prompt to
save the active data from the query as shown in Figure 12-20

Figure 12-20 Save Active Query Data

```
: ................................................................. :
:                            Exit                                  :
:                                                                  :
:  Type choice, press Enter.                                       :
:                                                                  :
:    Option  .  .  .  .  .   1      1=Exit saving active data      :
:                                   2=Exit without saving active data  :
:                                   3=Resume displayed report      :
:                                                                  :
:    F12=Cancel                                                    :
:                                                                  :
: ................................................................. :
```

That wraps up the Form creation section of the QM Query tutorial. Feel free to exercise this material over and over with different options and different saved names to get a good feel for what it is all about.

Figure 12-21 Back to the Select Report Format Panel

```
                         Select Report Format

Form . . . . . . . . :     FIRSTFORM

Type options, press Enter.   Press F21 to select all.
  1=Select


   Opt       Report Format
             Edit column formatting
             Edit page heading
             Edit page footing
             Edit final text
             Edit break text
             Specify formatting options

                                                           Bottom
F3=Exit F5=Display report  F13=Edit query    F18=Display SQL
F21=Select all    F22=QM Statement
RUN QUERY successful.
```

Now, it is time to end the SQL type queries that we have been using and let's see what it is like to use the prompted queries. Start by exiting. Hit F3 to get out of the QM Forms Manager and you will get the Exit prompt in Figure 12-22

Figure 12-22 Exit Prompt for Forms Manager

```
                               Exit

Type choices, press Enter.

   Option . . . . .   1               1=Save and exit
                                      2=Exit without save
                                      3=Resume without save
                                      4=Save and resume


   Form . . . . . .   FIRSTFORM       Name
      Library  . . .     SQLBOOK      Name, *CURLIB
   Description  . .



F5=Refresh    F12=Cancel
```

If you came in fresh, you will see the form name from the
Figure 12-8 displayed so you need only hit enter if the name is
OK. If you came in from F13, you get a chance to name the
form again or take the default form name, which would be the
name of the Query in which you were engaged when you took
the F13 prompt. Hit Enter and you will be taken to the panel in
Figure 12-23 on the way to an exit.

Figure 12-23 Back to QM Query Forms Panel on way out

```
                     Work with Query Manager Report Forms

   Library  . . . . . . . . . . .SQLBOOK      Name, F4 for list

   Type options, press Enter.
     1=Create   2=Change    3=Copy   4=Delete   5=Display
   6=Print    7=Rename          9=Run report

   Opt  Form          Description
    1   FirstForm
    __  FIRSTFORM


                                                 Bottom
   F3=Exit F4=Prompt F5=Refresh F11=Display form only    F12=Cancel
   F16=Repeat position to    F17=Position to    F22=QM Statement
```

Hit F3 from the panel in Figure 12-23 and you will continue
your exit at the Main QM panel in Figure 12-24.

Figure 12-24 Query Manager Main Panel

```
                    DB2 UDB for IBM i Query Manager

System:    SYSTEM3
Select one of the following:

     1. Work with Query Manager queries
     2. Work with Query Manager report forms
     3. Work with Query Manager tables

    10. Work with Query Manager profiles


Selection    1

F3=Exit    F12=Cancel    F22=QM Statement
```

D. Producing Default Qry with Qry Prompt.

Now, we can exit QM Forms Designer by hitting F3 one more
time. But, rather than do that, let's move on to create another
query but this time, let's use the prompter. You will find the
prompter to be a very powerful, Query/400-like means of
getting powerful queries operational without having to have all
of your SQL skills in tact before you venture out.

Using Prompted Input

For a moment, review Figure 12-3. Notice the keyword there is
PROMPT. To use the prompted Query, However the first time
through we chose to work with SQL. Now, to get restarted
with the Query Manager, go all the way out to the Query
Manager Main panel as shown in Figure 12-24 above.

We are going to take option 1 again from the panel in Figure
12-24 since we now want to build a query using the prompted
input. From there, we will be taken to the panel in Figure 12-

25 which right now is set to SQL sicne that is what we have
been using.

Figure 12-25 Prompt or SQL?

```
                  Work with Query Manager Queries

Library  . . . . . .  _____   Name, F4 for list
Query creation mode. SQL

Type options, press Enter.
1=Crt 2=Chg 3=Copy 4=Dlt 5=Dsply 6=Print 7=Rename
9=Run 10=Convert to SQL

 Opt   Query       Type       Description
 1     PQUERY
```

If the panel says SQL as in Figure 12-25, hit F19 and it will
toggle back to PROMPT. Now, with the panel at PROMPT,
take option 1 and type in the name of a new QM Query
PQUERY, and press the Enter key. You will see a panel that
looks like the one shown in Figure 12-26.

Figure 12-26 Define Prompted Query

```
                             Define Prompted Query

Query  . . . . . . . :     PQUERY

Type options, press Enter.  Press F21 to select all.
  1=Select

Opt       Prompted Query Selection
1         Specify files
__        Define expressions
1         Select and sequence fields
__        Select records
__        Select sort fields
__        Select summary functions
__        Specify duplicate records
__        Specify report formatting

Bottom
 F3=Exit          F5=Run report   F6=Run sample   F12=Cancel
F18=Display SQL
 F21=Select all   F22=QM Statement
```

From the panel shown in Figure 12-26, take option 1 in the first option area to specify the file(s) for the prompted query. We will return to this panel to discuss the 2nd area in which we have paced a 1 as shown in Figure 12-26.

Figure 12-27 Specify the Vendorp File

```
                          Specify Files

Type choices, press Enter.

File . . . . . . . . . . :   A    vendorp_____    Name, F4 for list
   Library  . . . . . . . :        SQLBOOK                Name, *LIBL

+ for more files . . . . .

                                                                    Bottom
F3=Exit            F4=Prompt    F5=Run report    F6=Run sample   F12=Cancel
F18=Display SQL    F20=Display entire name       F22=QM Statement
```

Type in "vendorp" for the file name and SQLBOOK for the library name. Then hit Enter. You will come back to the Define Prompted Query command as in Figure 12-26. Place a 1 next to the Select and sequence fields option as we have already done in Figure 12-26, and you will be taken to a panel similar to that shown in Figure 12-28 for field selection.

You will begin to notice if you are a Query/400 user that this regimen is very similar to how things are done with that product.

Figure 12-28 Select and Sequence Fields

```
                     Select And Sequence Fields

Type a sequence number (0-9999) for the name of each field to appear in the
   report, press Enter.

Seq   Field                          Seq    Field
1     SQLBOOK.VENDORP-- ALL
         A.VNDNBR
         A.NAME
         A.ADDR1
         A.CITY
         A.STATE
         A.ZIPCD
         A.VNDCLS
         A.VNDSTS
         A.BALOWE
         A.SRVRTG


                                                                    Bottom
F3=Exit    F5=Run report    F6=Run sample    F10=Duplicate column
F11=Display type            F12=Cancel       F18=Display SQL   F24=More keys
```

Pick option 1 for all the fields in as shown in Figure 12-28. This is basically the same as the "*" option in SQL. Then press the Enter key. From here, the panel numbers all the fields and places the ALL option at the bottom as shown in Figure 12-29.

Hit Enter again from Figure 12-29 to accept the default sequencing of the fields and you are taken back to the Define Prompted Query panel as shown in Figure 12-26. Of course, if you want to change the sequence of the fields as in Figure 12-29, you may just type over the sequence number with the number in sequence that you would like to assign to the field you want to move. You would type one field at a time. When you have made all your changes hit Enter and you will return to the Define Prompted Query panel shown in Figure 12-30.

Figure 12-29 Select and Seq. (Returned and Sequenced)

```
                        Select And Sequence Fields

Type a sequence number (0-9999) for the name of each field
to appear in the
  report, press Enter.


Seq    Field                          Seq     Field
  10      A.VNDNBR
  20      A.NAME
  30      A.ADDR1
  40      A.CITY
  50      A.STATE
  60      A.ZIPCD
  70      A.VNDCLS
  80      A.VNDSTS
  90      A.BALOWE
 100      A.SRVRTG
  __    SQLBOOK.VENDORP-- ALL



                                                         Bottom
F3=Exit    F5=Run report F6=Run sample F10=Duplicate column
F11=Display type   F12=Cancel  18=Display SQL   F24=More keys
```

Figure 12-30 Define Prompted Query – Two Selections

```
                          Define Prompted Query

Query  . . . . . . :    PQUERY

Type options, press Enter.  Press F21 to select all.
  1=Select

Opt      Prompted Query Selection
  __    > Specify files
  __      Define expressions
  __    > Select and sequence fields
  __      Select records
  __      Select sort fields
  __      Select summary functions
  __      Specify duplicate records
  __      Specify report formatting

                                                      Bottom
F3=Exit   F5=Run report   F6=Run sample   F18=Display SQL
F21=Select all      F22=QM Statement
```

As you look at the Define Prompted Query panel in Figure 12-30, you will notice that just like Query/400, the QM facility is nice enough to mark the fact that you have worked on that option by placing a greater than '>' sign next to it. As you can see, there are lots more options that you can pick and they are implemented as nicely as Query/400 so they should be familiar to most users.

Feel free to exercise all these options in this tutorial setting. When you are ready to get your report, hit F5 just as in the SQL based QM Query examples to run the prompted default report. You will see a report similar to that shown in Figure 12-31.

Figure 12-31 Display Report from Prompted Query

```
                              Display Report
Query . . . . .:    SQLTEST/PQUERY          Width . . .:        142
Form  . . . . .:    *SYSDFT                  Column . .:          1
Control  . . . .
Line
....+....1....+....2....+....3....+....4....+....5....+....6....+....7.
          VNDNBR  NAME                       ADDR1                    CITY
          -------  ------------------------  ------------------------  -----
-
000001       38  John B Stetz Clothier      3817 N. PULASKI          SCRANT
000002       40  Scranton Fabrics           2147 S MAIN ST           OLD FO
000003       42  Pass Pax Inc               1539 OAK HILL            OLD FO
000004       44  Cliffy Equipment Co.       2232 FOUEST              SCRANT
000005       46  Butts & Wallace Inc        2150 TOUGHY              SCRANT
000006       48  Denton and Ball            7934 S SCRANTON AVE      SCRANT
000007       49  John Studios               2040 N BELTWAY           SCRANT
000008       25  Macone Corp Of Chicago     1345 Prill Avenue        Chicag
000009       26  Lockhart Machinaws         45 Ginzo Lane            Wokego
000010       28  Charley Engraving Co       Pedulllion Avenue        Greghe
000011       30  Detweiller Controls        45 Fognetta Place        Kernst
000012       32  Irfing Power Machinery     56 Fineel La             Swingd
000013       34  Blind Robin Copany         11 Robin Lane            Robin
000014       36  Facile Steel Co            78 Engraved Rd.          Mattus

More...
 F3=Exit    F12=Cancel    F19=Left    F20=Right    F21=Split
```

If you press Enter, you will get the Exit panel. Take option 1 to save your work. You will again be at the Define Prompted Query Panel. From there, you will get another Exit panel where you can save the default prompted query and exit. When you get back to the Work with Query Manager Queries main panel, you have gone far enough. You can now select another query to be run or you can hit F3 to end the session. For now, we are done with reporting but we are still not finished with QM.

This action returns you to the main Query Manager Panel as shown in Figure 12-32. This is as far as we want to go at this point for Query Manager Reporting Options. Now, let's edit some data.

E. Using QM Edit--Create & Maintain DBs

Now that we have worked our way through the various query methods, SQL and PROMPT of the QM tool, we can proceed with a unique aspect of QM, the Edit facility.

Years ago when I developed my first course in End-User Computing for the early AS/400, SQL was just being introduced and not many users had the product. Now SQL is somewhat mature; it is strategic; it is well featured; and it comes with many of the smaller IBM i models and it is a feature purchased by many of the larger IBM i shops. Times have changed for the SQL product.

Prior to SQL and the perfection of QM as a powerful DB facility, I tried to piece together an en-user computing scenario for an AS/400 shop that would parallel the type of database functionality to which users had become accustomed with the Windows client databases of the day, including the infamous dBase, and the popular Paradox product. This was actually before Microsoft Access had achieved such popularity.

PC database packages enabled data structures to be built quite easily and to be altered with no sweat. When the db was altered, the data just automatically merged back into the altered file and only added fields needed to be touched with additional data. There were browse facilities to look and modify multiple rows of a PC database at a time and there were options to change one record at a time. You could also get reports very easily and you could structure nicely formatted reports with level breaks, headings, etc.

Hoping to convince small businesses that database on AS/400 was also easy, though there was no simple GUI to help me achieve this, I put together the ideal end user package for the AS/400 and I taught it as a module in some formal education classes that I delivered to IT professionals.

Though I was able to define end user computing facilities and how to get private databases up and running on an AS/400, I had to admit that it would be unwieldy at best to recommend turning this scenario over to real end users. So, IT professionals remained my target audience. The tools that were needed back then to provide simple, private database capability to AS/400 users included those defined in Figure 12-32.

Figure 12-32 DB Tools for IBM i Prior to Query Manager

Tool	Purpose
Program Development Manager (PDM)	Launch vehicle for other tools
Data Description Specifications (DDS)	Needed to define private databases
Library (CRTLIB)	Needed to store the DB and Source
Source file for storing DDS (QDDSSRC)	Needed to have a spot to store DB structures
Source File Member	Needed as a physical spot in a source file to store individual sets of DDS. Try explaining the concept of a QDDSSRC file member to an end user
Source Entry Utility (SEU)	Needed a means of entering DDS Db specs
Create Physical and Logical File commands (CRTPF / CRTLF)	Needed a means of creating DB objects in libraries
Data File Utility	Needed a tool to use for entering and maintaining the private database
Query/400	Needed a tool to be able to create reports from the private database
Remove Member, (RMVM) Delete File (DLTF) Reorganize Physical File Member (RGZPFM), etc.	Tools to help in the maintenance of the database environment.

I am pleased to say that those days are gone. Now, even with a green screen interface, the QM facility provides most of what is needed to create and maintain your private databases on the IBM i. I would be the last to suggest that an IT shop turn over the full QM toolset to the knowledge workers in the firm but prior to this facility existing, one look at the tools above and you know that it was more than security and data integrity notions that kept the IT shop from giving end users full access to their own databases.

With the IBM i database facilities that we are going to examine in Chapter 18, it is even easier than QM to create and maintain databases.

But, we are getting ahead of ourselves. It is now time to demonstrate the most radical capability of all that is packaged within the QM facilty. It is called Edit Table but it is the add-on to the package that really gives it the end-user capability that no IBM product ever delivered to an AS/400 end user in the past. Again, whether you choose to give this facility to an end user is up to you. But, it is certainly nice that it is in the product and it is reasonably easy to work with. Let's learn how:

Working with QM Tables

Figure 12-33 Query Manager Main Menu

```
                      DB2 UDB for IBM i Query Manager
                                    System:    SYSTEM3
Select one of the following:

    1. Work with Query Manager queries
    2. Work with Query Manager report forms
    3. Work with Query Manager tables

    10. Work with Query Manager profiles

Selection
     _3__

F3=Exit    F12=Cancel    F22=QM Statement
```

From the Query Manager main menu, take option 3 to launch the table facility.

From the main QM Menu, this time, lets take option 3 to use Query Manager to work with some SQL tables. A "pop-up" green screen menu overlay appears asking you to specify the library name to search for your database. This panel is shown in Figure 12-34

Figure 12-34 Start Edit Facility By Specifying Library Name

```
:.............................................................:
:                 Specify Collection or Library              :
:                                                            :
:   Type choice, press Enter.                                :
:                                                            :
:     Library . . . . . . . . .   SQLBOOK      Name, F4 for list :
:                                                            :
:                                                            :
:                                                            :
:   F4=Prompt   F12=Cancel                                   :
:                                                            :
:............................................................:
```

Press Enter and QM will give you an alphabetical list of all the
database files in the library to give you the opportunity to select
one to work with. Recognizing that all of the old PC database
tools provided a means to create a table right within the
package, option 1 of the display shown in Figure 12-35 below is
an option to create a table.

Figure 12-35 Work With QM Tables – Create Table
```
                       Work with Query Manager Tables

Library . . . . . . . . . .   SQLBOOK      Name, F4 for list

Type options, press Enter.
  1=Create table   3=Copy table     4=Delete table        5=Display table
  6=Print table    7=Rename table   8=Display definition   9=Add data
  10=Change data   11=Display data

Opt  Table                Description
1    PRIVATE
     ACP001
     ARMAST               DB Pocket Guide AR Master File
     BIDS
     CSCHGP
     CSCSFINP
     CSCSTP
     CSINVP
     CSORDP
     CSORDPRP
                                                              More...
F3=Exit   F4=Prompt    F5=Refresh   F11=Display table only   F12=Cancel
F16=Repeat position to   F17=Position to    F24=More keys
```

Of course, there is more than option 1 here to create a table.
There are 11 commands listed on the top, each activated by
typing as simple menu option (almost as easy as a mouse click)
to provide you whatever it is you need to create and manage a
database table. It takes IBM three lines just to list them and

besides that, there are more function keys at the bottom and even more if you press F24 for more keys. Of course, if you do not have a library or schema in which to place your new DB, you can get out of here and do a STRSQL and create a schema.

If you need a source file to put your CREATE Tables for keeps, then you still need to go out to a command line and use the trusty CRTSRCPF native system command. But, for the most part, there is an end user environment delivered to you within the panel that you see in Figure 12-35.

Looking at the panel in Figure 12-35, you can see that I already primed it with a 1 to create a table and the name PRIVATE to differentiate this from other databases. Of course it would be a good idea to isolate these private databases that a user creates from those in production schemas. SQLBOOK is our test library for this book so it is OK for us to create a PRIVATE table in SQLBOOK.

Press Enter to begin the table create from the panel in Figure 12-35 and you will see a very nice table definition facility as shown in the panel in Figure 12-36.

Figure 12-36 Create QM Table

```
                        Create Query Manager Table

Type choices, press Enter.
Table  .  .  .  .  .  .  .  .  .    Table  .  .  .  .  .  .       Name
Description  .  .  .  .  .  .   .  .  .     PRIVATE

                                                        Decimal
Column                         Type          Length     Places
CODE_NUMBER_____            CHARACTER     5_____   _____
DESCRIPTION_____            CHARACTER     30_____   _____
Dollars_and_cents_             _____     _____    _____
_____             _____     _____    _____
_____             _____     _____    _____
_____             _____     _____    _____
_____             _____     _____    _____
_____             _____     _____    _____
                                                                 Bottom
F3=Exit       F4=Prompt          F5=Refresh      F6=Insert line   F10=Copy line
F12=Cancel    F14=Delete line    F19=Add data    F24=More keys
```

At the point in table creation that you can observe in Figure 12-36, I have completed two fields of the three-field PRIVATE table, and now, I want to use a type of data that can hold numeric values and decimal points. Rather than guess what the exact spelling of the type needs to be, you can position your cursor to the column in which you have interest, such as the TYPE column above and when you hit the F4 key, you will be prompted with all of the field types from which you may select. So, hit F4 now and you will be presented a pop-up display that looks very much like the one shown in Figure 12-37

Figure 12-37 Data Type Pop-Up Menu

```
                         Create Query Manager Table
...........................................................................
:                         Select Data Type                                :
:                                                                          :
: Type option, press Enter.                                                :
:    1=Select                                                              :
:                                                                          :
:    Opt     Type         Description                                      :
:     __     BIGINT       Big integer                                      :
:     __     BINARY       Binary                                           :
:     __     BLOB         Binary large object                              :
:     __     CHARACTER    Any character                                    :
:     __     CLOB         Character large object                           :
:     __     DATALINK     Datalink                                         :
:                                                        More...   :
:     __     DATE         Date                                             :
:     __     DBCLOB       Double-byte large object                         :
:     _1     DECIMAL      Packed decimal                                   :
:     __     DOUBLE       Long floating point                              :
:     __     FLOAT        Floating point                                   :
:     __     GRAPHIC      Any graphic                                      :
:                                                        More...   :
:     __     INTEGER      Large integer                                    :
:     __     NUMERIC      Zoned decimal                                    :
:     __     REAL         Short floating point                             :
:     __     ROWID        Row identifier                                   :
:     __     SMALLINT     Small integer                                    :
:     __     TIME         Time                                             :
:                                                        More...   :
:     __     TIMESTAMP    Timestamp                                        :
:     __     VARBINARY    Variable binary                                  :
:     __     VARCHAR      Variable character                               :
:     __     VARGRAPHIC   Variable graphic                                 :
:                                                                          :
:                                                        Bottom    :
:  F12=Cancel                                                              :
:                                                                          :
:..........................................................................:
```

In the above panel, you see that there are three "Mores." That is because this panel is delivered in four sections. In section 2, the decimal type is given and that is what we want to use for our dollars and cents field. So, to select it, place a 1 next to DECIMAL as in Figure 12-37 and press Enter.. You will return

to the Create table panel as shown in Figure 12-38. When you
return to the panel, you will notice that the word DECIMAL
has been plugged into the type field. You will also notice that I
added the length of 6 and the decimal positions of 2 for this
numeric field.

Figure 12-38 Table Successfully Created

```
                    Create Query Manager Table

Type choices, press Enter.
Table  . . . . . . . . .    PRIVATE                  Name
Description  . . . . . .    Private Table for test private database


                                                    Decimal
Column                      Type          Length     Places
CODE_NUMBER                 CHARACTER     5
DESCRIPTION                 CHARACTER     30
DOLLARS_AND_CENTS           DECIMAL       6             2




Bottom
F3=Exit       F4=Prompt          F5=Refresh      F6=Insert line
F10=Copy line
F12=Cancel    F14=Delete line    F19=Add data    F24=More keys
Table successfully created. Press F19 to add rows.
```

At the bottom of Figure 12-38, you can see that I also pressed
the Enter key and the PRIVATE table was created successfully.
Since the library we typed in Figure 12-34 was SQLBOOK, that
is where this table was created. Following along with this
tutorial, do the same on your own systems.

Also on the bottom of Figure 12-38 is a suggestion to hit F19 to
add data. Take this option now and you will see a panel similar
to that shown in Figure 12-39.

Figure 12-39 Adding Data to a New Table

```
                    Add Data to Query Manager Table

Table . . . . . . . . :    PRIVATE
Description . . . . . :    Private Table for test private database


Type information up to (]), press Enter.

Column                    Value
CODE_NUMBER             [      ]
DESCRIPTION             [                                              ]
DOLLARS_AND_CENTS       [  0.00   ]




Bottom
F3=Exit   F5=Refresh      F11=Display type/length    F12=Cancel
F20=Display entire name   F22=QM Statement
```

Add a few records to this file and then exit by hitting F3. You
will return to the Work with Query Manager Tables menu as
shown in Figure 12-35. From this panel, roll until the
VENDORP file is shown as in Figure 12-40.

Figure 12-40 Work With Query Manager Tables

```
                    Work with Query Manager Tables

Library . . . . . . . . . .   SQLBOOK     Name, F4 for list

Type options, press Enter.
  1=Create table   3=Copy table     4=Delete table      5=Display table
  6=Print table    7=Rename table   8=Display definition 9=Add data
  10=Change data   11=Display data

Opt  Table              Description
 __   PRIVATE
 __   TPROJDTA
 __   TPROJORIG         Main Project FIle
 __   TRPROJAC
 __   UIINF             Job Information File For EOFDLY Send UI
 __   USRPWD            Security File for Web
 __   VCHP              Transaction File
 __   VENDDATA          Vendor Master File - Data Fo Refresh
 __   VENDOR
 10   VENDORP
                                                          More...
F3=Exit   F4=Prompt     F5=Refresh  F11=Display table only  F12=Cancel
F16=Repeat position to   F17=Position to   F24=More keys
```

Place a 10 next to VENDORP and Hit Enter to begin editing
data in the VENDORP file. You will be taken to the panel
shown in Figure 12-41.

Figure 12-41 Precursor to Select * from VENDORP

```
                       Find Data in Query Manager Table

Table . . . . . . . . :      VENDORP
Description . . . . . :


Type search conditions, press Enter.
No conditions entered will find all data.

AND,OR,
   (,)       Column                      Test     Value
   (

   )

Bottom
F3=Exit    F4=Prompt    F6=Insert line    F10=Copy line    F12=Cancel
F14=Delete line    F20=Display entire name        F22=QM Statement
```

Press Enter from this panel so that QM will bring back all of the records in the file so that you can see them, roll through them, and change them as in Figure 12-42.

Figure 12-42 Change Vendorp Data

```
                        Change Data in Query Manager Table

Table . . . :    VENDORP                 Current row  :    1
Description  :

Type information up to (]), press Enter.

Column                  Value
VNDNBR               [ 38      ]
NAME                 [ John B Stetz Clothier    ]
ADDR1                [ 3817 N. PULASKI          ]
CITY                 [ SCRANTON         ]
STATE                [ PA]
ZIPCD                [ 18503  ]
VNDCLS               [ 10   ]
VNDSTS               [ A]
BALOWE               [ 100.00      ]
SRVRTG               [ R]


                                                    Bottom
F3=Exit    F5=Refresh    F11=Display type/length   F12=Cancel
F14=Previous data row F15=Next data row F16=Find data F24=More keys
```

Notice the "Bottom" indicator in Figure 12-42. This means that all the fields are shown. The roll keys would get you back and forth between panels of fields if there were more fields in the file. Thus, the roll keys (page up / page down) are not used to roll through data records. QM has selected F14 to roll backwards and F15 to roll forward in the file. Unlike the BROWSE facility in the PC databases and the multiple row capability of the DFU product, QM presents just one record at a time. You can roll or go back and enter search criteria to narrow in on the record you want to change or delete.

Make the changes you want to the records in Vendorp. If you come across a record to be deleted, press F23 twice to remove the record from the database. To see PF23 (delete) on the bottom of the screen, you may hit F24 for More keys.

When you are finished changing data, hit F3 to exit and you will return to the Work with Query Manager Tables menu as shown in Figure 12-35. From here, hit F3 and this takes you back to the main Query Manager Menu as shown in Figure 12-33. That's it for the QM Query product.

Chapter Summary

QM provides a menu driven SQL based query facility that is both customized and prompted. It is a very nice tool to use for both queries and all SQL data manipulation.

In addition to standard SQL functions QM has a powerful Table Facility. This permits the user to create, display, and maintain tables. The latter is via a powerful table editor. Moreover, the user can also use QM to define QM profile data. The product is shipped with IBM's SQL Toolkit ID# 5722-ST1 as a licensed program.

With QM, users can perform the following tasks:

- ✓ Create and run QMQRY queries
- ✓ Create and manage QMFORM reports
- ✓ Create, manage, and report on DB files
- ✓ Create and Manage QM Profiles

With QM, Programmers can perform the following tasks:

- ✓ Perform all user functions
- ✓ Integrate queries into applications
- ✓ Pass PARM data into queries at RUN time
- ✓ Put any ISQL statement can be executed in a CL program
- ✓ Build a QM Query to manage, control, and manipulate data
- ✓ Perform QM updates insertion, and deletion of records

There are many facilities in QM that give you the feel of a full-function query product similar to those found in client PC environments. Though there was not enough space in a small chapter to review all of the facility in QM, the information that we covered in this chapter should give you enough to get a big jump start on your Query Management efforts

Key Chapter Terms

AS/400 Query
Averages
Break group
BREAK1
Calculate totals
Column headings
Command window
Control breaks
Control field
Control total
Create and change queries

Create table
Data File Utility
Default report form
Define prompted query
Descriptive text
Edit Panel
Final text
Footing
Formatted report
Grand totals
Level breaks
New Table
Order By
Page heading
PROMPT or SQL
Prompted query
Prompter, 15
query
Query Manager Menu
Query/400
Report
Report breaks
Reporting options
SQL query
SQL statements
STRQM
Summary functions
Summary values
Table editor
Table facility

Exercises

Use this chapter or look up information on the Web to answer
the following:

1. What are the functions of Query Manager for IBM i?

2. Does Query Manager use SQL? If so, how?

3. What are SQL queries in Query Manager?

4. What are prompted queries in Query Manager?

5. What is a report form in Query Manager?

6. How can you make reports easier to read?

7. What is a level break?

8. What is a default report?

9. How Does QM Query work?

10. What can be done with the usage column?

11. How can default queries be produced using the Query Prompter?

12. Describe the process of using the QM Edit Facility to create and

13. Use QM Query with a designed form and the SQL option to select the records from Vendorp in which the VNDNBR is in an inclusive range from 30 to 40.

14. Use QM Query with a prompted default report to select all of the records from VENDORP whose SRVRTG is R, P, or G.

15. Use QM Query with a prompted option and a designed form to select all of the records from Vendorp whose VNDNBR is greater than 1000, and whose VNDCLS is 20 or 30.

16. How would you use QM Query to add a record to the Vendorp File?

17. How would you use QM Query to change the person # in the Persons table to number 10.

Chapter 13   Embedded SQL in High Level Language Programs

SQL Works with IBM i Languages

The SQL coding that we have been working with in this book until this time is known as dynamic SQL. In other words, we place an SQL statement in ISQL or QM or RUNSQLSTM source files and without any preparation, the statements are immediately translated and executed with no need for compilation. This paradigm changes within the context of this new chapter. In this Chapter we introduce the notion of using SQL statements within your high level language programs to provide read, update, add, and delete capabilities.

SQL is available in IBM's high level languages that have been shipped with the WebSphere Development Studio product 5722-WDS since V5R1. The four languages provided with this product include the following:

- ✓ C
- ✓ C++
- ✓ RPG
- ✓ COBOL

IBM i also has three other languages in which SQL is supported. These are as follows:

- ✓ REXX
- ✓ FORTRAN
- ✓ PL/I

The biggest problem with FORTRAN and PL/I is that the compilers have been frozen for some time now and you need to do special things to get these languages.

In this chapter, we focus on embedding SQL in RPG language. In all cases, the theory is the same. After showing a simple program in RPG, we show the same program in COBOL. The second program that we demonstrate is in RPG and it uses SQL cursors to get the data from selected records into the program fields. This program is not repeated in COBOL. Once you get the sense of what embedded SQL actually is and how it can be deployed in one or several languages, performing additional functions such as inserts, updates, and deletes is just a matter of changing the SQL.

IBM has a great manual available for your most sophisticated use of embedded SQL with all host languages. The manual is called IBM i DB2 Universal Database for IBM i SQL Programming with Host Languages. It is available for free download from IBM's Web site. Just use a few keywords from the title and IBM will provide you a link to download the manual.

Create SQL Program Commands

The pre-compiler commands to read the SQL statements along with the program code written in the specific IBM i language for the pre-compiler are listed below along with an explanation of each command:

CRTSQLCBLI

The Create SQL ILE COBOL Object (CRTSQLCBLI) command calls the Structured Query Language (SQL) precompiler which precompiles COBOL source containing SQL statements, produces a temporary source member, and then optionally calls the ILE COBOL for IBM i compiler to create a module, create a program, or create a service program.

CRTSQLCI

The Create SQL ILE C Object (CRTSQLCI) command calls the Structured Query Language (SQL) pre-compiler which pre-compiles C source containing SQL statements, produces a temporary source member, and then optionally calls the ILE C compiler to create a module, create a program, or create a service program.

CRTSQLCBL

The Create SQL COBOL Program (CRTSQLCBL) command calls the Structured Query Language (SQL) pre-compiler which pre-compiles COBOL source containing SQL statements, produces a temporary source member, and then optionally calls the COBOL for IBM i compiler to compile the program.

If the Relational database (RDB) parameter is specified and a program is created, an SQL package will be created at the specified relational database.

CRTSQLCPPI

The Create SQL ILE C++ Object (CRTSQLCPPI) command calls the Structured Query Language (SQL) precompiler which precompiles C++ source containing SQL statements, produces a temporary source member, and then optionally calls the ILE C++ compiler to create a module.

Since this command only creates a module, the user must issue the CRTSQLPKG command after the CRTPGM or CRTSRVPGM command has created the program if an SQL package is needed.

CRTSQLPKG

The Create Structured Query Language Package (CRTSQLPKG) command allows you to create (or re-create) an SQL package on a relational database from an existing distributed SQL program. A distributed SQL program is a program created by specifying the Relational database (RDB) parameter on a CRTSQLxxx (where xxx = CBL, CBLI, CI, CPPI, PLI, RPG or RPGI) command.

CRTSQLPLI

The Create SQL PL/I Program (CRTSQLPLI) command calls the Structured Query Language (SQL) precompiler which precompiles PL/I source containing SQL statements, produces a temporary source member, and then optionally calls the PL/I compiler to compile the program.

If the Relational database (RDB) parameter is specified and a program is created, an SQL package will be created at the specified relational database.

CRTSQLRPG

The Create SQL RPG Program (CRTSQLRPG) command calls the Structured Query Language (SQL) precompiler which precompiles RPG source containing SQL statements, produces a temporary source member, and then optionally calls the RPG compiler to compile the program.

If the Relational database (RDB) parameter is specified and a program is created, an SQL package will be created at the specified relational database.

CRTSQLRPGI

The Create SQL ILE RPG Object (CRTSQLRPGI) command calls the Structured Query Language (SQL) precompiler which precompiles RPG source containing SQL statements, produces a temporary source member, and then optionally calls the ILE RPG compiler to create a module, create a program, or create a service program.

Writing SQL Code in Application Programs

This chapter assumes that you already know how to create plain old RPG programs and/or COBOL programs and that it is the SQL part that is new. So, now let's write s simple RPG program in Figure 13-1 that creates the VENDORP file with embedded SQL. Then we will create another RPG program in Figure 12-2 followed by a COBOL program shown in Figure 13-3 to do the same thing.

In the RPG program shown in Figure 13-1 take notice to the following:

1. The example is a complete RPG program that can be compiled
2. There are no "F" Specs or I Specs etc. required
3. If we were to remove the first and last two statements, the command could be pasted to run interactively with STRSQL or it would work with RUNSQLSTM if the code were first placed in a source file.

Figure 13-1 RPG SQL Code to Create a Table Vendorp

```
C/EXEC SQL
C+   CREATE TABLE SQLBOOK/VENDORP
C+      (VNDNBR       DEC(5,0),
C+       NAME         CHAR(25),
C+       ADDR1        CHAR(25),
C+       CITY         CHAR(15),
C+       STATE        CHAR(2),
C+       ZIPCD        DEC(5,0),
C+       VNDCLS       DEC(2,0),
C+       VNDSTS       CHAR(1),
C+       BALOWE       DEC(9,2),
C+       SRVRTG       CHAR(1))
C/END-EXEC
C                       SETON        ... LR
```

So, all you need to do is compile this code with either RPG
compiler and you have a functioning program that creates a
table in the SQLBOOK library. Now let's create an RPG
program that does a simple select as shown in Figure 13-2. The
COBOL version follows in Figure 13-4.

Figure 13-2 Select Single Row From a Table - RPG

```
I*      This is a complete RPG / SQL program:
I   DS
I                          1    50VNDNBR
I                          6    30 NAME
I                          30   31 CLASS
I                          32   402BAL
C*
C                 Z-ADD20      VNDNBR
C/EXEC SQL
C+    SELECT  VNDNBR, NAME, VNDCLS, BALOWE
C+      INTO  :VNDNBR, :NAME, :CLASS, :BAL
C+      FROM  VENDORP
C+     WHERE  VNDNBR = :VNDNBR
C/END-EXEC
C   ... 'NAME '   DSPLY     NAME
C   ... 'CLASS'   DSPLY     CLASS
C   ... 'BALOWE'  DSPLY     BAL
C                 SETON            ... LR
```

For those who can read RPG code, you can see the RPG/400
part here defines four fields VNDNBR. NAME, CLASS, and
BAL that will be used to store input in the program from the
embedded SQL SELECT statement. Then, a search argument

is primed to look up the vendor number. Vendor # 20 is in the file and this is moved with a Z-ADD operation into the field called VNDNBR that is already defined in the input specifications.

The SELECT statement reads in the four fields from the Vendorp file and using the INTO clause of the SELECT statement places the values into the corresponding program defined fields. When program fields are used in SQLRPG, they are prefixed by a colon. Notice the WHERE clause criteria is where the value from the program (:VNDNBR primed with 20) is equal to the value from the database (VNDNBR).

When the SELECT Statement is executed the four fields are in the input fields shown at the top of the program. To prove that this RPG/400 code works, I have chosen to use a DSPLY operation which takes the values and sends them out to the user of the terminal session to view.

The values retrieved from this record are as follows as shown in the display of the job log in Figure 13-3 below.

Figure 13-3 Results of Simple Select Program

```
Display Program Messages
DSPLY NAME   PHONDUS CORPORAT   2
DSPLY CLASS   20
DSPLY BALOWE 45000

Type reply, press Enter.
Reply_____
 F3=Exit    F12=Cancel
```

The program in COBOL is functionally the same and the appropriate pieces are shown in the panel in Figure 13-4 below

Figure 13-4 COBOL Program Pieces to Perform Simple Select

```
WORKING-STORAGE SECTION.
 77   VNDNBR    PIC   S9(5)   COMP-3.
 77   CLASS     PIC   S9(2)   COMP-3.
 77   NAME      PIC   X(25).
 77   BAL       PIC   S9(9.2) COMP-3.
 *
 *

 PROCEDURE DIVISION.
  MOVE   20   to VNDNBR.
  EXEC SQL
      SELECT   vndnbr, name, vndcls, balowe
      INTO   :vndnbr, :name, :class, :bal
      FROM   vendorp
      WHERE   vndnbr = :vndnbr
  END-EXEC.
```

Set Processing Only

It helps to recall that when using interpreted SQL (ISQL, QM, RUNSQLSTM) on the IBM i that one can only process data in sets. This is in contrast to the typical record at a time processing that IBM i programmers have used since the IBM i was called a System/38. The example in Figure 13-2 avoids the problem of having to deal with a set of data in a program as opposed to bringing in just one record at a time.

By searching just for the vendor # key of 20 in this program, we were assured to have just one record delivered. If instead of key value 20 for VNDNBR, we chose to select all the records that have a balowe filed greater or equal to $150.00, the program would bring back multiple records and bomb.

The simple program in Figure 13-2 has no idea of how to handle the storage of a set of data and it has no idea of how to get an individual record if a set of data is returned from a query rather than just one record. The trick in SQL programming to handle sets of data is to declare something that is called a cursor. Like a file cursor, the cursor we define will enable us to move from one record to another in the returned set of data.

Select and Process Multiple Rows

So, record by-record processing with embedded SQL requires the declaration of an SQL CURSOR. This notion can be accommodated in either a Stored Procedure or in SQL code embedded in a IBM i language such as one of those we noted above. One thing that all of these languages have in common is that all are compiled.

We know that once the source member containing the SQL statement is built, as long as it does not contain an SQL statement not supported by the RUNSQLSTM command, you can execute it in interpreted mode with the following: RUNSQLSTM SRCFILE(SQLBOOK/SQLSTMTS) SRCMBR(SQLMBR).

This CL command of course can be entered into any CL program. Once the SQL statement runs well in interpreted mode, then it is OK to embed it into a program. If you need to use the Select statement, then you would use the ISQL facility to prove the SQL works before moving it to the HLL program.

By defining a cursor in a IBM i program, the records returned from the embedded SQL select will be in memory and just like you process a subfile, the programmer can write code to read through the memory file that has been returned.

Unlike the memory subfile which gets defined in the DDS for a display file, the memory file for an embedded select is defined by the SELECT itself. The field names or the * for all selected fields are the columns that define the memory file. The number of records is obtained at execution time base upon the records that meet the WHERE clause criteria.

Figure 13-5 shows the functions that must be accomplished in order to process multiple records returned from a query.

Figure 13-5 Function and Meaning of Cursor Processing

Program Function	Meaning
1. Declare SQL cursor	Prepares the SELECT or other DML statement
2. Open the cursor	Process the SQL statement and position the cursor to record 1 of the memory file (returned set)
3. Fetch next record	Bring the data from the next memory record into the program fields for processing
4 Test for Last record	If no more records in the memory file, go to step 6 to close cursor.
5. Process record (program defined or SQL defined updates or inserts if part of spec)	Perform program functions as if this record arrived via normal record at a time processing.
6. Close Cursor	Remove the results of the SQL query that are in memory

Figure 13-6 Program Function I Pseudo Code Form

Program Function	Pseudo Code

1. Declare SQL cursor	DECLARE MYCURSOR CURSOR FOR
	  SELECT EMPNO, FIRSTNME, LASTNAME
	    FROM EMP
	      WHERE SEX = 'M'
	      ORDER BY LASTNAME

2. Open the cursor	OPEN MYCURSOR
3. Fetch next record	FETCH MYCURSOR INTO :EMPNO, :FNAME, :LNAME
4 Test for Last record	If last record: go to Step 6, else: go to Step 3
5. Process record	HLL Operations on retrieved data processing.
6. Close Cursor	CLOSE CURSOR MYCURSOR

Now, let's take the same functions and invent a pseudo code language in which to use these powerful SQL operations In Figure 13-6 we can see that the select returns the set of data in memory and then we keep moving through the data set in a forward direction fetching one record from memory at a time just like a plus 1 RRN with a subfile.

There are several new keywords and SQL terms that we introduced in this Chapter. They are shown in the table in Figure 13-7

Figure 13-7 New Terms and Purpose in Embedded SQL

Term	Purpose
Precompiler	A step before the compilation of an SQL high level language program which converts the SQl code to native language functions / calls.
/EXEC SQL	Starts block of SQL Code
/END-EXEC	Ends a block of SQL code
INTO	Used to place column values into program variables
DECLARE	Means of declaring a cursor for set at a time processing
CURSOR	The element in embedded SQL that positions Fetches to the proper next record.
OPEN	Brings the result set of the SQL query into memory
WHENEVER	A monitor condition function for embedded SQL
NOT FOUND	A condition to monitor – record not found by a fetch to the result set
GOTO	Spot in program to branch if a monitored error occurs such as no more records left in result set.
FETCH	Moral equivalent of a read. Performed agsinst the result set.
CLOSE	Closes the cursor; removes memory table (result set)

In Figure 13-8 we take the Pseudo from Figure 13-6 and we build a real RPG program from it. Rather than provide the DSPLY op code in this scenario, however, we used SQL's INSERT facility to send output to a new table we call HLDTABLE in SQLBOOK. It has just the VNDNBR, NAME, VNDCLS, and BALOWE fields defined and that is just enough. The program does a select of all rows with the BALOWE field column being greater or equal to $150.00. Then the RPG program cursors through the result table in memory and processes each record, one at a time, sending

the output via the INSERT statement into the new
HLDTABLE file.

In Figure 13-9, we show the same program in RPGIV after
having done the CVTRPGSRC command. Notice that the
CVTRPGSRC understands SQL syntax and lets it ride just
as it was in the RPG/400 code.

Figure 13-8 RPG/400 Cursor Program

```
*************** Beginning of data ***********************
0001.00 F* THIS PROGRAM SELECTS RECORDS & WRITES LAST RCD FETCHED
0002.00 I           DS
0003.00 I                                    1   50VND
0004.00 I                                    6   30 NAM
0005.00 I                                   31   32 CLASS
0006.00 I                                   33  410BAL
0007.00 I*
0008.00 C*
0009.00 C*  RIGHT HERE STEP 1 IS ACCOMPLISHED
0010.00 C*
0011.00 C*  SET SOME OPTIONS
0012.00 C/EXEC SQL
0013.00 C+ SET OPTION COMMIT=*NONE,
0014.00 C+                  DATFMT=*ISO
0015.00 C/END-EXEC
0021.00 C/EXEC SQL
0022.00 C+ DECLARE MYCURSOR CURSOR FOR
0023.00 C+ SELECT VNDNBR, NAME, VNDCLS, BALOWE
0024.00 C+  FROM SQLBOOK/VENDORP
0025.00 C+    WHERE BALOWE >=  150
0026.00 C+     ORDER BY NAME
0027.00 C/END-EXEC
0028.00 C*
0029.00 C* RIGHT HERE, STEP 2 IS ACCOMPLISHED
0030.00 C*
0031.00 C/EXEC SQL
0032.00 C+ OPEN MYCURSOR
0033.00 C/END-EXEC
0034.00 C*
0035.00 C          SQLCOD    DOWEQ0
0036.00 C* RIGHT HERE, STEPS 4 & 5 ARE ACCOMPLISHED
0037.00 C/EXEC SQL WHENEVER NOT FOUND GO TO NF
0038.00 C/END-EXEC
0039.00 C*
0040.00 C*
0041.00 C/EXEC SQL
0042.00 C+ FETCH MYCURSOR
0043.00 C+ INTO :VND, :NAM, :CLASS, :BAL
0044.00 C/END-EXEC
0045.00 C* DO SOMETHING WITH CODE HERE!!- WRITE TO HLDTABLE FILE
0046.00 C* EACH RECORD IS WRITTEN TO HLDTABLE TO SHOW CODE WORKS
0047.00 C/EXEC SQL
0048.00 C+               INSERT INTO SQLBOOK/HLDTABLE
0049.00 C+               ( VNDNBR, NAME, VNDCLS, BALOWE)
0050.00 C+               VALUES( :VND,:NAM,:CLASS,:BAL)
0051.00 C/END-EXEC
0052.00 C               ENDDO
0053.00 C*
0054.00 C*
0055.00 C* RIGHT HERE STEP 6 IS ACCOMPLISHED
0056.00 C*
0057.00 C          NF        TAG
0058.00 C/EXEC SQL
0059.00 C+ CLOSE MYCURSOR
0060.00 C/END-EXEC
0061.00 C               SETON                    LR
*********** End of data*************************
```

Figure 13-9 RPGIV (ILERPG) Cursor Program

```
********** Beginning of data *********************************
0001.00 F* THIS PROGRAM SELECTS RECS & WRITES LAST RECORD FETCHED
0002.00 D                    DS
0003.00 D   VND              1      5  0
0004.00 D   NAM              6     30
0005.00 D   CLASS           31     32
0006.00 D   BAL             33     41  0
0007.00 I*
0008.00 C*
0009.00 C*  RIGHT HERE STEP 1 IS ACCOMPLISHED
0010.00 C*
0011.00 C*  SET SOME OPTIONS
0012.00 C/EXEC SQL
0013.00 C+ SET OPTION COMMIT=*NONE,
0014.00 C+                  DATFMT=*ISO
0015.00 C/END-EXEC
0021.00 C/EXEC SQL
0022.00 C+ DECLARE MYCURSOR CURSOR FOR
0023.00 C+ SELECT VNDNBR, NAME, VNDCLS, BALOWE
0024.00 C+   FROM SQLBOOK/VENDORP
0025.00 C+   WHERE BALOWE >=  150
0026.00 C+    ORDER BY NAME
0027.00 C/END-EXEC
0028.00 C*
0029.00 C* RIGHT HERE, STEP 2 IS ACCOMPLISHED
0030.00 C*
0031.00 C/EXEC SQL
0032.00 C+ OPEN MYCURSOR
0033.00 C/END-EXEC
0034.00 C*
0035.00 C      SQLCOD        DOWEQ     0
0036.00 C* RIGHT HERE, STEPS 4 & 5 ARE ACCOMPLISHED
0037.00 C/EXEC SQL WHENEVER NOT FOUND GO TO NF
0038.00 C/END-EXEC
0039.00 C*
0040.00 C*
0041.00 C/EXEC SQL
0042.00 C+ FETCH MYCURSOR
0043.00 C+ INTO :VND, :NAM, :CLASS, :BAL
0044.00 C/END-EXEC
0045.00 C* DO SOMETHING WITH CODE HERE!  -- WRITE TO HLDTABLE FILE
0046.00 C* EACH RECORD IS WRITTEN TO HLDTABLE TO SHOW CODE WORKS
0047.00 C/EXEC SQL
0048.00 C+              INSERT INTO SQLBOOK/HLDTABLE
0049.00 C+              ( VNDNBR, NAME, VNDCLS, BALOWE)
0050.00 C+              VALUES( :VND,:NAM,:CLASS,:BAL)
0051.00 C/END-EXEC
0052.00 C              ENDDO
0053.00 C*
0054.00 C*
0055.00 C* RIGHT HERE STEP 6 IS ACCOMPLISHED
0056.00 C*
0057.00 C      NF           TAG
0058.00 C/EXEC SQL
0059.00 C+ CLOSE MYCURSOR
0060.00 C/END-EXEC
0061.00 C              SETON                                LR
         ***************** End of data  *********************
```

Figure 13-10- HLDTABLE File after a Run.

```
                              Display Physical File Member
File . . . . . . . :    HLDTABLE         Library  . . . . :   SQLBOOK
Member . . . . . . :    HLDTABLE         Record . . . . . :   1
Control  . . . . .      _____         Column . . . . . :   1
Find . . . . . .        _____
*...+....1....+....2....+....3....+..
07030ATG Dynamo
FFFFFCEC4CA98994444444444444444440000320
07030137048514600000000000000002F0050F

08020Bings Music             `ø
FFFFFC898A4DAA88444444444444444440007700
08020295720442930000000000000002F0900F

00034Blind Robin Copany
FFFFFC98984D98894C9989A44444444440000130
000342395409629503671580000002F0050F

00046Butts & Wallace Inc      &
FFFFFCAAAA454E8998884C984444444440000500
00046243320006133135095300000003F0000F
                                                              More..
F3=Exit    F12=Cancel   F19=Left    F20=Right    F24=More keys
```

Check out the six documented stages of a cursor program in each of the RPG programs to see how the cursor-ing is accomplished in RPG. Notice the first SQL execution does something that makes it all work. In the Set option area at the top of the code in line 13, we set commitment control off because in this program we are not demonstrating how to achieve commitment control in SQL HLL languages.

Chapter Summary

Once you get your SQL code verified with RUNSQLSTM or ISQL, it is time to place it in a program and give it a whirl. The SQL code in both COBOL and RPG and RPGIV is basically the same and it is learning how to deal with the host compiler's variables and nuances that make the difference.

There are a host of compiler commands available for whatever language you choose and the editors from PDM to WDSc Eclipse have the necessary formats for SQL language derivatives.

The code to process a set of data is at first annoying but as you learn what it is doing, it is no more annoying than OPNQRYF and quite frankly, the code is easier to read. When you open the cursor, the SQL statement is executed and the result set is in your program. Then, you cursor through the result set (memory file) and process one record at a time just like in subfile programming.

One of the first things that everybody notices when looking at the RPG code to create the table is that there really is no RPG code. And, there would not be any COBOL code if the program was in COBOL. There are no F specs or I specs. The only thing needed is the C specs for the SQL precompiler directives.

The same applies to the bigger programs in RPG and RPG IV. Though the RPG program is reading a file and writing a file, there are no F specs in the program and there is no RPG I/O involved. There is so little RPG code that it is easy to consider the language in this instance as merely a place for SQL to execute. There is nothing better than getting your feet wet just to find out whether it is miserable out or not. Though there is not much RPG in this code, there is no C and no Java either – just RPG and SQL. That's not really a bad combination.

Key Chapter Terms

/END-EXEC /EXEC SQL
5722-WDS
CLOSE
Create SQL Program
CRTSQLCBL
CRTSQLCBLI
CRTSQLCI
CRTSQLCPPI
CRTSQLPKG
CRTSQLPLI

CRTSQLRPG
CRTSQLRPGI
Cursor
CVTRPGSRC
Declare
DSPLY
Embedded SQL
Fetch
GOTO
High level languages
INTO
Memory table
OPEN
Precompiler
Pseudo code
Result set
RPG compiler
RPG program
RPG/400
RPGIV
Set option
Set Processing
SQL cursor
SQL programming
SQL query
Subfile
Whenever

Exercises

Use this chapter or look up information on the Web to answer the following:

1. When creating a table through RPG, why is there no File Description specification required for the table being created?

2. Are there any SQL statements that you can think of that are not permitted within an RPG program?

3. What re the two compile commands to run the RPG SQL and RPG ILE SQL compilers?

4. What is a cursor?

5. Why is a cursor necessary in some programs and not in others?

6. What would have to change in the last RPG programs if we wanted to process only the records in the Vendorp file that are in VNDCLS 20??

Chapter 14   Advanced SQL, Special Facilities, Select, Join, Sub-Query, Update, Insert and Delete.

SQL Special Facilities

So far, we have touched on just about everything basic that you might want to do with the SQL language. In this chapter, we take a number of those notions a lot further and we explore more of the clauses in DML with a powerful set of examples to capture both the imagination and the coding pad. You'll like some of the spiffy examples that we use to make SQL come alive in this chapter.. Before we get into the examples, let's take a look at a very powerful operator, LIKE.

Like Operator

You use the Like operator when you are looking for a partial match inside a column. It is used with the WHERE Clause and helps you provide powerful selection options for SQL queries. With the like operator are several powerful wild card functions to provide a means of getting at data that is typically not intuitive with field selects.

The format of the Select statement with the LIKE predicate is as follows:

```
SELECT "column_name"
    FROM "table_name"
        WHERE "column_name"
            LIKE {PATTERN}
                [:wildcard])
```

The {PATTERN} in the above format often consists of
wildcards. An indicator variable is returned by Like to show
whether the string contains the requested pattern. The wildcard
parameter is optional; if unspecified, the percent sign (%) will
be assumed. The wild card options include the following

%   **Any string of 0 or more chars**
_   **Exactly one single character**

The % wildcard is especially powerful in that you can place it
before, after, or both before and after a set of text that you
would like to find a string of characters inside of a column – but
not the whole column. The % itself represents a string of
columns that are ignored.

If you place the % before the text you are using as a search
argument, then the LIKE operator ignores all text until it finds
that string. Then it compares the string, character by character
until it hits the end of the field. If all characters in the search
string match the string found from that point on in the field
then the record is selected. The caution of course is that if there
are blanks or any other characters in the field after the text
value is found, it will not result in a match unless your search
value also contains the trailing blanks or other characters.

If you place the % after a group of characters then the Like
operator compares from the beginning of the field to the
wildcard and if it gets a match against the search argument the

record is selected. If you are off by one character, the record will not be selected.

The "%" before and "%" after "Like" arguments are handy when you are looking for a string of text that begins a field or ends a field. If the string is in the middle, the use of one wildcard before or after requires exact precision. But, there is a solution, and a nice solution at that. If you want to select the records in a database that contain a string of characters anywhere in the record, you can use a % before and % after the text for which you are searching.

There are some SQL implementations by some vendors that support the use of a "CONTAINS" predicate, which is basically what you get when you sandwich the search text within two % wild cards.

The "_" wildcard is a substitute for just one character and does not need the same level of explanation as the % wildcard.

Now, to make sure we have this down right, let's look at some examples and make sure you try them on your own machines:

Where Fieldname LIKE ('A%')

This returns all of the values in the column that start with A.

Where Fieldname NOT LIKE ('KE_LY')

This returns all of the records for column that do not match KELLY or any other letter than L for the third character.

'A_Z':

This combo returns the records in a column that matches a string that starts with 'A,' then has any character and finally ends with a 'Z'. Valid combinations are 'ABZ' and 'A2Z'

Note: In the above example, 'AKKZ' would not cause a match because there are two characters between A and Z instead of one.

'ABC%':

This string search argument would return a record for any string in which this field starts with 'ABC,' such as 'ABCD' and 'ABCABC." Both of these satisfy the condition.

'%XYZ':

This would return those records in which the column values end with 'XYZ.' Both 'WXYZ' and 'ZZXYZ' satisfy the condition.

'%AN%':

This is a double wildcard text search string. The search is looking for string in the specified column that contains the pattern 'AN' anywhere in the column. Examples that fit are 'LOS ANGELES' and 'SAN FRANCISCO'
Both satisfy the condition.

Null Fields

Null fields contain null values. They are truly empty. They are not blank or filled with zeroes. They are not populated with any data. As such, as you will see, they are not included in functions such as averages. However, you can search for a null since it is its own character value. An example is the following:

Where Fieldname IS NULL

Concat – Concatenate Two or More Strings

The concatenation operator (concat) permits you to concatenate two strings into one field. For example, take a column called FIRSTNME, concatenate it with a blank and a column called LASTNME:

FIRSTNME CONCAT ' ' CONCAT LASTNAME

Substr – Substring

The Substring operation permits you to pick a string out of a larger string. In other words, the SUBSTR operation returns a substring of a string.. An example would be to select all rows from a PROJECT table for which the project name (PROJNAME) starts with the word 'OPERATION '

**SELECT * FROM PROJECT WHERE
SUBSTR(PROJNAME,1,10) = 'OPERATION '**

Now, let's move on to some spiffier SQL example using what we have learned already in this book. In Chapter 5 we created the PERSON table with the RUNSQLSTM command. Let's do a few selects from this table:

Select Exercise 1

Select every column and every row from the PERSON table:

```
SELECT *  FROM PERSON
```

Result: Retrieves all data from PERSON table

Select Exercise 2

```
SELECT FIRSTNME, LASTNAME FROM
PERSON WHERE EDLEVEL = 12
```

Result: Retrieves the names of those who are seniors from the person table.

Select Exercise 3

Select the name, balance, vendor class from the vendor p file.

```
Select name, balowe, vndcls from
vendorp
```

Result – projection of three fields, all records included.

Select Exercise 4

Select vendor number and balowe minus $200 and the first 15 positions of name from VENDORP

```
Select VENDNR, balowe - 200,
SUBSTR(name, 1,15) FROM vendorp
```

The results from this query are included below or on the next page:

VENDOR NUMBER	BAL-200	SUBSTR
7,000	190.46-	Microsoft Corpo
7,010	105.00-	Oracle Corporat
7,020	7,800.00	Sun MicroSystem
7,030	152.56	ATG Dynamo
7,040	199.75-	Education Direc

Select Exercise 5

Select vendor name, balance owed, from VENDORP if balowe is greater than 200 and the vendor class is one of the following: 4,6,10.

```
SELECT name, balowe FROM vendorp
WHERE balowe > 200 AND vndcls
IN(4,6,10)
```

The results from this query are included below:.

```
....+....1....+....2....+...+....4
NAME                    BALANCE
                        OWED
Sun MicroSystems        8,000.00
McFadyen Consulting       250.00
********  End of data  **
```

Using SQL Built-In Functions

SQL has a ton of functions that help make the language very rich and powerful. These are broken down into two groups, Scalar functions, and Column functions.

Scalar Functions

A scalar function can be used wherever an expression can be used. The restrictions on the use of column functions do not apply to scalar functions, because a scalar function is applied to single parameter values rather than to sets of values. The argument of a scalar function can be a function.

However, the restrictions that apply to the use of expressions and column functions also apply when an expression or column function is used within a scalar function. For example, the argument of a scalar function can be a column function only if a column function is allowed in the context in which the scalar function is used.

The list of scalar functions available is very large and is shown in Figure 14-1. The column functions are included at the bottom of Figure 14-1.

Column Functions

The following information applies to all column functions other than COUNT(*) and COUNT_BIG(*). Sometimes the rules actually make SQL more confusing than the reality. But all SQL developers must play by the rules.

The argument of a column function is a set of values derived from an expression. The expression may include columns but cannot include another column function. The scope of the set is a group or an intermediate result table. If a GROUP BY clause is specified in a query and the intermediate result of the FROM, WHERE, GROUP BY, and HAVING clauses is an empty set, then the column functions are not applied.

Figure 14-1 Scalar and Column Functions

See tables together on next two pages. I admit, being my own formatter. It was tough trying to get this table on this page. Sorry about that. It is a great list nonetheless.

Scalar Functions

ABS	DIFFERENCE	LOR	SIN
ACOS	DIGITS	LOWER	SINH
ANTILOG	DLCOMMENT	LTRIM	SMALLINT
ASIN	DLLINKTYPE	MAX	SOUNDEX
ATAN	DLURLCOMPLETE	MICROSECOND	SPACE
ATANH	DLURLPATH	MIDNIGHT_ SECONDS	SQRT
ATAN2	DLURLPATHONLY	MIN	STRIP
BIGINT	DLURLSCHEME	MINUTE	SUBSTRING or
BLOB	DLURLSERVER	MOD	SUBSTR
CEILING	DLVALUE	MONTH	TAN
CHAR	DOUBLE_PRECISION or DOUBLE	NODENAME	TANH
CHARACTER_ LENGTH	EXP	NODENUMBER	TIME
CLOB	FLOAT	NOW	TIMESTAMP
COALESCE	FLOOR	NULLIF	TIMESTAMPDIFF
CONCAT	GRAPHIC	PARTITION	TRANSLATE
COS	HASH	PI	TRIM
COSH	HEX	POSITION or POSSTR	TRUNCATE or
COT	HOUR	POWER	TRUNC
CURDATE	IDENTITY_VAL_ LOCAL	QUARTER	UCASE
CURTIME	IFNULL	RADIANS	UPPER
DATE	INTEGER or INT	RAND	VALUE
DAY	JULIAN_DAY	REAL	VARCHAR
DAYOFMONTH	LAND	ROUND	VARGRAPHIC
DAYOFWEEK	LCASE	ROWID	WEEK
DAYOFWEEK_ISO	LEFT	RRN	WEEK_ISO
DAYOFYEAR	LENGTH	RTRIM	XOR
DAYS	LN	SECOND	YEAR
DBCLOB	LNOT	SIGN	ZONED
DECIMAL or DEC	LOCATE		
DEGREES	LOG10		

Column
Functions

AVG	COUNT_BIG	MIN	SUM
COUNT	MAX	STDDEV_POP or STDDEV	VAR_POP or VARIANCE or VAR

If a GROUP BY clause is not specified in a query and the intermediate result of the FROM, WHERE, and HAVING clauses is an empty set, then the column functions are applied to the empty set. For example, the result of the following SELECT statement is the number of distinct values of JOB for employees in department D01:

```
SELECT COUNT(DISTINCT JOB)
   FROM EMPLOYEE
   WHERE WORKDEPT = 'D01'
```

The keyword DISTINCT is not considered an argument of the function, but rather a specification of an operation that is performed before the function is applied. When DISTINCT is specified, duplicate values are eliminated. If ALL is implicitly or explicitly specified, duplicate values are not eliminated.

A column function can be used in a WHERE clause only if that clause is part of a sub-query of a HAVING clause and the column name specified in the expression is a correlated reference to a group. If the expression includes more than one column name, each column name must be a correlated reference to the same group.

Using Group By and Having

GROUP BY allows grouping of selected columns. It can be based on a criteria in the HAVING clause.

HAVING provides the selection criteria for the GROUP BY clause.

ORDER BY is specified after GROUP BY and HAVING. It can specify order of rows. Results are sorted in ascending or descending collating sequence based on one or more column values.

The SELECT statement has a number of built-in scalar functions for grouping such as the original big five as following

- ✓ AVG   (numeric columns)
- ✓ SUM   (numeric columns)
- ✓ MAX   (num or char columns)
- ✓ MIN   (num or char columns)
- ✓ COUNT (count selected rows)

Let's try these out with some examples.

Select Exercise 6

Using a subset of the VENDORP file, give me the count of all the records and the average balance in each state.

```
SELECT COUNT(*), AVG(balowe), state
FROM vendorp GROUP BY state
```

Results

COUNT (*)	AVG (BALOWE)	STATE
1	78.50000000000000000000000	NY
1	19.00000000000000000000000	MI
1	4.99000000000000000000000	FL
1	1,495.55000000000000000000000	OK
1	250.00000000000000000000000	IN
1	352.56000000000000000000000	MA
3	2,833.41666666666666666666666	IL
1	56.00000000000000000000000	AZ
1	66.54000000000000000000000	MS
1	29.83000000000000000000000	OR
1	9.54000000000000000000000	WA
2	4,047.50000000000000000000000	CA
1	256.00000000000000000000000	OH
14	2,996.98214285714285714285142	PA
2	12.47500000000000000000000	TX
1	79,700.00000000000000000000000	VA

Scalar functions such as SIN and COS are listed in the table in Figure 14-1 but are not covered in this presentation.

Select Exercise 7

In this example, we need to display all the records in the EMP file which we created in Chapter 8. The EMP file is the basis of some queries to come. Before we start doing involved queries, let's get a look at some of the records in the EMP File so we know what we're sampling

SELECT * from SQLBOOK/EMP

Figure 14-2 Left side of EMP Table

EMPNO	FIRSTNME	MIDINIT	LASTNAME	WDEPT	PHONENO	HIREDATE
1451	Dernit	Q	Pitt	D13	421	07/12/81
112	Brian	U	John	D11	422	04/21/74
145	Dan	A	Patterson	D13	423	02/22/65
145	Dino	G	Lella	D12	322	03/17/84
190	Lisa	A	Maria	D11	425	09/12/88
763	Michelle	L	Dente	D11	426	04/12/86
120	Linda	A	Bates	D17	334	05/17/81
169	Morpheus	T	Zion	D16	439	07/20/88
1458	Darla	D	Debroskin	D13	449	01/23/86
1449	Clarence	G	Wunnerful	D12	657	09/12/86

******** End of data ********

Figure 14-2 Right Side of EMP Tablee

JOB	EDLEVEL	SEX	BIRTHDATE	SALARY	BONUS	COMM
D12	18	M	03/21/57	22.50	55.50	.14
D11	12	M	05/30/78	17,000.00	250.00	.20
D16	17	M	01/21/56	21.50	55.00	.12
D45	11	M	11/21/68	31.50	65.00	.13
56	16	F	05/12/89	64.50	30.00	.16
57	20	F	02/16/68	107.50	40.00	.13
58	12	F	03/23/76	10.75	80.00	.14
D16	16	M	12/12/88	537.50	690.00	.15
D16	20	F	01/21/66	26.50	75.00	.11
D12	18	M	01/21/56	54.50	23.00	.13

******** End of data ********

Select Exercise 8

In this example, we would like to determine the maximum pay rate value and minimum pay rate value from the EMP Table..

SELECT MAX (rate), MIN (rate) FROM emp

```
                                    Display Data
                                             D
    Position to line  . . . . .      Shift
    ....+....1....+....2....+....3
    MAX ( SALARY )  MIN ( SALARY )
        17,000.00           10.75
    ********  End of data  ********
```

Select Exercise 9

For each department within the company, what is the number of employees and the total salary paid to them? – Show Dept #, Employees, and Total Salary

```
SELECT WORKDEPT, SUM(salary),COUNT (*)
FROM emp
GROUP BY WORKDEPT
ORDER by WORKDEPT
```

```
                          Display Data
                                    Data width . . . . . :
Position to line  . . . . .         Shift to column  . . . . .
....+....1....+....2....+....3....+....4....+....5....+....6....+..
WORKDEPT                            SUM ( SALARY )    COUNT ( * )
    D11                                 17,172.00              3
    D12                                     86.00              2
    D13                                     70.50              3
    D16                                    537.50              1
    D17                                     10.75              1
********  End of data  ********
```

Select Exercise 10

Select the department, the sum of its salaries, and the # of employees in the department from the employee file.

```
SELECT WORKDEPT,SUM(salary),COUNT (*)
FROM emp
GROUP BY WORKDEPT
HAVING COUNT (*) > 1
ORDER by WORKDEPT
```

```
                        Display Data
                                Data width . . . . . .
Position to line  . . . .        Shift to column  . . . . .
...+....1....+....2....+....3....+....4....+....5....+....6....+...
ORKDEPT                          SUM ( SALARY )    COUNT ( * )
 D11                                17,172.00               3
 D12                                    86.00               2
 D13                                    70.50               3
*******  End of data  ********
```

Select Exercise 11

Sub Query

Now, we are about to move from simple queries to queries
within queries. These are also known as Sub Queries. In order
for you to fully see what is going on, we are going to do some
setup queries so you can see the data as it unfolds in the
subquery. So, let's look at some more data in the EMP file

```
SELECT LASTNAME, FIRSTNME, HIREDATE,
WORKDEPT
  FROM emp
  WHERE WORKDEPT IN ('D11','D12')
  ORDER BY LASTNAME
```

```
                        Display Data
                                      Data
Position to line  . . . . .           Shift to
....+....1....+....2....+....3....+....4....+....
LASTNAME          FIRSTNME     HIREDATE   WORKDEPT
Dente             Michelle     04/12/86   D11
John              Brian        04/21/74   D11
Lella             Dino         03/17/84   D12
Maria             Lisa         09/12/88   D11
Wunnerful         Clarence     09/12/86   D12
********  End of data  ********
```

Select Exercise 12

We are still setting up for the sub query. Let's now take a look at the values in the department file.

Select * from dept

```
...+....1....+....2....+....3....+....4....+....5....+
DEPTNO   DEPTNAME                          MGRNO   ADMRDEPT
 D11     Spiffy Computer Service DEPT      -
 D12     Planning Dept                     -
 D16     Information Center                -
 D13     Manufacturing Systems             -
 D17     Administrative Systems            -
 D19     Support Services                  -
 D18     Operations                        -
 D20     Software Support                  -
********   End of data   ********
```

Select Exercise 13

Select Employees who work in dept names starting with "S"

```
SELECT LASTNAME, FIRSTNME, WORKDEPT
FROM emp
WHERE WORKDEPT IN (SELECT DEPTNO FROM
DEPT
WHERE DEPTNAME    LIKE 'S%' )
ORDER BY LASTNAME
```

SELECT statement run complete.

```
                    Display Data

Position to line  . . . . .                    Shift
....+....1....+....2....+....3....+....
LASTNAME            FIRSTNME         WORKDEPT
Dente              Michelle         D11
John               Brian            D11
Maria              Lisa             D11
********  End of data  ********
```

Select Exercise 14

Produce an employee list showing the name and monthly salary, of those employees who have a double "t" or 'tt" in their last name.

Another Example From ISQL

SELECT LASTNAME, (SALARY / 12) AS MONTHLY_SALARY FROM EMP WHERE LASTNAME LIKE '%tt%' ORDER BY 2

```
                              Display Data
                                           Data wi
Position to line  . . . . .               Shift to co
....+....1....+....2....+....3....+....4....+....5..
LASTNAME                        MONTHLY_SALARY
Patterson              1.791666666666666666666666
Pitt                   1.875000000000000000000000
********  End of data  ********
```

Update Exercise 15

Now, let's use some SQL statements other than SELECT to demonstrate the data manipulation facility built into SQL's DML. We'll demonstrate two examples of the Update statement. The first will be simple but the second one will take some thinking.

Set the vendor status of all records in the vendorp backup file to "S" if the vendor class is "03"

```
UPDATE vendorpin2 SET vndsts = 'S'
WHERE vndcls = 10
```

26 rows updated in VENDORPIN2 in
SQLBOOK.

Update Exercise 16

Now, let's move on to something really spiffy. It is called the scalar Subselect. With this function, we can update rows in one table based on the values in another table. To do this example we create a duplicate of the EMP file and we change the column name of the salary in this file to csal. We name the file SALFILE. Here is a scalar subselect function within an Update SQL statement.

```
UPDATE EMP A1 SET salary =
    (SELECT csal FROM salfile A2
        WHERE A1.EMPNO  = A2.EMPNO)
```

10 rows updated in EMP in SQLBOOK

In this scalar sub-select, the notations, "A1" and "A2" within the UPDATE statement are abbreviations for the two files. This is a very, very powerful operation. To make sure this works without a hitch, you must be sure that you get a hit on item #. In other words, there needs to be a record in the SALFILE for every record in the EMP file. If there is not a record, some bad things can happen.

The subselect comes after the words salary = as you can see in the above UPDATE function. That means that the second half of the query runs for each record read in the first half. If there is no hit in the second query, there is nothing to prevent the SALARY field from being updated with a zero or null value signifying that it is now nothing.. To prevent this with better SQL coding you would have to add some additional tests to be sure you got a hit.

Insert Exercise 17

Insert one row of constant data into the emp file. Add the contents of the eleven fields

LASTNAME	Anstett,
FIRSTNME	Borregard
WORKDEPT	D13
SALARY	59000.00
Etc.	

The SQL for this is as follows:

```
INSERT INTO SQLBOOK/EMP (EMPNO, FIRSTNME,
MIDINIT, LASTNAME,
WORKDEPT, PHONENO,  EDLEVEL, SEX,  SALARY,
BONUS,COMM) VALUES(596,'Borregard','A',
'Anstett', 'D13',456,
17, 'M', 5900000, 23000, 17)
```

1 rows inserted in EMP in SQLBOOK.

Insert Exercise 18

So we've done some fancy selects, a nice scalar sub-select for update and now, let's do a repopulation (refresh of a database with another database that has good data. When you are messing with data in a lab environment refreshing data is a normal task. In this insert sub-select we will access all of the

fields from a refresh file called VENDORPIN1 and we will
insert these rows into the file VENDORPIN2.

```
INSERT INTO VENDORPIN2
(VNDNBR, NAME, ADDR1, CITY, STATE,  ZIPCD,
VNDCLS, VNDSTS, BALOWE, SRVRTG)
SELECT  VNDNBR, NAME, ADDR1, CITY, STATE,
ZIPCD, VNDCLS, VNDSTS, BALOWE, SRVRTG
FROM VENDORPIN1
33 rows inserted in VENDORPIN2 in SQLBOOK.
```

Delete Exercise 19

If you have concluded in Exercise 19 that this will not refresh
anything, you are 100% correct. It will actually add thirty-three
more rows to the file and not replace any of them. So, to get an
SQL way of doing a native clear physical file member
(CLRPFM), we look no further than the DML DELETE
statement. To delete all of the rows in VENDORPIN2 prior to
running the INSERT in Exercise 18, use the following cure-all
for data.

delete from VENDORPIN2

SQL warns with this message panel

delete from VENDORPIN2

```
                    Confirm Statement

You are about to alter (DELETE or UPDATE) all of the records in
your file(s).
```

When you issue the unconditional delete against all fields and
all records in a file, the file will be cleared just as if you had
issued a CLRPFM native command.

Advanced SQL Exercise 20

For the piece d' resistance, Write an SQL SELECT statement
which will retrieve the last name, job code, education level,
salary, and the work department of each employee in either
work department D11 or E21 who also has an education level
of 12, 16, 17, or 18, and has a salary between 0 and 23700.
Please make sure that the job code is not null for any rows
selected.

The SQL Code

```
SELECT LASTNAME, JOB, EDLEVEL, SALARY,
WORKDEPT FROM EMP
WHERE
(WORKDEPT = 'D11' or WORKDEPT = 'E21')
AND (EDLEVEL IN (17, 12, 16, 18))
AND (SALARY BETWEEN 0   AND 23700)   AND (JOB
IS NOT NULL)
```

SELECT statement run complete.

```
                        Display Data
                                       Data width . . .
  Position to line  . . . . .          Shift to column  . .
  ....+....1....+....2....+....3....+....4....+....5....+....6
  LASTNAME         JOB       EDLEVEL        SALARY   WORKDEPT
  John             56           12      17,000.00   D11
  Denrock          56           16          64.50   D11
  Dente            57           12         107.50   D11
  ********  End of data  ********
```

Advanced SQL Exercise 21 - Having

Write an SQL SELECT statement which will retrieve the work
department, maximum salary, minimum salary, and average
salary from departments with at least one male employee
whose maximum salary is greater than $2,000. Group the
results by workdept.

SQL – Having

```
SELECT WORKDEPT, MAX(SALARY),
MIN(SALARY),
AVG(salary)
FROM EMP
Where SEX = 'M'
Group by workdept
HAVING MAX(SALARY) > 2000

SELECT statement run complete.
```

Results

```
                            Display Data
                                Data width . . . . . . :     77
Position to line  . . . . .          Shift to column  . . . . . .
....+....1....+....2....+....3....+....4....+....5....+....6....+....7....+..
WORKDEPT  MAX ( SALARY )  MIN ( SALARY )                    AVG ( SALARY )
  D11        17,000.00       17,000.00     17,000.00000000000000000000000000
  E21      5,900,000.00    5,900,000.00  5,900,000.00000000000000000000000000
********  End of data  ********
Another Exercise - Subselect
```

Advanced SQL Exercise 22 - SubQuery

Write an SQL SELECT statement with a subquery statement
included that will retrieve the last name, first name, and birth
date from the employee file for all employees in which their
salary is greater than the average salary of all employees.

Objective: find all of the employees whose salary is greater than
the average salary

Looking for All Employees > AVG

```
Select lastname, firstnme, birthdate
from emp
where   salary  >
Select avg(salary) from emp)
```

```
                     Display Data
                         Data width . . . . . . :     40
Position to line  . . . . .          Shift to column  . . . .
 . .
....+....1....+....2....+....3....+....4
LASTNAME          FIRSTNME      BIRTHDATE
Gwolf             Dnzel         11/05/56
Anstett           Borregard     08/14/83
********  End of data  ********
 •
 •     ********  End of data  ********
```

Join

A join is a query that combines rows from two or more tables, or views SQL performs a join whenever multiple tables appear in the query's FROM clause. The query's select list can select any columns from any of these tables. If any two of these tables have a column name in common, you must qualify all references to these columns.

There a re a number fo different types of joins. The most common join is called the inner join and the second most used join is clled the left outer join. In this section, we will provide a definition for all of the join types and then provide two examples. One each for the inner join and the left outer join.

The seven types of joins supported on IBM i are the following:

- ✓ Inner Join
- ✓ Left Outer Join
- ✓ Right Outer Join
- ✓ Left Exception Join
- ✓ Right Exception Join
- ✓ Cross Join
- ✓ Full Outer Join

An Inner Join returns only the rows from each table that have matching values in the join columns. Any rows that do not have a match between the tables will not appear in the result table. If a customer file and an order file are joined and there are no orders for the customer, the customer will not be selected in the join view.

A Left Outer Join returns values for all of the rows from the first table (the table on the left) and the values from the second table for the rows that match. Any rows that do not have a match in the second table will return the null value for all columns from the second table. Nulls can be monitored and be defaulted with an IFNULL clause For example: IFNULL(OPERATIONS , 0) will replace the value of OPERATIONS with a 0 if a NULL is detected. This type of join comes in handy in a payroll operation in which a person who did not submit a time card record for example would appear on the edit list but would have no time card.

A Right Outer Join return values for all of the rows from the second table (the table on the right) and the values from the first table for the rows that match. Any rows that do not have a match in the first table will return the null value for all columns from the first table. This is the opposite of the left outer join.

A Left Exception Join returns only the rows from the left table that do not have a match in the right table. Columns in the result table that come from the right table have the null value. This is another way of finding errors where there must be matches to process properly.

A Right Exception Join returns only the rows from the right table that do not have a match in the left table. Columns in the result table that come from the left table have the null value. It is the opposite of the Left exception join.

A Cross Join or a product join returns a row in the result table for each combination of rows from the tables being joined (a Cartesian Product)

A Full Outer Join which IBM calls a Simulating Full Outer Join, like the left and right outer joins, a full outer join returns matching rows from both tables. However, a full outer join also returns non-matching rows from both tables; left and right.

Inner join using JOIN syntax

To use the inner join syntax, both of the tables you are joining are listed in the FROM clause, along with the join condition that applies to the tables. The join condition is specified after the ON keyword and determines how the two tables are to be compared to each other to produce the join result. The condition can be any comparison operator; it does not need to be the equal operator. Multiple join conditions can be specified in the ON clause separated by the AND keyword. Any additional conditions that do not relate to the actual join are specified in either the WHERE clause or as part of the actual join in the ON clause.

Join Exercise 23

Create a list of employees showing the number, employee last name and the department last name where the lastname starts with a letter higher in the alphabet then the letter 'L'.

```
SELECT EMPNO, LASTNAME, DEPTNAME
   FROM SQLBOOK/EMP
INNER JOIN SQLBOOK/DEPT
         ON WORKDEPT = DEPTNO
   WHERE LASTNAME > 'L'
```

In this example, the join is done on the two tables using the WORKDEPT and DEPTNO columns from the EMP and DEPT tables. Since only employees that have last names starting with at least 'L' are to be returned, this additional condition is provided in the WHERE clause.

```
                                    Display Data
                                    Data width
Position to line  . . . . .              Shift to column
...+....1....+....2....+....3....+....4....+....5....
MPNO   LASTNAME        DEPTNAME
45     Lella           Planning Dept
449    Wunnerful       Planning Dept
69     Zion            Information Center
451    Pitt            Manufacturing Systems
45     Patterson       Manufacturing Systems
*******  End of data  ********
```

Left Outer Join

A left outer join returns all the rows that an inner join returns plus one row for each of the other rows in the first table that did not have a match in the second table.

Join Exercise 24

Suppose you want to find all of the departments with a starting letter higher than L and all the employees who are assigned to those departments. You also want to see those departments' with no assigned employees as well. The following query will return a list of all departments whose names are greater than 'L', along with their assigned employees.

```
SELECT DEPTNO,DEPTNAME,EMPNO,LASTNAME
    FROM SQLBOOK/DEPT
LEFT OUTER JOIN SQLBOOK/EMP
    ON DEPTNO = WORKDEPT
WHERE DEPTNAME  > 'L'
```

```
                         Display Data
                       Data width . . . .
Position to line  . . . . .        Shift to column  . . .
...+....1....+....2...+...3....+....4....+....5....+....6..
EPTNO   DEPTNAME                        EMPNO   LASTNAME
D11     Spiffy Computer Service DEPT    112     John
D11     Spiffy Computer Service DEPT    190     Denrock
D11     Spiffy Computer Service DEPT    763     Dente
D11     Spiffy Computer Service DEPT    558     Gwolf
D12     Planning Dept                   145     Lella
D12     Planning Dept                   1449    Wunnerful
D13     Manufacturing Systems           1451    Pitt
D13     Manufacturing Systems           145     Patterson
D13     Manufacturing Systems           1458    Debroskin
D19     Support Services                -       -
D18     Operations                      -       -
D20     Software Support                -       -
*******   End of data   ********
```

Union Exercise 25

The purpose of the SQL UNION command is to combine the results of two queries together. In this respect, UNION is somewhat similar to JOIN in that they are both used to relate information from multiple tables. One restriction of UNION is that all corresponding columns need to be of the same data type. Also, when using UNION, only distinct values are selected so it is similar to SELECT DISTINCT.

In this scenario, as you have witnessed our files have a bit more data in them from our exercises and we have made backups of the Vendorp called VENDORPIN1 and VENDORPIN2. For this join view we are going to select from the IN1 file where the balance owed is greater than 150 and the SRVRTG is equal to 'A''. To this, we are going to Union the records in IN2 in which the SRVRTG column is equal to 'R' At this point, there are over 90 records in these two files. The SQL to accomplish this UNION is as follows:

```
SELECT * FROM VENDORPIN1
WHERE BALOWE > 150 AND SRVRTG ='S'
UNION ALL SELECT *
FROM VENDORPIN2  WHERE SRVRTG = 'A'
ORDER BY NAME
```

SELECT statement run complete.

The results are in the table below:

Union

```
                        Display Data
                              Data width . . . . . . :      134
Position to line  . . . . .          Shift to column  . . . . . .
 ....+....1....+....2....+....3 |
 .9....+...10....+...11....+...12....+...13....
VNDNBR    NAME              |  ZIPCD   VNDCLS  VNDSTS      BALOWE
SRVRTG
  7,030   ATG Dynamo        |  2,141     20      A         352.56      A
  7,030   ATG Dynamo        |  2,141     20      A         352.56      A
     34   Blind Robin Copany|  18,702    20      A         153.00      A
     34   Blind Robin Copany|  18,702    20      A         153.00      A
  7,040   Education Direct  |  18,515    20      A          14.50      A
  7,040   Education Direct  |  18,515    20      A          14.50      A
 77,777   Left Outer Join   |  18,515    10      S         500.00      A
 77,777   Left Outer Join   |  18,515    10      S         500.00      A
  7,130   McFadyen Consulting| 98,523    10      S         250.00      A
  7,130   McFadyen Consulting| 98,523    10      S         250.00      A
  7,070   Red Hat Club      |  85,743    10      S          78.50      A
  7,070   Red Hat Club      |  85,743    10      S          78.50      A
******** End of data   ********
                                                             Bottom
F3=Exit      F12=Cancel      F19=Left      F20=Right     F21=No split
Last column of data.
```

Notice there are just twelve records in the unioned output view.
This is because we selected only a few records to be combined
from each of the underlying files.

Chapter Summary

SQL's Powerful DML statements – Select, Update, Insert, and
Delete were used in well over 20 exercises in this chapter to
both drive home how to use the SQL statements that you have
learned in preceding chapters as well provide an opportunity for
more advanced learning regarding the nuances that make the
SQL language so elegant and powerful.

We continue to find new things to discuss regarding the where
clause and in this chapter it gains much facility with the use of
the underscore and the percentage wildcards with the Like
predicate. This combination permits single and multiple
characters or character strings to be searched and found at the
beginning, middle, end, or anywhere within large or small
character string. For the array programmer this saves
substantial work in programming to be able to use these
features that are natural to the SQL language.

The concat and substring operations are also highlighted as very powerful operators available in this free format language. A number of exercises focused on the utility of the column functions with the Group By and Having clauses providing powerful capabilities in summarizing, averaging, and counting column values and providing additional values to be selected in the Having clause.

These exercises took us to the very powerful sub query facility that typically is not viewed as the easiest of all SQL capabilities to learn. Besides this, we demonstrated just how powerful the IBM i SQL can be and how powerful some sub query operations can be. Besides a standard sub query, we also developed a scalar sub query in which two tables were involved and values from one table selectively updated values in another table. .

The rest of this chapter was exercises with the last set of tutorials, text, and exercises focusing on the facility of two multi-file powerful operators – Union and Join and the many flavors of Join. The flavors of Join are always very interesting and the examples we covered were right to the point.

Key Chapter Terms

%

_
Advanced SQL
AVG
Between
Column Functions, 6
Concat
COS
COUNT
Cross Join
Delete
Double wildcard

Full Outer Join
GROUP BY
HAVING
Inner Join
Insert
INTO
Join
Left Exception Join
Left Outer Join
Like
MAX
MIN
NOT
Null
OR
Right Exception Join
Right Outer Join
Scalar Functions
SIN
SQL Built-In Functions
Sub Query
Substr
SUM
Union
Update
Values
Where Clause
Wildcard

Exercises

Use this chapter or look up information on the Web to answer the following:

1. What is a Null capable field?

2. Describe how the SUBSTR and CONCAT operations work?

3. Create a table for the Voucher file that can link to the vendor file on vendor number. A voucher is an accounts payable disbursements record that is assigned a unique "voucher number" when a vendor invoice is accepted for payment.

4. Populate the voucher file to provide for the join operations that are requested in exercises 5 through 12.

5. Use the description of the vendor file plus create a description for a voucher file Construct tow Concat – Concatenate Two or

6. Write an Inner Join Select on the Vendor file and the voucher file to include all records in a joined format designed by you.

7. Write a Left Outer Join Select on the Vendor file and the voucher file to include all records in a joined format designed by you.

8. Write a Right Outer Join Select on the Vendor file and the voucher file to include all records in a joined format designed by you.

9. Write a Left Exception Join Select on the Vendor file and the voucher file to include all records in a joined format designed by you.

10. Write a Right Exception Join Select on the Vendor file and the voucher file to include all records in a joined format designed by you.

11. Write a Cross Join Select on the Vendor file and the voucher file to include all records in a joined format designed by you.

12. Write a Full Outer Join Select on the Vendor file and the voucher file to include all records in a joined format designed by you.

Chapter 15   AS/400 and IBM i Database Concepts

AS/400 & IBM i Basic Nomenclature

Let's take a closer look at what IBM originally built in as the System/38 and then the AS/400 native database.

In a book, the focus of which is SQL, on a system that stores even its SQL objects in native form, one of the challenges is presenting the SQL language in the right sequence without dwelling on the native facility that exists with or without SQL. It was about 28 years ago in 1978 that IBM invented the native mechanism for defining tables and views. Still today, this natural, free and integrated method of defining databases on IBM i is called Data Description Specifications or simply, DDS.

Relational tables and views built with DDS have been implemented all these years using what IBM calls physical and logical files. Physical files are regular old data files with data as you would expect them to be, though internally they have a few extra bells and whistles, such as metadata to accommodate record and field information as well as other object information. SQL tables are stored internally as physical file objects with a few extra defining characteristics, which give away their source.

Logical Files are also called Logical Views, or just Views. A logical file is really just a view of one or up to 32 physical files. It has a similar object structure as a physical file, but there is no physical data. It is a superset of an SQL view in that it can also define an index (access path) to the data. The area of the file object in which the data would be referenced, points to physical data files outside of the object instead of to internal data, since there is none. The point is that the structure of the physical and logical file objects is the same. The physical file references its data as part of the same object whereas the logical references data in other physical file objects.

A logical view enables data access via presentation rules, which come into play when the logical file is used in a program or query. These rules govern how the data in the "based-on" physical files is to be presented, when accessed via the logical view. Again, the logical file itself contains no data. Its access paths and / or indices point to data in up to 32 separate physical files. In many ways a logical file mimics the capability of an SQL view and its ability to carry an index mimics the SQL index capability. SQL views and SQL indexes are physically implemented on IBM i using the native logical file structure.

This information is germane even to an AS/400 shop that has decided to use SQL as its major database language. All SQL data manipulation operations can be performed on AS/400 databases built from DDS just as well as those built using SQL commands. Whether you code your programs in C++, COBOL, RPG/400 or RPGIV, unless you are depending on keyed access, they will work with SQL views in the same fashion as do logical files, and vice-versa.

Keyed Access Issues with DDL

Though tables are implemented as physical files and views are implemented as logical files, until IBM chooses to violate the SQL standard, there are actually lots of issues to deal with if you one day choose to create all of your tables (files) with DDL. The problem is simple to explain but difficult to solve for a programmer. SQL treats views and indexes as two separate entities. An index is created as a keyed logical, and a view is a non-keyed logical and neither will ever be given the other's capabilities. All of those nice logical views that provide keyed access to programs that you may have created with DDS over the years can still be used but you cannot create anything like that with SQL. The logical file and the index are one and the same with DDS while with SQL they are separate SQL objects.

Without some major work on the standard and at the lab, you cannot and will not be able to define a key for an SQL view. Yes, that does mean that all of those goodies that are available when defining SQL views are of little or no benefit if your high-level language programs depend on keyed access through an index that is a part of the view. Such an animal does not exist in SQL. An SQL view then is useful to the native implementer only if you do not need a key sequence or you do not need to access records by key or if you choose to remove record level access from your programs (CHAIN, READE, etc.) and you choose to move to embedded SQL.

Physical Files

Since an SQL table becomes an AS/400 physical file object when it is created, we will now take a closer look at what makes up a physical file. In addition to data records, a physical file contains a definition of the fields in the file (a description of the data a.k.a. a format or database structure). It also contains an access path, so the data can be stored either in arrival sequence (plus one access path), or in keyed sequence, such as customer number. Unlike an SQL table that has no keyed access, a native physical file as created with DDS is the equivalent of an SQL table but it also has an access path.

The IBM i is an object oriented system. The operating system supports many object types. Yet, there is no object type of index on the IBM i and there has never been an object type of index with System/38 or AS/400. So, if SQL has the ability to create indexes, and the operating system has not been tweaked to support an index object type, then what exactly is an index on the IBM i?

As noted previously, SQL tables are not built with indexes within the same object structure. Instead, when an index is created with SQL, the IBM i builds an object type that has been part of the OS from day one – an object type with far more native capabilities than a mere index. The object is a logical file, which inherently has the ability to store an index. When an SQL index is stored in such a file, SQL markings in the object prevent the logical file from being anything other than an index for SQL activity.

The data in a physical file or that data referenced by a view or logical file is packaged in a sub-object, called a member, which we say is contained in the file object. Though we like to say that, it is really not true. The physical structure of the data container is separate from the file object itself and is usable only through its reference in the file object.

Members

File members can at first appear to be an elusive notion so we will take the time to discuss them since they are very usable with SQL. For a further explanation, please review Chapter 7. First of all, it helps to know up front that there can be many members "in" a physical file. Each member segregates a portion of the data from all other members. In normal database processing, one member is accessed at a time. The first member is the default used when no member is specified.

A file can be overridden to provide data from all members, one at a time to a calling program. This helps in transaction-based systems. For example, it helps when data needs to be segregated by transaction date, and it helps at month end, when the data is easily merged for reporting. Thus, we can envision that as part of every file, there is a list of members as an integral part of the file object. The members can be accessed specifically by file name / member name.

Though the default in IBM i/OS with SQL or native DDS is to create a file with just one member, a file can contain thousands of members. In fact, because of this special structure, IBM uses members to store individual source programs, such as those written in RPG and COBOL. IBM also uses source file members to store DDS to build native physical files. More importantly to the SQL student, experts in AS/400 systems recommend that SQL developers place their create commands in source members as a "permanent" area from which tables, views, indexes etc. can be rebuilt or modified as needed. There is a nice Q & A on members in Chapter 7.

DDS / SQL Is Not Always Needed

As you learned in prior chapters, data description specifications (DDS) are typically used to create a native database. The native command to create a physical file (CRTPF) can create a physical database file without the developer providing a description of the data. The term used for these DB files is internally described since they must be described inside of programs in order to be used. Structurally, without DDS, the command creates a single field file with the field being the same size as the file record length as specified in the command.

Logical Files

AS/400 logical file objects are structured similarly to physical file objects, and they behave in the same way as described above, but, they contain (reference) no private data within the object itself. Well, then what do they contain? They contain nothing more than a definition, or view, or set of rules as to how to retrieve records from a physical file or files, and how to format fields when the dependent physical file is used. Through the native logical file, the AS/400 database is able to implement the relational operators, and send a view of the results of those operations to the requesting program or user.

A single logical file can be built over one to 32 physical files. In other words, up to 32 physical files can be brought together, with JOIN or non-JOIN DDS operations, to create one logical file. The same capabilities exist with SQL Views. Many (any number of) logical files can be built over (specify) the same physical file, just as any number of views can be built against a specific SQL table.

Logical files are also implemented with an internal access path that points to the data container in a physical file member. Therefore, just as a physical file, it has an efficient means of getting at the data in the based-on physical file. The access path contains an index of key values and locations as to where the actual data records reside in the based-on physical file. When a logical file or SQL view is used, the logical file object's access path governs how physical file data is presented / retrieved from data manipulation operations.

Just as physical files can be used with either internally described data or externally described data, logical files work the same way. In fact, a logical file or SQL view, with all fields defined can often be substituted in a program for its underlying physical file, and the program would produce the same results as with the physical file. Of course, because data would be retrieved via a separate view and perhaps a separate index, the program timings would more than likely be a bit slower.

Logical files and therefore SQL views are used to make new relationships in the data base from the existing database. As noted in prior chapters, the operations include Order, Union, Selection, Projection, Join, and others. Records can therefore be referenced, and/or selected based on data content, and/or subdivided (projected) based on data fields desired.

Data Currency

The implementation of DB2 UDB for IBM i, with or without SQL is done to accommodate data currency and immediacy. For example, any change to data can be immediately reflected in all views, regardless of how the view was created. Moreover, there are no embedded pointers or linkage records used to order the records, so there is not a big chain of events necessary when index fields are originally entered or later updated. All links are done based on the relationships of data, not by external, unnatural means.

Data and Index Currency

Changes to an AS/400 database can be immediately reflected or can be deferred. When new records are added or when key values are updated in records, the access path must be maintained to reflect the changes. The system automatically updates the access path in all logical files and SQL indexes either (1) immediately one at a time, (2) delayed, after the job is over, or (3) on a rebuild basis - the database rebuilds the index before every use. Based upon file usage, one of these approaches typically fits the database.

When you create your physical file or logical file, when you change the file object using either a Change Physical File (CHGPF) command, or the Change Logical File command (CHGLF), you can specify your choice for access path maintenance. The parameter is used to govern all members of the file, regardless of how the file object was crated – SQL or native. Of course, since SQL table and View objects are built with arrival access paths, they never have an index within the internal object. Thus, this notion does not really matter for SQL created objects. The index object is a native keyed logical file so it is affected by access path maintenance. The SQL Create Index function establishes the index with an *IMMED access path. However, it can be altered using a change logical file command (CHGLF) to any of the following values.

The possible values are:

*IMMED   The access path is updated each time a record is changed, added, or deleted from a member. *IMMED must be specified for files that require unique keys.

*REBLD   The access path is completely rebuilt each time a file member is opened. The access path is maintained until the member is closed, then the access path is deleted. *REBLD cannot be specified for files that require unique keys.

*DLY   The maintenance of the access path is delayed until the logical file member is opened. Then, the access path is updated only for records that have been added, deleted, or changed since the logical file was last opened.

Creating Physical and Logical Files

How do you create physical and logical files? We have already discussed two ways. There is a third method on the AS/400 and IBM i which was more or less imported from the System/36 to make migrations from that platform even easier. The three ways to create physical files are as follows:

- ✓ IDDU Interactive Data Definition Utility (used in S/36 environment)

- ✓ SQL Structured Query Language

- ✓ DDS Data Description Specifications - AS/400 native interface to the database.

- ✓ Interactive Data Definition Utility (IDDU)

Physical files can be described using IDDU. However, you will
have to use DDS or SQL in order to build logical files or to
build views.. You would choose to use IDDU if you are
looking for a menu driven, interactive method of describing
data. You might also choose IDDU if you are already familiar
with describing data, using IDDU, on a System/36. If this
were a Java topic, we might say that IDDU has been
deprecated.

SQL Structured Query Language

Of course SQL is the way everybody else does a relational
database. On the IBM i, it is an optional, separately orderable,
separately licensed program. It uses the ANSI data definition,
data manipulation, and data control language. SQL is
characterized by its simplicity and lack of verbosity. You tell
the system what you want. You do not tell the system how to
get it. One of the precepts of Ted Codd's relational design was
that the implementation details are unnecessary to the use of
the database.

SQL is a very nice, fee-based alternative to DDS on the AS/400
and IBM i. It has been well-adopted by the newer breed of
developer, whose roots often spring from other platforms such
as Unix and Windows. On every other platform but IBM i, you
either take relational database the way Codd envisioned it, and
that means SQL is the standard . . . or you don't take the
database.

The following is an example of a CREATE TABLE command,
which is the equivalent of building and compiling DDS into a
database file. By now, you should know the syntax of this
command cold.

```
CREATE TABLE STUDENT
       (STUDENT_NO   DECIMAL(10)      NOT NULL,
        STUD_NAME    CHAR(30)         NOT NULL,
        STUD_ADDR    CHAR(30)         NOT NULL)
```

This SQL command creates an arrival sequence physical file,
named STUDENT, with no key, in the user's current library.
The Create Table command is explained in detail in Chapter 8.

Data Description Specifications

Data Description Specifications (DDS) is the most frequently
used method for describing AS/400 databases. DDS is the
language of the native database. Although we show some DDS
examples in this book, it is only to help relate SQL to those
who already know DDS. For more information on the native
database, please see The IBM i Pocket Database Guide from
Lets Go Publish! at www.letsgopublish.com.

Physical files are defined to the system as fields comprising
physical records of data and access to data. The definition of a
physical file contains information about the file itself such as:
File by name, Record format by name, Fields by name, and
access by arrival sequence or keyed sequence.

The CRTPF Command

When DDS is used to create any database file in a particular
library, such as SQLBOOK, by default, a member with the
same name is created within the created file at the same time.
As noted previously, it is these members that actually "hold"
the data when it arrives. The physical file is built with a
description of all the data elements (fields) – contained within
the file object itself. To put this in perspective, any newly
created physical file, with CRTPF or SQL's Create Table, with

its field definitions is equipped with the data definitions within the object itself.

A sample CRTPF command with the English keyword prompts is shown in Figure 15-1

Figure 15-1 Create Physical File

```
                        Create Physical File (CRTPF)

Type choices, press Enter.

File . . . . . . . . . . . . . . > ARMAST          Name
  Library . . . . . . . . . . . > SQLBOOK          Name, *CURLIB
Source file . . . . . . . . . . > QDDSSRC          Name
  Library . . . . . . . . . . . > SQLBOOK          Name, *LIBL,
*CURLIB
Source member . . . . . . . . . > ARMAST          Name, *FILE
Record length, if no DDS . . . .                   Number
Generation severity level . . . > 20               0 30
Flagging severity level . . . . > 0                0 30
File type . . . . . . . . . . . > *DATA            *DATA, *SRC
Member, if desired . . . . . . . > *FILE           Name, *FILE, *NONE
Text 'description' . . . . . . . > *SRCMBRTXT

                        Additional Parameters

Maximum members . . . . . . . . > 1                Number, *NOMAX
Access path maintenance . . . . > *IMMED           *IMMED, *DLY,
*REBLD
Force keyed access path . . . . > *NO              *NO, *YES
Member size:
  Initial number of records . . > 10000            1 2147483646,
*NOMAX
  Increment number of records . > 1000             Number
  Maximum increments . . . . . . > 3               Number
Allocate storage . . . . . . . . > *NO             *NO, *YES
Contiguous storage . . . . . . . > *NO             *NO, *YES
Preferred storage unit . . . . . > *ANY            1 255, *ANY
Records to force a write . . . . > *NONE           Number, *NONE
Maximum file wait time . . . . . > *IMMED          Seconds, *IMMED,
*CLS
Maximum record wait time . . . . > 60              Seconds, *NOMAX,
*IMMED
Share open data path . . . . . . > *NO             *NO, *YES
Max % deleted records allowed . > *NONE            1 100, *NONE
Reuse deleted records . . . . . > *NO              *YES, *NO
Record format level check . . . > *YES             *YES, *NO
```

Dissecting CRTPF Parameters

Now, let's dissect the first part of this command just a bit so we have a better understanding of what we are telling the compiler when we create a physical file.

```
File . . . . . . . . . . . > ARMAST
   Library . . . . . . . . > SQLBOOK
Source file . . . . . . . > QDDSSRC
     Library . . . . . . . .> SQLBOOK
Source member . . . . . . > ARMAST
Record length, if no DDS . > _____
```

In this section of the command, you tell the compiler to create a file object named ARMAST and that it should be built in the SQLBOOK library. You then tell it the DDS is in the QDDSSRC source file which is in the SQLBOOK library. In the second last line, you tell the compiler that the specific DDS for this file are located in the ARMAST member of the QDDSSRC source file. The last line shows on the prompt but is not used. If no DDS were used for the file, this is where you would specify the record length.

In Figure 15-1, you can see that there are many other parameters that can be applied at create time. Most affect performance and structure.

Creating Logical Files

Logical files are defined to the system as a bunch of rules in much the same fashion as physical files. In addition to the create logical file parameters, the rules in logical file DDS cause record Selection, Projection, and other relational operations upon records from a physical file. In addition to the rules for access, the logical file also contains the means to accessing the data.

Defined with DDS

The definition of a logical file is provided in DDS in much the same fashion as a physical file. In other words, you specify file by name, record by name, and fields by name (optional). Fields are optional because if you choose to have all of the fields from the physical exist in the logical file, you don't specify any logical fields. If you specify any fields – that is all you get. When you specify fields in a simple, logical file, based on one physical file, you are performing relational projection. Unless you explicitly specify each of the fields in the physical file, you get a subset of the fields available. Thus, you are projecting a smaller image (# of fields) of the physical file than actually exists in the physical file.

Using DDS, you define the access path in a logical file. You specify whether the path is in arrival sequence or keyed sequence. You also specify whether all of the records will be included in the view, using DDS select/omit criteria. Figure 15-2 shows the components involved in a logical file creation.

Figure 15-2 Compile Diagram with PF and FieldREF

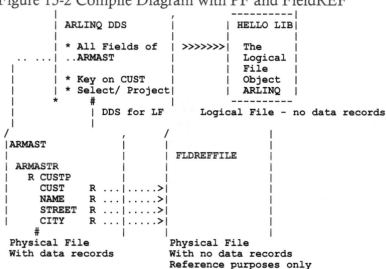

Collecting the Attributes

As you can see in the diagram, at compile time, which is also known as logical file creation time, the DDS compiler uses the physical file (ARMAST in this instance) to obtain the record and field attributes for use in the logical file build. SQL views are constructed under the covers in much the same way.

The "dictionary," on the bottom right has no real role at logical file creation time. The diagram merely demonstrates that the physical file originally got its descriptions from the reference file. During the logical file compilation process, as shown in Figure 15-2, the logical file receives all of its information from the physical file ARMAST, upon which it is based.

In DDS systems, the field reference file provides a passive data dictionary to the native database.

The CRTLF Command

Just as with a physical file, when DDS is used to create a logical file in a particular library, such as SQLBOOK, a member is created at the same time. The member in the logical file does not "hold" the data, as you can visualize in a physical file. However, the logical member built via CRTLF or SQL Create View does access the data in the physical file by pointing to the member component in the "based-on" physical file.

The CRTLF command to create a logical file is shown below with many of its first page of default parameters. Following this command, we will briefly examine some of these parameters, so that you can get a good feel about the information you must provide, and that which the system provides as defaults for the file creation process. Now, let's take a closer look at the CRTLF command as shown in Figure 15-3

Dissecting CRTLF Parameters

Now, let's dissect the first part of this command just a bit, so we have a better understanding of what we are telling the compiler, when we create a logical file.

```
File . . . . . . . . . . . > ARLINQ
   Library . . . . . . . . > SQLBOOK
Source file . . . . . . . > QDDSSRC
   Library . . . . . . . .> SQLBOOK
Source member . . . . . . > ARLINQ
```

In the section above, you tell the compiler to create a logical file object named ARLINQ, and that it should be built in the SQLBOOK library. You then tell it that the DDS is in the QDDSSRC source file which is in the SQLBOOK library. In the second to last line, you tell the compiler that the specific DDS for this file are located in the ARLINQ member of the QDDSSRC source file.

Figure 15-3 Create Logical File

```
                        Create Logical File (CRTLF)

Type choices, press Enter.

File . . . . . . . . . . . . . > ARLINQ       Name
  Library . . . . . . . . . . >   SQLBOOK     Name, *CURLIB
Source file . . . . . . . . . > QDDSSRC       Name
  Library . . . . . . . . . . >   SQLBOOK     Name, *LIBL,
*CURLIB
Source member . . . . . . . . > ARLINQ       Name, *FILE
Generation severity level . . . > 20          0 30
Flagging severity level . . . . > 0           0 30
File type . . . . . . . . . . > *DATA         *DATA, *SRC
Member, if desired . . . . . . > *FILE        Name, *FILE, *NONE
Physical file data members:
  Physical file . . . . . . .    *ALL         Name, *ALL
    Library . . . . . . . . .                 Name, *CURRENT
  Members . . . . . . . . . .                 Name, *NONE
              + for more values
              + for more values
  Text 'description' . . . . . . > *SRCMBRTXT

                      Additional Parameters

Maximum members . . . . . . . . > 1           Number, *NOMAX
Access path maintenance . . . . > *IMMED      *IMMED, *DLY,
*REBLD
Force keyed access path . . . . > *NO         *NO, *YES
Preferred storage unit . . . . . > *ANY       1 255, *ANY
Records to force a write . . . . > *NONE      Number, *NONE
Maximum file wait time . . . . . > *IMMED     Seconds, *IMMED,
*CLS
Maximum record wait time . . . . > 60         Seconds, *NOMAX,
*IMMED
Share open data path . . . . . . > *NO        *NO, *YES
Record format level check . . . > *YES        *YES, *NO
                                                        Bottom
  F3=Exit   F4=Prompt   F5=Refresh   F10=Additional parameters
F12=Cancel
  F13=How to use this display      F24=More keys
```

DB2/400 Database Characteristics

The AS/400 database automatically accommodates data
sharing by multiple users – concurrent access to physical files /
SQL Tables and/or logical files / SQL Views. The system
maintains data integrity and provides data independence.

Unique DB Characteristics

There are a number of unique database characteristics, which
are contained as attributes of a physical file. In essence, they
define the rules of behavior for the DB file. One might call these
data management rules, since they are implementation-
oriented, not definition-oriented. In other words, Ted Codd
would not care about them because they are implementation
details and are not part of relational theory.

Despite the efforts of the great master, Ted Codd, whose
database ideal was for developers and users to have no concern
for the underlying system implementation and attributes, of any
computer system deploying a relational database, the fact is that
every database runs on a computer with its own personality.
When you deploy your database on any type of hardware, or
operating system, you will find some different knobs to turn.
There will be some different bells to ring. And, there will be
some different whistles to blow, in order for you to get
everything the way you want – and still have a fine-performing
machine. It is simply unavoidable, though you can, in most
cases, ignore the underlying AS/400 and IBM i options and just
take the defaults.

Defining Behavioral Rules

Most of the file attributes we are about to examine are
originally placed in the file as a result of the Create Physical
File command – CRTPF command or the CRTLF. After the
file is created, physical or logical, most of these attributes can
be changed permanently by the right Change Command –
CHGPF or CHGLF. Changes to the file made with these
commands are permanent until changed again.

A smaller number of attributes can also be changed,
temporarily, during execution, using the Override with

Database File command - OVRDBF. There are also some attributes, which are invisible in the object, but affect the file object only during execution. These attributes are given in the form of overrides, with the Override Database File (OVRDBF) command.

Database attributes most often pertain to your physical database files, although some attributes, such as index characteristics / maintenance, are part of a logical file. However, the number of attributes in the file object is always the same, regardless of how the file is built - SQL, IDDU, or DDS.

Let's start taking a look at these very powerful attributes, one at a time. It helps to remember that these database attributes collectively form the rules for a database file, and are in fact stored within the object itself.

Records to Force a Write (FRCRATIO)

The AS/400 and IBM i are boxes, which use the notion of Single Level Storage. Inherent in this implementation, is the concept that virtual memory and virtual disk are one and the same, and present the image of single-level storage to the system. All objects, therefore, are addressed at the same level, using their single-level storage address. They are ultimately resolved (located) to real memory or disk. Neither the user, nor the implementer controls what may be in memory and what may not be in memory at any given moment.

Virtual Programs and Data

By default, on your AS/400 or IBM i, both programs, and data are virtualized. Long after a program thinks that it has updated or written a new disk record, depending on system and file characteristics, the record may still be hanging around in memory. To developers who have chosen to implement without journaling, commitment control, and perhaps, without RAID5 disks, the idea that an order record, as an example, may not actually be "really" updated on disk, causes some level of consternation. And it should!

If the system were to crash. . . . Yes, the probability is low that the disk will crash tomorrow. However, it is very high that one or more disks will crash during the life of your system. If you use RAID5, or mirroring, you are in reasonably good shape for preserving records that have been written.

But what about those records that have not yet been written to disk? Well, without journaling, you may not get the more recently-written records back. If the system powers off, without a Universal Power Source (UPS) available for you to do an orderly shutdown, un-journaled records in memory disappear, with the rest of memory's contents, as soon as the system is deprived of power. If your journals are on disk drives that are managed independently of your main disk storage pool, (separate auxiliary storage pool - ASP), you can get your data back up-to-date, as well as withstand a disk crash.

This book does not teach you sophisticated techniques, such as commitment control and journaling, nor does it deal with other implementation topics, such as RAID disk protection, or auxiliary storage pools (ASPs). Most non-AS/400 relational databases use journaling and commitment control, because, quite frankly, their systems do not have the same reliability as an AS/400 or IBM i. Please note that it is best, even with AS/400 and IBM i to use journaling and commitment control in your applications. Regardless of how your system is set up, however, you need to be familiar with the Records to Force a Write (FRCRATIO) attribute of the physical file.

Protecting Data

The FRCRATIO attribute determines the number of Insert, Delete, or Update operations that can occur on records in memory before those records are forced into auxiliary (permanent) storage. If the physical file is being journaled, IBM suggests a very large number or the use of the value *NONE. There is a caveat with *NONE, in that it may cause long synchronization of the journal and physical files. More detailed IBM information on this topic is available in the CL reference information in the AS/400 Information Center.

The Force Write Ratio of course is most important if your data is unprotected by RAID or mirroring. The term itself means the number of program database writes necessary to force an actual write to disk. It is like blocking at a system level vs. a program level. . If you have three records in the memory block that are not written when the system crashes, they are gone. A FRCRATIO of one minimizes the impact of lost data since no more than one update can be lost, but it also keeps the disk drives lots busier, thereby impacting performance.

Maximum File Wait Time (WAITFILE)

Since the AS/400 is an object-oriented system, there is code within the object itself to give information about the object, even when the object otherwise cannot be used. One such attribute which delivers a response to a program is the WAITFILE parameter. This attribute determines the number of seconds that a requesting program will wait for the file resources to be allocated when the program attempts to open the file.

Maximum Record Wait Time (WAITRCD)

There is another WAIT attribute, which is also very helpful in finding problems and in terms of providing work-arounds while the problems are being investigated. This attribute has to do with how long a file will wait, after being requested by a program to fetch a record, before it gives up and sends an error message. This is what will happen if the record is locked by another process.

Wait, Don't Crash!

The WAITRCD parameter permits you to specify the number of seconds that any program is going to wait for a record to be updated or deleted, or for a record read in the commitment control environment with LCKLVL(*ALL) specified. If the record is not allocated in the specified wait time, the file complains by sending an error message to the program.

Records Retrieved at Once (NBRRCDS)

This parameter specifies the number of records read from auxiliary storage as a unit and written to main storage as a unit. The amount of data actually read is equal to the number of records times the physical record length, not the logical record length. Valid values range from 1 through 32767.

This parameter is valid for sequential or random processing and is specified only when the data records are physically located in auxiliary storage in the sequence in which they are processed. This parameter overrides the number of records value specified in the program, or in other previously issued OVRDBF commands.

In this land of web programming and client-server code, we sometimes forget about all of the batch processes which are designed, and must be designed, into systems. Along with batch processes comes sequential processing. Along with sequential processing comes the AS/400 and IBM i sort program, as invoked via the Format Data command (FMTDTA). Yes, even with an integrated database, there is ample need to sort records into a particular sequence before running a program.

OVRDBF NBRRCDS

The Records Retrieved at Once (NBRRCDS) attribute is not specified in the file itself and thus cannot be changed. It is invoked only via the OVRDBF, and lasts until the job has ended or the override is deleted.

EOF Retry Delay in Sec (EOFDLY)

Another processing setting carried by the file object and triggered only by an OVRDBF command, is the End-Of-File Retry Delay in Seconds (EOFDLY) attribute. With this parameter, you specify the number of seconds of delay, before the system will try to read additional records when an end of file condition is reached, in a program reading the overridden file. The typical happening for a program, when it fetches a record after the end of file is reached, is that the request is denied. No more records can be read from the file, until the program either closes and reopens the file, or the program ends and restarts. In both of these cases, however, in order to get to newly added records while processing sequentially, the program must read through all of the beginning records, one at a time, and it must have information about where the new records begin.

No EOF Message

EOFDLY prevents the typical file close logic in programs. The file does not send an EOF message to the program. The program is disconnected from the file, and the program then sleeps for a period of time. The database physical file object wakes up periodically (1 second to 99999 seconds) as set by the EOFDLY parameter and it checks to see if there are more records to process. If there are more records, it starts shipping the newly retrieved records to the program for processing.

When you choose to use this technique, the delay time is used to allow other jobs in the system an opportunity to add records to the file, and have the new records processed without having to start the program again. Instead the program sits on the READ statement. When the delay time ends, the job is made active, and data management determines whether any new records were added. If no new records were added, the job waits for another time delay without informing the application program. When a number of seconds is given, no end of file occurs on the given database file until an End Job (ENDJOB) command or Forced End of Data (FEOD) occurs

Record Format Level Check (LVLCHK)

We've looked at performance attributes and program facility attributes, and now we are going to look at an integrity attribute. The Record format level check (LVLCHK) attribute specifies whether the level identifiers for the record formats of the database file should be checked when the file is opened by a program. For this check, which is done while the member is opened, the system compares the record format identifiers of each record format used by the program with the corresponding identifiers in the database member. Level checking cannot be done unless the program contains the record format identifiers. You cannot use an override to change level checking from *NO to *YES, but you can go from *YES to *NO to turn it off.

An Indelible Mark

When a database file is created (logical or physical), the compiler prints some identifying information within the created file object. A unique stream of data is associated with each of the different formats in the file during the process. It is known as "level information," or more formally as record format identifiers.

When a program is compiled that uses a database file, the compiler copies this unique "level information" into the created program object. In this way, the program "knows" the shape of the file as it was on the day the program was compiled. The object program is built to accommodate that shape. If you go ahead and change that database file, the system will reward you by building a new set of "level information" into the file object. This will make your program bomb. It will bomb with a level check error at file open time, since the file signature is not the same as when the program was compiled. If the program is based on one shape of data and you change the shape, you want the program to bomb before it messes something up. This is exactly what happens. It serves to protect program and database integrity.

How Do You Get the Levels in Synch?

So, this is good overall. But it may be bad temporarily. Let's say, for argument purposes, that you added a field to the end of a record and you recreated the database. Let's also say that the program you are working with does not need the additional field or fields you added. If you do nothing extra, your program will bomb. However, if you compile the database with LVLCHK(*NO), or you override it (OVRDBF) at execution time, you can avoid the costly level check and your program will run fine.

The down side is that you will have degraded the value of the level mechanism, and you will have lost a valuable means of protecting program and database integrity. The right thing to do, for integrity purposes, after a major database change, is to recompile all affected programs. This recaptures the level information and gives the compiler the opportunity to assure that all is OK before building the new program object.

Share Open Data Path (SHARE)

Now, we come to an attribute that helps us control file sharing. Again, not exactly! The Share Open Data Path (SHARE) attribute determines whether the open data path (ODP) is shared with other programs in the same routing step. When an

ODP is shared, the programs accessing the file share facilities such as the file status information and the data buffer.

What is an open data path ODP?

You can think of an ODP as the information in a job about a file. For example, one of the things a job knows about a file it is processing is the address of the current record, and, if processing is consecutive, it knows which record will be processed next. When an ODP is shared, more than one program in a job stream is aware of the processing information, such as the file cursor (the "which record" pointer).

Suppose program A opens up a file with a shared ODP. Let's say it then reads two records and calls program B. Program B in turn, opens the same file with a shared ODP. When program B reads the file, it is presented with record 3 of the file, not record 1, since it has elected to share the open data path with program A.

There are a few choices when specifying whether you want the ODP shared or not. If the value is *NO, then the ODP is not shared with other programs in the routing step (job). A new ODP for the file is both created and used every time a program opens the file. On the other hand, if you select *YES for the attribute, the same ODP is shared with each program in the job.

Limit to Sequential Only (SEQONLY)

The Limit to Sequential Only (SEQONLY) is another processing-only attribute. It has some similarities to the number of records (NBRRCDS) parameter discussed above, but it is not the same. In fact, it takes over after the NBRRCDS parameter finishes doing its thing. Moreover, as you will soon see, the SEQONLY parameter has its own number of records sub-parameter. Its job, when specified in the OVRDBF command, is to stage the physical file for sequential-only processing. In other words, it specifies, for database files whose records are processed in sequential order only, whether sequential only processing should be used with this file. It will help avoid confusion if I show you how this thing looks in a prompted override (OVRDBF) as follows:

```
Limit to sequential only:
SEQONLY
        Sequential only  .  . . . . > *YES
  Number of records   . . ..        > 100
```

From Disk to Virtual Memory and Back

This parameter also specifies the number of records transferred as a group to or from the database (virtual memory) if sequential only processing is used. If a number is not specified, a default number is handily determined by the system. You are better off specifying your own number. This parameter is used to improve the performance of programs that process database files in a sequential manner. It overrides any blocking value specified in the program or in any other previously issued OVRDBF commands.

Chapter Summary

Every database takes on some of the characteristics of the system that it grew up on. The IBM i database grew up integrated and originally came into being from one of the easiest to use file systems every created – the System/3. So, lots of ease of use is built-in to the natural database objects on every IBM i..

The IBM i database system is made up of libraries, physical files, logical files and members. The IBM i has always optimized data currency over all database attributes. When you update a record, it ought to be updated and its access path ought to be updated also so that all keys are in order and all records are accessible by any keys that are on the system – even if a key was just added or deleted or changed. SQL is a direct beneficiary of IBM's care in making its internal DB objects so all-encompassing. It's nice that SQL runs on a system that demands so much of itself.

The whole idea of database on an integrated machine is to have a base facility that every facet of the machine can use. So, it is no wonder that when SQL came to the integrated database box, it would be positioned to use the powerful objects that had already been established for it, even unknowing of its imminent arrival.

The physical file structure has already been discussed and various facets of this remarkable object have been amplified in this chapter. What is not obvious in this book but which is obvious in native books about the IBM i is that this DDS phenomenon that continues to be pervasive on the box is not just a database thing. DDS is also used to describe communications files, display files, printer files, and others. It is the native descriptor language for the IBM i and database is just one piece of that need.

Each IBM i physical and logical file has an access path. For a non-keyed logical file, it is an arrival key of sorts that gets pinned to the record as a slot keeper. Some files have keyed access paths. Physical and logical files may have keys. An SQL index is not implemented as an independent object on a IBM i but rather it uses a logical file structure with an access path to get its job done.

Thus, to make an index facility within SQL, parts of the logical file object had to be "dumbed" down from its native capabilities. The same goes for the SQL view. A logical file object can contain an index and an SQL View cannot. A logical file index can also have select omit logic built within an index but SQL cannot. An SQL view cannot have an index bound to any view. DDS does not have a link to an optimizer but SQL does and IBM attests that the SQL optimizer does a good job of figuring out an access approach when and if indexes should be used.

Additionally, because of this access path notion – even non keyed IBM i records can be processed by relative record number. In fact, there is a command called INZPFM which goes ahead and pre-writes default records to a "direct" file so that the file can be processed by relative record #.

Members are the vehicle that IBM has chosen to contain the data for SQL or DDS-built files. This is a step up on the notion of a partitioned data set but it has many of the same characteristics. IBM has been improving SQL with notions to help make the anomalies go away. Member access can now be achieved in SQL by the Alias facility. As time passes, more anomalies and differences between SQL and Native will be smoothed out. Let the better method win in all cases. Adjust the standards rather than pin the database to an inferior method.

There are lots of attributes that can be created along with a physical or logical file objects. There are many parameters. If you miss the opportunity to do it right at create time, however, there are also lots of ways to make it right after the fact. These commands are part of the IBM i/OS operating system. They are part of the integrated database.

The first level of change are the change commands such as Change Physical File (CHGPF) or Change Logical File CHGLF). These enable the implementer to modify parameters in an object permanently without having to delete and recreate the object. This facility has been there since day one on the System/38. These commands can even change the record allocations. You practically cannot run out of room on a file anyway as the operating system continually permits more and more records to be added with operator intervention after the initial allocations are made. Operator intervention may not be desirable, however, so the Change operation permits the allocation to be updated on the fly.

Then again, if you just want to make a change for today or the next hour or for your terminal session, you can do that also with the override with database file CL command (OVRDBF). With this command, you can change the specs until you sign off or until the job that you changed finishes executing. The system gives great flexibility and top level integrity, full sharing, and currency. This chapter gave you a nice look at a lot of those features of which SQL takes advantage because it sits on top of the IBM i/OS operating system on the IBM i.

Key Chapter Terms

*DLY
*IMMED
*REBLD
Access path
Index
CRTPF
Index currency
Data Currency
EOFDLY
File Wait Time
FRCRATIO
IDDU
Keyed access
Keyed logical
Logical files
LVLCHK
Members
NBRRCDS
Object oriented system
Object type
ODP
Open Data Path
Physical file object

Exercises

Use this chapter or look up information on the Web to answer the following:

1. When customer number 2 and customer number 4 exist in a database that is keyed by customer number and a user types in a record for new customer number 3, what happens to the index in terms of access path mainteanance choices?

2. Describe the three methods of maintaining an access path, *DLY, IMMED, or *REBLD.

3. When an SQL index is created, what physical object is used and why? What else can be done with that object in high level language programs?

4. What parameters on the CRTPF command have to do with data and index currency?

5. Does FRCRATIO as a parameter give a programmer the opportunity to use natural system caching? If not, what happens if there is no forced write to update ratio?

6. Is EOFDLY a way of delaying operations so that other operations complete or is it a programmer tool? Explain?

7. Can an SQL view support record level access in an RPG program? If yes, how? If no, why?

8. Is there a file parameter that prevents a program from using a database object that it has been bound to if that object is altered or deleted and recreated?

9. What parameter permits a program to wait a period of time to get a file lock? Record lock?

10. What is meant by an object type? How can physical and logical files both be *file object types when they are different?

11. What is an open data path? Why would you care about such a thing?

12. Is the FRCRATIO for performance or for protecting data or neither or both?

13. Should SQL tables be created with IDDU?

14. Can AS/400 data be blocked when used in programs?

15. Why would I want to limit processing to sequential only?

16. If a program is written to be able to update a million record file processed sequentially by record, and later the need to update is taken away from the program by a switch that gets set in the program each time it is run, if the program were rewritten so that the file open was for input and not for update would there be any difference in performance? Explain.

Chapter 16   Relational Database Theory

Theory behind DB Reality

There is a notion in formal relational database design theory called Entity Relationship Diagramming, E-R. It has great value in helping analysts design databases without anomalies. We'll get back to some E-R principles shortly. First, let's examine a concept of which most DB practitioners are aware – Data Normalization. E-R and Data Normalization are complimentary theories and methodologies.

Database Normalization

Database normalization can be summarized by this one cute phrase:

"Every field in a record design must depend on the key, the whole key and nothing but the key."

If you have a design that mirrors this statement, then your data is probably, at least in third normal form. When a field in a record does not depend on the primary key, then normalization rules dictate that the field, and other fields that depend on the same field, should be removed from the record being built and moved to another or a new file. That is one way in which files come into being in formal database design

There are three popular forms of database normalization as follows:

1st Normal Form
2nd Normal Form
3rd Normal Form

Objective of Normalization

The objective of normalization is to re-structure data base records in files to third normal form. Then, once the data is in third normal form, you may choose a lesser form based on anticipated performance and usability for queries etc. If you want to be relationally correct, however, at a minimum, you will take your database design to third normal form before you make any other decision.

Many IT folks like normalization, but they don't like normalization at the same time. Though most of the production database problems are solved with normalization, developers very soon miss those big, chub-ball sized records that existed in a small number of files. They remember that it was not much work once it was set up to get all kinds of good information from just one file, even though the design may have been a time bomb ticking.

The only real problem besides a possible performance hit is that full normalization most often results in atomic, single fact, teeny weenie records and many files. This is great for production data processing but it does not server end users well. So, a corollary to teeny weenie records is that to accommodate end user computing, Humpty Dumpty sometimes has to be put back together again – either in the production database or in an adjunct data warehouse.

First Normal Form - Removing Repeating Groups

Many new files are created during the normalization process because an initial first-cut record design most often comes with its share of repeating groups of fields. The biggest culprit is data that is designed to be processed in a group such as arrays and various multiple occurrence data structures. This data most often looks like it is perfectly designed for the repeating group scenario but the trained DB designer will resist the temptation and will go ahead and move each repeating group into its own file.

Problems with Repeating Groups

Suppose, for example you have a file that somebody designed years ago that has twelve sales fields, one for each month. Like it or not, this is a repeating group. You may see it as an array and as such it should be treated as one element but the facts do not support that reasoning. Let's say your company changes to four week intervals from monthly intervals so that each period is approximately twenty-eight days. In the "repeating group scenario," you would then need a thirteenth field to store the new period's sales.

But there is no thirteenth spot available. Your database was designed to supports just twelve fields in a big wad with no concern that legislation or company decree would disrupt this notion. Thus, without a redesign of your database and a prior impact analysis of all the programs that depend on the current design, you cannot accomplish the new requirement. You must restructure the data to accommodate the company's dictates because someone violated the 1st normal form rule.

You have the same problem, but perhaps even worse if the company decides to go to weekly sales tracking and reporting. In this scenario, you would need fifty-two-fields to store the weekly data for a year. However, your database still has only twelve fields. It gets even worse, when the company decides to keep two years of data in the file for better analysis, how do you accommodate this?

Perhaps even before you get there, somebody says to management that the company ought to track daily sales for a five year period and now your single record bucket number is up close to 2000 buckets If you cannot accommodate all of these changes, then your data is not in First Normal Form.

How to Fix Repeating Groups

You solve this problem by putting these repeating groups in their own file / relation. If there would be twelve repeating fields in the original record design, then the new file would have twelve records, one for each amount, along with the proper key identifiers. If you needed another sales bucket to give you thirteen, you would just add another record to the file. No record re-design is necessary.

If you need 40 more to accommodate weekly, just add more records. If you need 104 records to accommodate a two-year weekly strategy, just add the records. You are never shut out when you design to first normal form. There's always room. Just add another record.

Get Rid of Repeaters

Many database designers design their files with no repeating groups because they intuitively know that it is wrong. Their intuition more than likely came from being burned some time in their DB design life and many of us who toiled in the file systems of the 1970's and 1980's had the same problem with file system record design. This is not really a database phenomenon. The DB role in this issue is that with virtual files, such as join Views, you can actually reconstruct some of the good old days when repeating groups were in, without having to deal with repeating groups.

As you may believe by now, even if the DB designer missed a few repeating groups here and there in initial design; the process of normalization would find them. And, that helps the rest of us explain why the great DB designers do what they do. Normalization is a mental process that all great database designers pick up as a skill even without formally going through the process. Otherwise, they would not be great DB designers.

So, a lot of files come into being by their data having been cast off from a repeating group scenario from initial record designs. Eventually even the newest DB designer runs out of repeating groups. When all repeating groups of fields are removed, you have achieved the First Normal Form of database design.

So, how do you remove repeating groups? First, you have to recognize the fields as repeating fields, and secondly, you move them to a new file. If the file in which the group belongs does not already exist, then you create a new file design for each repeating group.

So, how then do you think files such as an Address Master file or an Earnings Master file or a Deduction Master file in a payroll application came into being? If formal database design were used, they would come to being because of Database Normalization and its first cousin, Entity Relationship Mapping / Diagramming.

Second Normal Form - Remove Functional Dependencies

To achieve Second Normal Form, the design objective is to remove functional dependencies to assure that all of the non-key fields functionally depend on all of the key fields in those files in which there is more than one key field (called a composite key). To be in Second Normal Form, data must first have a composite key.

Spotting Functional Dependencies

To give you a feel for how to spot functional dependencies, we will use an INVOICE file as an example. Its initial design is shown below: You will note that it shows several Functional Dependencies. These must be removed to put the Invoice file in Second Normal Form.

```
Invoice File:
```

Field Name	Dependent on	Action
CUST_NO (Key)		
INVOICE_NO (Key)		
CUST_NAME	Cust#	*REMOVE
CUST_ADDR	Cust#	*REMOVE
AMOUNT	Cust#, Inv#	*none
DATE_DUE	Cust#, Inv#	*none

There are two fields in this file that are functionally dependent on just one of the two fields that are part of the composite primary key. The fields with functional dependency are the CUST_NAME and CUST_ADDR fields. They do not depend on the whole key (CUST_NO and INVOICE_NO). They depend only on part of the key - CUST_NO (customer number). This field represents just ½ of the composite primary key.

The CUST_NAME and CUST_ADDR fields do not depend on the INVOICE_ NO field at all so they should exist in some database file, but not the INVOICE file, regardless of whether there are any invoices for customers or not. It is somewhat obvious in this example that the removed fields belong in a file such as a customer master.

As you can see at the bottom, the AMOUNT and DATE_DUE fields depend on the INVOICE NO for a particular CUST NO. Therefore, these columns in this design depend on both fields of the composite key. Thus, they belong in the Invoice file.

Solving Functional Dependencies

To solve the functional dependency anomaly, the customer data fields, CUST_NAME, and CUST_ADDR need to be placed in a separate file. Thus, the Customer file is born through normalizing to second normal form. Of course, there might already be a customer file. You do not want to create a new customer file for your application if it already exuists. That may be a worse scenario than the non composite key dependency that you just eliminated.

No Lost Data

This removal of functional dependencies removes the natural potential for lost data. For example, if there were no longer open invoices for a customer, and there were no customer file, there would no longer be a record in the system that would show that the customer ever existed.

Moreover, there would be more work to process invoices. For example, each new invoice would require that the customer data be keyed in anew, rather than be referenced from the customer file.

Less Work

Having a customer file built as a result of the Second Normal Form process brings other time savings and benefits besides new customers getting keyed just once or the potential loss of date. Without a customer file, for example, what happens when customer data changes? If a customer address changes, for example, with a customer file, the data needs to be changed in just one place. However, if we held the customer information in an Invoice file as in the original non-normalized design, if there were twenty-five open invoices for a customer, the customer-data would exist in 25 invoice records. To change the customer data in this scenario, twenty-five records would have to be updated.

Third Normal Form

To achieve Third Normal Form, the objective is to remove all transitive dependencies to assure that all of the non-key fields in the record design depend on the primary key, and only the primary key. Those attributes that are dependent on non key fields are known as transitive dependencies. Let's look at a sample of a Parent / Child database as shown below:

Record Structure of Child File

Fields	Dependent on	Action
Child SS# (key)		
Child Data ...	Child SS#	
Other child data		
...		
Parent 1 SS#	Child SS#	
Parent 1 Name	Parent SS#	**Remove
Other parent data	Parent SS#	**Remove

Spotting Transitive Dependencies

You can immediately see in the example above, that the Parent's name is not dependent on the child's SSN. It is dependent on the Parent's SSN. The parent's SSN is in the Child File and that is OK. To solve the dependency a Parent file would be created ad it would relate back to the Parent SSN. Thus, the Parent SSN would be known as a foreign key, since it would relate to the primary key of the new Parent's file.

However, the Parent's key is not the primary key to the Child file as shown above. From the Child file's perspective, the Parent 1 (mom or dad) SS# field is a non key field. Thus. The Parent 1 (mom or dad) Name field depends on a non key field, thereby indicating a transitive dependency.

Solving Transitive Dependencies

Thus the parent's name and other information should be placed in its own file. By creating a parent file and having a record for each parent, you solve the transitive dependencies, and the file morphs almost immediately into Third Normal Form.

Problems Solved

Many of the same problems are solved as noted in the second normal form example, such as the ability to lose parent information if the child record is gone. Additionally, if a parent has ten children and changes his or her address, the parent address information in child records would need to be changed with the new parent information. By providing a foreign key in the child record, a change to the one parent record changes all the child record relations.

Reaching Third Normal Form

In summary, when you have driven out the repeating groups, the functional dependencies, and the transitive dependencies, you have a situation in which every field depends on the key, the whole key, and nothing but the key. The data is then in Third Normal Form.

Data Normalization Steps

The steps that you follow to reach Third Normal Form to achieve acceptable data normalization are as follows:

1. Create a conceptual data structure
2. Remove any repeating groups -- 1NF
3. Remove any functional dependencies -- 2NF
4. Remove any transitive dependencies -- 3NF

When you've done this, you will have a situation that can, again, be characterized by the cute little phrase that we showed at the beginning of this section - Author unknown:

"Every field in a record design must depend on the key, the whole key and nothing but the key."

Entity Relationships / Cardinality

Now, let's get a little technical for a little while. I will try to make this as painless as possible. Though we have not defined too much yet regarding Entity-Relationship (E-R) diagramming, we have been discussing some ways in which E-R mapping and diagramming can help us design databases. These simple notions can help us in our role of DB designer to know what goes into which file. Let's define a few things now so that we have a general notion of E-R techniques.

There are three basic elements in ER models:

✓ Entities are the "things" about which we seek information.

✓ Attributes are the data we collect about the entities.

✓ Relationships provide the structure needed to draw information from multiple entities.

✓ Entities are the people, places, things, events and concepts of interest to an organization. In short, anything which an organization needs to store data about can be called an entity.

An entity can also be defined as an object (not necessarily a IBM i object) that exists and is distinguishable from other objects. To be less abstract, let's say that the term entity represents the people, places, things, events, and concepts of interest to somebody.

For instance, John Smith, with Social Security Number (SSN) 490-11-2368, is part of some entity. He is part of the entity called persons. He may also be part of the entity called food shoppers, and of course from the grocery store's perspective, he may also be part of the entity called customers. And, yes if each of these entities in their respective organizations chose to store data bout John Smith, he would be nothing more than part of the contents of that entity

An entity may be concrete, such as a person, a car, or a magazine, for example, or the entity can be abstract, such as a holiday, a concept, or an event. The actual content of the entities is not as important as how the entities relate with each other. Thus, it is only necessary that each record in each entity (e.g., each person or organization) be identifiable by some code, called a primary key.

An entity is represented by a set of attributes. An attribute can be thought of as a defining property. Attributes of a person include a name, a social security number, an employee number, etc. Attributes of a customer include a customer number, a street, a city, a credit limit, an amount owed, etc. You may recall in a few sections of this book, we acknowledged another name for a field or a column in a database table. The name attribute takes on more meaning the more theoretical we get. The word certainly has relevance in our study. Thus, a database attribute is a field in a database file. If entities are represented by attributes, then, it follows that the entities in a database are files, which some call tables and others call relations. And the attributes of that relation are stored in the columns which we like to call fields.

All of this work we are doing in this chapter is conceptualizing a data model. A data model shows the entities, attributes and the various relationships between the entities involved. In DB theory there is always a store of data involved. It's important to realize that a database model is not a flow chart or a process flow diagram. There is no beginning and there is no end, there is just a relationship.

It would be reasonably easy to spot that there are really just three types of models that work in the DB arena. The first may be seen as a conceptual model. It operates at the top of the DB chain. When it is diagrammed it shows the basic entities alone and how they relate to each other. It may even give a general clue as to how the entities are used by management in the process.

Working your way down the detail chain, the second type of model is the logical model. When diagrammed, this model contains more detail, and this kind of diagram often maps nicely to the symbols and processes used for a logical ERD.

The bottom of the detail chain is where the disk drives are spinning but if we come up just a bit from there, the final type of DB diagram that we might examine is the physical ERD. This model cares about whether Linux or Unix or IBM i/OS or DB2 or Oracle, or MySQL or SQLServer is dictating the rules. Thus, there is a great deal of detail. After we add some body to the logical ERD, it naturally morphs into the physical ERD, and then at least theoretically, you can create your database.

For the academic purists and for those who actually invented these notions, an. An Entity Relationship Diagram (ERD) is the formal (neutral) term for a Chen-Diagram. Peter Chen defined this notion in 1976. He was not alone as other graphical diagrams such as the Yourdon model developed by Ed Yourdon shows the shape of the database as well. Regardless of the form you choose to use, the diagramming is just about the same. Most database texts give both Chen and Yourdon their stake in the history of this powerful notion .

E-R Diagramming

In E-R diagramming, as you would expect, the relationships among entities are diagrammed, in an attempt to make sense of their various relationships in a relational database. The E-R diagram then can be used as both a design tool, and a map that shows how to use the data. Many designers believe that the construction of an Entity Relationship Diagram is essential for the design of tables, of extracts, and even metadata (data about data).

This book is intended to be a practical, example-oriented tool for you to be able to learn and to work well with relational databases, using SQL. E-R diagramming at a detailed level is not the object of this study but it is very germane to designing proper data records and being able to describe that design to other interested parties.

A good exercise for students wanting to learn more about the formal notion of database design would be to take a trip out the world wide web with your browser. The masters are mostly all published on the subject and you can get some great diagrams, explanations and practical tips to help you formalize your approach to database design.

learly E-R helps us better present, and therefore better understand, the relationships of files (entities) in a relational database system. The notion of cardinality is also a great aid in this study.

Cardinality Relationships

E-R diagrams represent database files and the relationships among files. By having to diagram your database relationships before your design is complete, especially their cardinality relationships (one to one, one to many, etc.) you quickly get a perspective as to the shape your files must take.

Parent & Child Example

Whenever you have a one to one relationship of an attribute with an entity, not one to many, or many to many, you can expect that the attribute belongs with at particular entity. We can use a person entity (say a child) again as an example. A person has one first name. Therefore, there is a one to one relationship of a person to a name. In database terms now, if we substitute the primary key (unique identifier), for a personnel record, such as social security number, then we can say that the name has a one to one relationship with the primary key of social security number. For each SSN, you will have just one name.

Which Parent?

OK, now let's take a look at another attribute. How about parent's first name. Uh oh? Which parent? See the problem? There is a one to many relationship between the primary key (SSN) of the child and the parent's first name. You may not like this example. You may say that at worse there is a one to two relationship - one child SSN to two parent sets of information. That's still one too many!

Am I Wrong?

You may challenge me by saying that there would be a one to one relationship if we had used mother's first name and father's first name instead of parent's first name. If we have a one to one relationship in database design, then the attribute belongs in the same record format as the primary key. If, on the other hand, we have a one to many relationship, then our data relationship modeling tells us we need to create a new file for the new entity, which we have discovered — which is Parents. In database design, we devise a primary key for the parents (perhaps SSN again, though such use of SSN is getting to be illegal) and we move all of the associated information about the parents, such as address information, to the parent's file.

But, you may say, for a maximum of a one to two relationship, maybe we are better off keeping the parent's information in the child file. If this were a university, we might even call it a student file for universities all have this DB relation issue big-time. So maybe there are ten new fields we need, to describe each parent, which adds twenty fields to our database record. Maybe this is OK? But it is not relationally correct.

Parents Must Go!

No matter which analytical tool you choose, the vote is that the parents must go from the child (student) record design. Let's now look at some of the database design tools, which we have been studying, to see, just why, mom and dad are o-u-t.

Cardinality Says "Go!"

Using the cardinality relationships, a one to many relationship should be split into its own files. Now we see how files are called relations in relational database theory. Based on cardinality, the parents must go.

First Normal Form also Says "Go!"

How about the idea of first normal form, which says that there should be no repeating groups? Aren't two-sets of ten fields a repeating group? According to first normal form, the Parents gotta go!

One would conclude that if the conclusion of a cardinality analysis suggests a separate file for a one-to- many relationship such as parents, and the first normal form rule of no repeating groups suggests that a second set of parents in the student file represents a repeating group, then clearly, the Parents must go — to their own file. Now, let's look at some other relationships.

Second and Third Normal Form Say "Go!"

The second and third normal data normalization form starts looking at each field, one by one, to be assured that each field in the record design depends on the primary key. If we were walking through the parent's attributes in the child record (doesn't even sound right - does it?), we might find a parent's social security number and a parent's street address.

Is the street address for the parent an attribute of the child? No, it is not! It depends on the social security number (primary key - unique identifier) of the parent, not the social security number of the child. It does not depend on the primary key of the child entity, the whole key, and nothing but the key. Therefore, the second and/or third normal form test says that each of the parents' fields should be moved to a separate file, so they can depend on the proper primary key for the proper entity.

Three For Three – Gotta Go!

So far, we are three for three against stuffing parent information in the child's file. Let's say you are stubborn, and you just don't want a lot of files cluttering up your application. So, you go ahead and implement, with the design as is. You do not create a Parent's file. Will it work? Well . . . maybe! But, it certainly won't work well for parent things, since parents remain non-entities.

What About Divorce?

Now let us move the file into the twentieth century - the century where divorce became almost as common as marriage. Now what? You have designed two parent slots into your child record. What about mommy's new husband? Do you add ten more fields? What about daddy's new wife? Do you add another ten more fields? How many divorces are you going to permit each parent in your child database design? Can database design be the next big inhibitor to divorce? If it can, you may soon be on the Oprah Winfrey show or the Doctor Phil show!

Give Parents Own File

Of course, according to basic DB design principles, parent data wasn't supposed to be in the child file in the first place. Maybe you had a one-to-many relationship all along, and maybe you should have designed for it – from the start! Give the parents their own file. Make sure that the primary key of the child is in each parent record. That way the data can be accessed from child or from parent. It's relational, right?

Many to Many Relationship

Is this really a many-to-many relationship? Whoah Nelly! That's one step up from a one to one relationship. Might a particular parent have more than one child? (That's any of the fifteen parents, to which you might have limited the child record in the prior design.) If this were a doctor's office, a hospital, a school or a church database application, would you expect that a parent might have more than one child involved? That's a many-to-many relationship. A parent may have many children and a child may have many parents. If we split the parents into their own file, this works both ways. Doesn't it? The many-to- many relationships are satisfied! Right?

Nope! It is not, and it does not. The design works from child to parent since the common chord is child SSN. We are sticking it in each parent's record - regardless of how many parents. Unfortunately, it does not work the other way around — from parent to child. If there is a second child, it messes it up. The second child number cannot be rammed into the one child SSN slot in the parent record. Oh! Just add another child number to the parent record! That's a convenient solution. Whoops – the repeating group rule applies - No can do! Then what?

Just Make Some Rules?

Well! You could make rules such that the parents and the children have to use different doctors or go to different schools or hospitals but you know this would not work. If you do could this, it might make a bad design last longer. You could use dummy social security numbers for a second set of records for the same parents - as many parents as there may be. You could relate the second child to the second set of parents through the new number. But, then you have data redundancy and you don't know that the second child and the first child are related. Wow! This gets complicated!

What Is the DB Design Solution?

How would you solve it? You could create a link file between the parents and the children. Its key would be a composite of the parents and the children's SSN. Each parent would have a field in the link record with his or her SSN and a child's SSN. The parent's number references the key in the parent information record. The child # references the child information record.

If a parent has four children, that parent would have four records in the file. Each record in the link file would have the same parent SSN and the SSN of a different child. The beauty of this scenario is that you never run out of room. Another kid brings in another record in the link file. Another parent brings in another link. It's OK when you design it right.

What About the Kids?

What about the kids? If all the parent link records are completed, then all the kids' records are automatically completed! Right? Yes, Indeedy! If you were to sort the link file on the kids' SSN, most of them would probably have two records in the link file provided, one each, from each parent. Some may have one, some three, etc. depending on how many parents. This solves the parent child link! But does it do it well?

Linking DB Child to Child

How do we link child to child? This starts to hurt my head at this point. Can you use the parent/child link file for this? Theoretically you can! You could join sibling records with parent records.

The view of the Join could have a child's SSN, parent's SSN, and a record in the file for each of the siblings of each parent. For each child in a Join like this, there would be enough records to handle each parent and all of the siblings of each parent. Since, by definition, there would be duplicates in the view, in that a brother would show up under both parents, as would his sister, there would be some additional DB design tuning necessary. But, the deed is theoretically accomplishable.

Don't ask me to code the SQL or DDS for this now. But, it would be fun! By the way, there are a number of examples that can show how to join a file to itself. In essence we would be doing this to accommodate the child to child solution. Don't worry, we're not going to do that now.

Since it hurts all of our heads to go there, we will stop here and say that — if you read all this, you should have a real appreciation for database design and how important it is – even if you don't know it all . . . yet!

Different Methods Can Be Used

Just a few more comments now before the pain is over completely. There are many ways to skin a briefcase. Being bits-and-bytes efficient is not always the right approach. For example, a Child - Sibling file might be the best bet in addition to the Parent-Child file. All the machinations to join a file to itself and then to other records may not be worth the pain and the performance. In this file, you could have the SSN of each child on the left and right side of a table. A family of four children would have twelve records in this table such as the following:

Child	Sibling
SSN#1	SSN#2
SSN#1	SSN#3
SSN#1	SSN#4
SSN#2	SSN#1
SSN#2	SSN#3
SSN#2	SSN#4
SSN#3	SSN#1
SSN#3	SSN#2
SSN#3	SSN#4
SSN#4	SSN#1
SSN#4	SSN#2
SSN#4	SSN#3

As the theme from the old TV program suggests: "There are many different designs available in the Naked Database, this has been one of them."

Parent and Child File

One final note regarding the parent information file and the child information file. Theoretically, both sets of data can be in one file, but in different records. There would be child records and parent records commingled. Each record would be shaped the same. Parents have SSNs. Children have SSNs. If SSN is the key, remember that a file can be joined to itself, and the link file could be joined multiple times to the parent/child file, as long as all the records are the same.

If we did this, of course, we would no longer have a child or parent entity, we would have a person entity instead. Moreover, we would have to classify people as child, parent, or both. It would become so much fun that you might even say, "Two or three files are better. That idea doesn't hurt my head."

Good DB Design Can Tax Your Mind

Many of the design situations you get into can hurt your head big-time. It is always best to keep the design simple and understandable. The next time you look at your own DB work, if it is complex, it may take you a long time to come up to speed to understand your own design. The other possibility, of course is that you won't necessarily see anomalies right away, and if you implement with unseen data anomalies, you will get big time headaches.

Chapter Summary

An entity is a person, place, or thing that we choose to collect data about. When we design systems, we initially try to group our data within a particular entity, when we find that we have things like repeating groups indicating a cardinality issue or we have functional or transitive dependencies in some of our first-shot record designs, we now know that the solution always is to remove the offending group or attribute from the record design of the entity in question and move it to another file. If there is no file waiting for that particular attribute, then the rule says we create a new file.

In many DB designs, that is how new files get created.

Take your design to third normal form and then depending on how your performance is, you may need to back up a bit. The simple notion about data normalization is that every attribute should depend on the primary key and nothing but the key. If it doesn't, you are not yet in third normal form and you've got more work to do.

Key Chapter Terms

1st Normal Form
2nd Normal Form
3rd Normal Form
attribute,
Cardinality
Data normalization steps
DB design
DB theory
Entity
Entity Relationship Diagram
Entity Relationship Diagramming
Entity Relationships
E-R techniques
Foreign key
Functional dependencies
Lost data,
Many to many
MySQL
Objective of normalization
One to one
One to many
Record,
Transitive dependencies

Exercises

1. What is meant by the term, Relational Database Theory?

2. What is the purpose of Entity Relationship Diagramming?

3. Who are two of the top proponents of ERD?

4. What is database normalization?

5. What is the objective of database normalization

6. What is the principle of cardinality?

7. Does cardinality have anything to do with recognizing repeating groups?

8. How can a many to many cardinality relationship be explained?

9. What form of normalization is your database when there are just a few "necessary" repeating groups?

10. What is First Normal Form?

11. How do you f ix repeating groups in record design?

12. What types of objects increase as the number of attributes are removed from entities during database normalization?

13 What is a functional dependency?

14. How do you solve functional dependencies?

15. What does it mean to have data in second normal form?

16. What is a transient dependency?

17 How do you solve transient dependencies?

18. How is it that data that is not normalized can have lost data? How can this happen?

19 What does it mean to have data in third normal form?

20.Should DB design go to fourth or fifth normal form? Explain?

21. Should DB design ever come back to 1st normal form after having created a DB with atomic records? Explain.

22. Why aren't production databases in third normal form not appropriate for end user read-only access?

23. Data warehousing applications like to work with denormalized data. What does this mean and how far would you go back to provide a denormalized record design for a data warehouse? Does this mean planned data redundancy?

24. What is second normal form?

25. What is third normal form?

Chapter 17   Advanced SQL – Constraints and Isolation Levels

Powerful Rule-Based Capabilities

Constraints are a very powerful capability of SQL dating back to its invention. They are enforced by DB2 UDB for IBM i to assure that the constraint rules as applied function as defined. The types of constraints that are offered are as follows:

- ✓ Unique constraints
- ✓ Referential constraints
- ✓ Check constraints

Unique constraints

A unique constraint is the rule that the values of the key are valid only if they are unique. They can be created using the CREATE TABLE and ALTER TABLE statements.

Enforcement

Unique constraints are enforced during the execution of INSERT and UPDATE DML statements. A PRIMARY KEY constraint is a form of UNIQUE constraint. The difference between this and non-primary use is that a PRIMARY KEY cannot contain any null-able columns.

Referential Constraints

A referential constraint is the rule that the values of any foreign key are valid only if they also appear as values of a parent key; or some component of the foreign key is null.

Enforcement

Referential constraints are enforced during the execution of INSERT, UPDATE, and DELETE statements.

Check Constraints

A check constraint is a rule that limits the values allowed in a column or group of columns. Check constraints can be added using the CREATE TABLE and ALTER TABLE statements.

Enforcement

Check constraints are enforced during the execution of INSERT and UPDATE statements. To satisfy the constraint, each row of data inserted or updated in the table must make the specified condition either TRUE or unknown (due to a null value).

Note: the examples in this chapter and the data as well come from IBM's DB2 UDB for IBM i SQL Programming Concepts V5R2 book. We thank IBM for the use of this material in this book.

Adding and Using Check Constraints

A check constraint assures the validity of data during inserts and updates by limiting the allowable values in a column or group of columns.

In this example, the following statement creates a table with two columns and a check constraint over COLUMN2 that limits the values allowed in that column to positive integers:

```
CREATE TABLE T1 (COLUMN1 INT, COLUMN2 INT
CHECK (COL2>0))
```

If we tried to insert a row with a negative value for COLUMN2 into this table, it would fail because the value to be inserted into COL2 does not meet the check constraint; that is, -1 is not greater than 0.

The insertion of a positive value, however, would be successful:

Referential Integrity Constraints

Referential integrity is the condition of a set of tables in a database in which all references from one table to another are valid. IBM has supplied a series of sample tables in Appendix A of its Reference Guide, DB2 UDB for IBM i Sample Tables. For our examples, we will assume that these tables are in the schema named SQLBOOK.

- ✓ SQLBOOK/EMPLOYEE serves as a master list of employees.
- ✓ SQLBOOK/DEPARTMENT acts as a master list of all valid department numbers.
- ✓ SQLBOOK/EMP_ACT provides a master list of activities performed /for projects.

Other tables may refer to the same entities described in these tables. When a table contains data for which there is a master list, such as a customer number column in an order file that data should actually appear in the master list, such as a customer table. If not, the reference is not valid. The table that contains the master list is the parent table, and the table that refers to it is a dependent table.

When the references from the dependent table to the parent table are valid, the condition of the set of tables is called referential integrity. So, if there is a reference in the order table for a customer, the customer must exist in the master list.

Stated another way, referential integrity is the state of a database in which all values of all foreign keys are valid. Each value of the foreign key must also exist in the parent key or be null. IBM supplies definitions to these terms in its SQL Reference Guide. Understanding these terms is essential in understanding the notion of referential integrity:

- ✓ A unique key is a column or set of columns in a table which uniquely identify a row. Although a table can have several unique keys, no two rows in a table can have the same unique key value.
- ✓ A primary key is a unique key that does not allow nulls. A table cannot have more than one primary key.
- ✓ A parent key is either a unique key or a primary key which is referenced in a referential constraint.
- ✓ A foreign key is a column or set of columns whose values must match those of a parent key. If any column value used to build the foreign key is null, then the rule does not apply.
- ✓ A parent table is a table that contains the parent key.
- ✓ A dependent table is the table that contains the foreign key.
- ✓ A descendent table is a table that is a dependent table or a descendent of a dependent table.

Enforcement of referential integrity prevents the violation of the rule which states that every non-null foreign key must have a matching parent key.

Adding or Dropping Referential Constraints

Use the SQL CREATE TABLE and ALTER TABLE
statements to add or change referential constraints.

- ✓ When you define a referential constraint, you specify:
- ✓ A primary or unique key
- ✓ A foreign key
- ✓ Delete and update rules that specify the action taken with respect to dependent rows when the parent row is deleted or updated.
- ✓ Optionally, you can specify a name for the constraint. If a name is not specified, one is automatically generated.

Example 1 Adding Referential Constraints

The rule that every department number shown in the sample employee table must appear in the department table is a referential constraint. This constraint ensures that every employee belongs to an existing department. The following SQL statements create the CORPDATA.DEPARTMENT and CORPDATA.EMPLOYEE tables with those constraint relationships defined.

Example 1A

```
CREATE TABLE SQLBOOK/DEPARTMENT
   (DEPTNO    CHAR(3)       NOT NULL
                            PRIMARY KEY,
    DEPTNAME VARCHAR(29) NOT NULL,
    MGRNO    CHAR(6),
    ADMRDEPT CHAR(3)       NOT NULL


CONSTRAINT REPORTS_TO_EXISTS
REFERENCES SQLBOOK/DEPARTMENT (DEPTNO)
ON DELETE CASCADE)
```

Example 1B

```
CREATE TABLE SQLBOOK/EMPLOYEE
    (EMPNO        CHAR(6)       NOT NULL
                                PRIMARY KEY,
     FIRSTNAME VARCHAR(12) NOT NULL,
     MIDINIT      CHAR(1)       NOT NULL,
     LASTNAME  VARCHAR(15) NOT NULL,
     WORKDEPT  CHAR(3)

CONSTRAINT WORKDEPT_EXISTS
REFERENCES SQLBOOK/DEPARTMENT (DEPTNO)
ON DELETE SET NULL ON UPDATE RESTRICT,

        PHONENO    CHAR(4),
        HIREDATE   DATE,
        JOB        CHAR(8),
        EDLEVEL    SMALLINT    NOT NULL,
        SEX        CHAR(1),
        BIRTHDATE DATE,
        SALARY     DECIMAL(9,2),
        BONUS      DECIMAL(9,2),
        COMM       DECIMAL(9,2),

CONSTRAINT  UNIQUE_LNAME_IN_DEPT
UNIQUE (WORKDEPT, LASTNAME))
```

In this case, the DEPARTMENT table has a column of unique department numbers (DEPTNO) which functions as a primary key, and is a parent table in two constraint relationships:

The constraint named *REPORTS_TO_EXISTS* is a self-referencing constraint in which the DEPARTMENT table is both the parent and the dependent in the same relationship. Every non-null value of ADMRDEPT

The constraint named WORKDEPT_EXISTS establishes the EMPLOYEE table as a dependent table, and the column of employee department assignments (WORKDEPT) as a foreign key.

Thus, every value of WORKDEPT must match a value of DEPTNO. The DELETE SET NULL rule says that if a row is deleted from DEPARTMENT in which the value of DEPTNO is n, then the value of WORKDEPT in EMPLOYEE is set to null in every row in which the value was n.

The UPDATE RESTRICT rule says that a value of DEPTNO in DEPARTMENT cannot be updated if there are values of WORKDEPT in EMPLOYEE that match the current DEPTNO value.

The constraint named UNIQUE_LNAME_IN_DEPT in the EMPLOYEE table causes last names to be unique within a department. While this constraint is unlikely, it illustrates how a constraint made up of several columns can be defined at the table level.

Removing Referential Constraints

The ALTER TABLE statement can be used to add or drop one constraint at a time for a table. If the constraint being dropped is the parent key in some referential constraint relationship, the constraint between this parent file and any dependent files is also removed.

DROP TABLE and DROP SCHEMA statements also remove any constraints on the table or schema being dropped.

Example 2 Removing Constraints

The following example removes the primary key over column DEPTNO in table DEPARTMENT. The constraints REPORTS_TO_EXISTS and WORKDEPT_EXISTS defined on tables DEPARTMENT and EMPLOYEE respectively will be removed as well, since the primary key being removed is the parent key in those constraint relationships.

Example 2A

```
ALTER TABLE SQLBOOK/EMPLOYEE
DROP PRIMARY KEY
```

You can also remove a constraint by name, as in the following example:

Example 2B

```
ALTER TABLE SQLBOOK/DEPARTMENT
DROP CONSTRAINT UNIQUE_LNAME_IN_DEPT
```

Update Considerations with Referential Constraints

If you are updating a parent table, you cannot modify a primary key for which dependent rows exist. Changing the key violates referential constraints for dependent tables and leaves some rows without a parent. Furthermore, you cannot give any part of a primary key a null value.

Update Rules

The action taken on dependent tables (EMPLOYEE in this example set) when an UPDATE is performed on a parent table depends on the update rule specified for the referential constraint. If no update rule was defined for a referential constraint, the UPDATE NO ACTION rule is used. Let's take a look at the various actions that can occur when such an update occurs that affects a referential constraint:

UPDATE NO ACTION Specifies that the row in the parent table can be updated if no other row depends on it. If a dependent row exists in the relationship, the UPDATE fails. The check for dependent rows is performed at the end of the statement.

UPDATE RESTRICT Specifies that the row in the parent table can be updated if no other row depends on it. If a dependent row exists in the relationship, the UPDATE fails. The check for dependent rows is performed immediately.

There is a subtle difference between the RESTRICT rule and the NO ACTION rule. This difference is best seen when looking at the interaction of triggers and referential constraints. Triggers can be defined to fire either before or after an operation (an UPDATE statement, in this case).

A before trigger fires before the UPDATE is performed and therefore before any checking of constraints. An after trigger fires after the UPDATE is performed, and after a constraint rule of RESTRICT (where checking is performed immediately), but before a constraint rule of NO ACTION (where checking is performed at the end of the statement). The triggers and rules would occur in the following order:

A before trigger would be fired before the UPDATE and before a constraint rule of RESTRICT or NO ACTION.

An after trigger would be fired after a constraint rule of RESTRICT, but before a NO ACTION rule.

If you are updating a dependent table, any foreign key values (non-null) that you change must match the primary key for each relationship in which the table is a dependent. For example, department numbers in the employee table depend on the department numbers in the department table. You can assign an employee to no department (the null value), but not to a department that does not exist.

If an UPDATE against a table with a referential constraint fails, all changes made during the update operation are undone. A number of these constraint rules are implemented via the automatic journaling that is established when tables are built within schemas rather than libraries. It would help to have an appreciation for commitment control and journaling to best understand how the system reacts to an update that violates a constraint

Example 3 UPDATE Rules

For example, you cannot update a department number from the department table if it is still responsible for some project, which is described by a dependent row in the project table.

The following UPDATE fails because the PROJECT table has rows that are dependent on DEPARTMENT.DEPTNO having a value of 'D01' (the row targeted by the WHERE statement). If this UPDATE were allowed, the referential constraint between the PROJECT and DEPARTMENT tables would be broken.

```
UPDATE SQLBOOK/DEPARTMENT
  SET DEPTNO = 'D99'
  WHERE DEPTNAME = 'DEVELOPMENT CENTER'
```

The following statement fails because it violates the referential constraint that exists between the primary key DEPTNO in DEPARTMENT and the foreign key DEPTNO in PROJECT:

```
UPDATE CORPDATA.PROJECT
  SET DEPTNO = 'D00'
  WHERE DEPTNO = 'D01';
```

The statement attempts to change all department numbers of D01 to department number D00. Since D00 is not a value of the primary key DEPTNO in DEPARTMENT, the statement fails.

Deleting from Tables with Referential Constraints

If a table has a primary key but no dependents, DELETE operates as it does without referential constraints. The same is true if a table has only foreign keys, but no primary key. If a table has a primary key and dependent tables, DELETE deletes or updates rows according to the delete rules specified in the constraint. All delete rules of all affected relationships must be satisfied in order for the delete operation to be successful. If a referential constraint is violated, as you would expect, the DELETE fails.

The action to be taken on dependent tables when a DELETE is performed on a parent table depends on the delete rule specified for the referential constraint. If no delete rule was defined, the DELETE NO ACTION rule is used.

DELETE NO ACTION Specifies that the row in the parent table can be deleted if no other row depends on it. If a dependent row exists in the relationship, the DELETE fails. The check for dependent rows is performed at the end of the statement.

DELETE RESTRICT Specifies that the row in the parent table can be deleted if no other row depends on it. If a dependent row exists in the relationship, the DELETE fails. The check for dependent rows is performed immediately. For example, you cannot delete a department from the department table if it is still responsible for some project that is described by a dependent row in the project table.

DELETE CASCADE Specifies that first the designated rows in the parent table are deleted. Then, the dependent rows are deleted. For example, you can delete a department by deleting its row in the department table. Deleting the row from the department table also deletes: (1)The rows for all departments that report to it (2) All departments that report to those departments and so forth.

DELETE SET NULL Specifies that each null-able column of the foreign key in each dependent row is set to its default value. This means that the column is only set to its default value if it is a member of a foreign key that references the row being deleted. Only the dependent rows that are immediate descendants are affected.

DELETE SET DEFAULT Specifies that each column of the foreign key in each dependent row is set to its default value. This means that the column is only set to its default value if it is a member of a foreign key that references the row being deleted. Only the dependent rows that are immediate descendants are affected.

For example, you can delete an employee from the employee table (EMPLOYEE) even if the employee manages some department. In that case, the value of MGRNO for each employee who reported to the manager is set to blanks in the department table (DEPARTMENT). If some other default value was specified on the create of the table, that value is used. This is due to the REPORTS_TO_EXISTS constraint defined for the department table.

If a descendent table has a delete rule of RESTRICT or NO ACTION and a row is found such that a descendant row cannot be deleted, the entire DELETE fails.

When running this statement with a program, the number of rows deleted is returned in SQLERRD(3) in the SQLCA. This number includes only the number of rows deleted in the table specified in the DELETE statement. It does not include those rows deleted according to the CASCADE rule. SQLERRD(5) in the SQLCA contains the number of rows that were affected by referential constraints in all tables.

The subtle difference between RESTRICT and NO ACTION rules is easiest seen when looking at the interaction of triggers and referential constraints. Triggers can be defined to fire either before or after an operation (a DELETE statement, in this case). A before trigger fires before the DELETE is performed and therefore before any checking of constraints. An after trigger is fired after the DELETE is performed, and after a constraint rule of RESTRICT (where checking is performed immediately), but before a constraint rule of NO ACTION (where checking is performed at the end of the statement).

The triggers and rules would occur in the following order: A before trigger would be fired before the DELETE and before a constraint rule of RESTRICT or NO ACTION. An after trigger would be fired after a constraint rule of RESTRICT, but before a NO ACTION rule.

Example 4 DELETE Cascade Rule

Deleting a department from the DEPARTMENT table sets WORKDEPT (in the EMPLOYEE table) to null for every employee assigned to that department. Consider the following DELETE statement:

Example 4A

```
DELETE FROM SQLBOOK/DEPARTMENT
      WHERE DEPTNO = 'E11'
```

Given the tables and the data as defined in IBM's tables, one
row is deleted from table DEPARTMENT, and table
EMPLOYEE is updated to set the value of WORKDEPT to its
default wherever the value was 'E11'. A question mark ('?') in
the sample data below reflects the null value. The effects of the
delete operation to the department file would appear as follows:

Figure 17-1 Department Table Data

Contents of the table after the DELETE statement is complete.

DEPTNO	DEPTNAME	MGRNO	ADMRDEPT
A00	SPIFFY COMPUTER SERVICE DIV.	000010	A00
B01	PLANNING	000020	A00
C01	INFORMATION CENTER	000030	A00
D01	DEVELOPMENT CENTER	?	A00
D11	MANUFACTURING SYSTEMS	000060	D01
D21	ADMINISTRATION SYSTEMS	000070	D01
E01	SUPPORT SERVICES	000050	A00
E21	SOFTWARE SUPPORT	000100	E01
F22	BRANCH OFFICE F2	?	E01
G22	BRANCH OFFICE G2	?	E01
H22	BRANCH OFFICE H2	?	E01
I22	BRANCH OFFICE I2	?	E01
J22	BRANCH OFFICE J2	?	E01

Note that there were no cascaded deletes in the
DEPARTMENT table in SQLBOOK because no department
reported to department 'E11'.

Below are snapshots of one affected portion of the
EMPLOYEE table in SQLBOOK before and after the
DELETE statement is completed.

Figure 17-2 Partial Employee Table Before snapshot

```
Partial contents before the DELETE statement.
EMPNO    FIRSTNME MI   LASTNAME WORKDEPT PHONENO  HIREDATE
000230   JAMES    J    JEFFERSON D21     2094     1966-11-21
000240   SALVATORE     MARINO   D21      3780     1979-12-05
000250   DANIEL   S    SMITH    D21      0961     1960-10-30
000260   SYBIL    P    JOHNSON  D21      8953     1975-09-11
000270   MARIA    L    PEREZ    D21      9001     1980-09-30
000280   ETHEL    R    SCHNEIDER E11     0997     1967-03-24
000290   JOHN     R    PARKER   E11      4502     1980-05-30
000300   PHILIP   X    SMITH    E11      2095     1972-06-19
000310   MAUDE    F    SETRIGHT E11      3332     1964-09-12
000320   RAMLAL   V    MEHTA    E21      9990     1965-07-07
000330   WING          LEE      E21      2103     1976-02-23
000340   JASON    R    GOUNOT   E21      5696     1947-05-05
```

Figure 17-3 Partial EMPLOYEE Table After snapshot

```
Partial contents after the DELETE statement.
EMPNO    FIRSTNME MI   LASTNAME WORKDEPT PHONENO  HIREDATE
000230   JAMES    J    JEFFERSON D21     2094     1966-11-21
000240   SALVATORE     MARINO   D21      3780     1979-12-05
000250   DANIEL   S    SMITH    D21      0961     1960-10-30
000260   SYBIL    P    JOHNSON  D21      8953     1975-09-11
000270   MARIA    L    PEREZ    D21      9001     1980-09-30
000280   ETHEL    R    SCHNEIDER ?       0997     1967-03-24
000290   JOHN     R    PARKER   ?        4502     1980-05-30
000300   PHILIP   X    SMITH    ?        2095     1972-06-19
000310   MAUDE    F    SETRIGHT ?        3332     1964-09-12
000320   RAMLAL   V    MEHTA    E21      9990     1965-07-07
000330   WING          LEE      E21      2103     1976-02-23
000340   JASON    R    GOUNOT   E21      5696     1947-05-05
```

DB2 UDB for IBM i Trigger Support

A trigger is a set of actions that are run automatically when a specified change operation is performed on a specified table. The change operation in this case is said to have "fired a trigger." The change operation can be an SQL INSERT, UPDATE, or DELETE statement, or an insert, update, or delete high level language statement in an application program. Triggers are useful for tasks such as enforcing business rules, validating input data, and keeping an audit trail. Triggers can be defined in two different ways:

✓ SQL triggers
✓ External triggers

For an external trigger, the CRTPFTRG CL command is used. The program containing the set of trigger actions can be defined in any supported high level language including the RPG/400, COBOL, and RPGIV. External triggers can be insert, update, delete, or read triggers.

For an SQL trigger, the CREATE TRIGGER statement is used. The trigger program is defined entirely using SQL. SQL triggers can be insert, update, or delete triggers.

Once a trigger is associated with a table, the trigger support calls the trigger program whenever a change operation is initiated against the table, or any logical file or view created over the table. SQL triggers and external triggers can be defined for the same table. Up to 200 triggers can be defined for a single table.

Each change operation can call a trigger before or after the change operation occurs. Additionally, you can add a read trigger that is called every time the table is accessed. Thus, a table can be associated with many types of triggers.

- ✓ Before delete trigger
- ✓ Before insert trigger
- ✓ Before update trigger
- ✓ After delete trigger
- ✓ After insert trigger
- ✓ After update trigger
- ✓ Read only trigger (external trigger only)

SQL Triggers

The SQL CREATE TRIGGER statement provides a way for the DB2 UDB for IBM i to actively control, monitor, and manage a table or group of tables whenever an insert, update, or delete operation is performed. The statements specified in the SQL trigger are executed each time an SQL insert, update, or delete operation is performed. An SQL trigger may call stored procedures or user-defined functions to perform additional processing when the trigger is executed.

Unlike stored procedures, an SQL trigger cannot be directly called from an application. Instead, an SQL trigger is invoked by the database management system upon the execution of a triggering insert, update, or delete operation. The definition of the SQL trigger is stored in the database management system and is invoked by the database management system, when the SQL table, within which the trigger is defined, is modified.

Creating an SQL Trigger

An SQL trigger can be created by specifying the CREATE TRIGGER SQL statement. The statements in the routine-body of the SQL trigger are transformed by SQL into a program (*PGM) object. The program is created in the schema specified by the trigger name qualifier. The specified trigger is registered in the SYSTRIGGERS, SYSTRIGDEP, SYSTRIGCOL, and SYSTRIGUPD SQL Catalogs.

Example 5 BEFORE SQL triggers

BEFORE triggers do not modify tables, but they can be used to verify input column values, and also to modify column values that are inserted or updated in a table. In this example the trigger is used to set the fiscal quarter for the corporation prior to inserting the row into the target table. We first create the simple table called TransactionTable and then we create the trigger for it

```
CREATE TABLE TransactionTable
(DateOfTransaction DATE,
 FiscalQuarter SMALLINT)


CREATE TRIGGER
TransactionBeforeTrigger
BEFORE INSERT ON TransactionTable

REFERENCING NEW AS new_row
FOR EACH ROW MODE DB2ROW

BEGIN
  DECLARE newmonth SMALLINT;
  SET newmonth =
MONTH(new_row.DateOfTransaction);
  IF newmonth < 4 THEN
    SET new_row.FiscalQuarter=3;
  ELSEIF newmonth < 7 THEN
    SET new_row.FiscalQuarter=4;
  ELSEIF newmonth < 10 THEN
    SET new_row.FiscalQuarter=1;
  ELSE
    SET new_row.FiscalQuarter=2;
  END IF;
END
```

For the SQL insert statement below, the "FiscalQuarter" column would be set to 2, if the current date is November 14, 2000.

```
INSERT INTO
 TransactionTable(DateOfTransaction)
 VALUES(CURRENT DATE)
```

Note: SQL requires all tables, user-defined functions, procedures and user-defined types to exist prior to creating an SQL trigger. In the examples above, all of the SQL objects are defined before the trigger is created. Now. Let's look at AFTER SQL triggers

Example 6 AFTER SQL Triggers

The WHEN condition can be used in an SQL trigger to specify a condition. If the condition evaluates to true, then the SQL statements in the SQL trigger routine body are executed. If the condition evaluates to false, the SQL statements in the SQL trigger routine body are not executed, and control is returned to the database system. In the following example, a query is evaluated to determine if the statements in the trigger routine body should be run when the trigger is activated.

The first step is to create two simple tables. The first is called TodaysRecords and the second is called OurCitysRecords. The third event is the creation of the SQL trigger to fire after an update of a column of the TodaysRecords table. The fourth event is the creation of another SQL trigger to fire after the update of a different column in the same table.

```
CREATE TABLE TodaysRecords
  (TodaysMaxBarometricPressure FLOAT,
   TodaysMinBarometricPressure FLOAT)
```

```
CREATE TABLE OurCitysRecords
  (RecordMaxBarometricPressure FLOAT,
   RecordMinBarometricPressure FLOAT)
```

If today's maximum barometric pressure is greater than the maximum barometric pressure in our city's records, then we want to update the city's records with the new maximum

Example 6A

```
CREATE TRIGGER
UpdateMaxPressureTrigger
AFTER UPDATE OF
TodaysMaxBarometricPressure
ON TodaysRecords

REFERENCING NEW AS new_row
FOR EACH ROW MODE DB2ROW

WHEN
(new_row.TodaysMaxBarometricPressure>
SELECT
MAX(RecordMaxBarometricPressure)
FROM OurCitysRecords))
   UPDATE OurCitysRecords
     SET RecordMaxBarometricPressure =
     new_row.TodaysMaxBarometricPressure
```

If today's minimum barometric pressure is less than the minimum barometric pressure in our city's records, then we want to update the city's records with the new minimum.

Example 6B

```
CREATE TRIGGER
UpdateMinPressureTrigger
AFTER UPDATE OF
TodaysMinBarometricPressure
```

```
ON TodaysRecords

REFERENCING NEW AS new_row
FOR EACH ROW MODE DB2ROW

WHEN
(new_row.TodaysMinBarometricPressure<
(SELECT
MIN(RecordMinBarometricPressure)
FROM urCitysRecords))
   UPDATE OurCitysRecords
     SET RecordMinBarometricPressure =
     new_row.TodaysMinBarometricPressure
```

To get the action started we first initialize the current values for the tables with the following INSERT statements.

```
INSERT INTO TodaysRecords
VALUES(0.0,0.0)


INSERT INTO OurCitysRecords
VALUES(0.0,0.0)
```

For the SQL update statement below, the RecordMaxBarometricPressure in OurCitysRecords is updated by the UpdateMaxPressureTrigger.

```
UPDATE TodaysRecords
SET
TodaysMaxBarometricPressure = 29.95
```

But tomorrow, if the TodaysMaxBarometricPressure is only 29.91, then the RecordMaxBarometricPressure is not updated.

```
UPDATE TodaysRecords
SET
TodaysMaxBarometricPressure = 29.91
```

SQL allows the definition of multiple triggers for a single triggering action. In the previous example, there are two AFTER UPDATE triggers: UpdateMaxPressureTrigger and UpdateMinPressureTrigger. These triggers are only activated when specific columns of the table TodaysRecords are updated.

AFTER triggers may modify tables. In the example above, an UPDATE operation is applied to a second table. Note that recursive insert and update operations should be avoided. The database management system terminates the operation if the maximum trigger nesting level is reached. You can avoid recursion by adding conditional logic so that the insert or update operation is exited before the maximum nesting level is reached. The same situation needs to be avoided in a network of triggers that recursively cascade through the network of triggers.

Isolation level

The notion of isolation level is another simple idea but with so many variations that it appears to be complex. The isolation level used during the execution of SQL statements determines the degree to which the activation group (ILE – See Sidebar on Activation Groups at the end of this chapter) is isolated from all other concurrently executing activation groups. Thus, when activation group X executes an SQL statement, the isolation level determines:

The degree to which rows retrieved by X and database changes made by X are available to other concurrently executing activation groups.

The degree to which database changes made by concurrently executing activation groups can affect X.

Isolation is only important where databases get modified by DELETE, INSERT, SELECT INTO, and UPDATE. Since a SELECT of data may be for update, it is important also. The actual level of isolation can be explicitly specified on a DELETE, INSERT, SELECT INTO, UPDATE, or SELECT-statement. If the isolation level is not explicitly specified, the isolation level used when the SQL statement is executed is the default isolation level.

DB2 UDB for IBM i supports five different isolation levels. For all isolation levels except No Commit, the database manager places exclusive locks on every row that is inserted, updated, or deleted. In other words, to protect records from being updated by other processes, the database manager locks each and every record that is included in the return set. This ensures that any row that a user or a program chooses to change during a unit of work is not changed by any other activation group in the meantime. The protection prohibits any other activation group (typically in another job) that uses a different commitment definition from updating the data that your process has read until the unit of work is complete. The five isolation levels are as follows:

Repeatable Read

The IBM IBM i Repeatable Read (RR) isolation level ensures:

- ✓ Any row read during a unit of work is not changed by other activation groups that use different commitment definitions until the unit of work is complete.

- ✓ Any row changed (or a row that is currently locked with an UPDATE row lock) by another activation group using a different commitment definition cannot be read until it is committed.

- ✓ In addition to any exclusive locks, an activation group running at level RR acquires at least share locks on all the rows it reads. Furthermore, the locking is performed so that the activation group is completely isolated from the effects of concurrent activation groups that use different commitment definitions.

- ✓ This facility is also defined in the SQL 1999 Core standard, Repeatable Read in which it is called Serializable.

DB2 UDB for IBM i supports repeatable-read through COMMIT(*RR). Repeatable-read isolation level is supported by locking the tables containing any rows that are read or updated.

Read stability

Like level RR, level Read Stability (RS) assures that:

- ✓ Any row read during a unit of work is not changed by other activation groups that use different commitment definitions until the unit of work is complete.

- ✓ Any row changed (or a row that is currently locked with an UPDATE row lock) by another activation group using a different commitment definition cannot be read until it is committed.

✓ Unlike RR, RS does not completely isolate the activation group from the effects of concurrent activation groups that use a different commitment definition. At level RS, activation groups that issue the same query more than once might see additional rows. These additional rows are called phantom rows.

For example, a phantom row can occur in the following situation:

Activation group P1 reads the set of rows n that satisfy some search condition.

Activation group P2 then INSERTs one or more rows that satisfy the search condition and COMMITs those INSERTs.

P1 reads the set of rows again with the same search condition and obtains both the original rows and the rows inserted by P2.

In addition to any exclusive locks, an activation group running at level RS acquires at least share locks on all the rows it reads.

In the SQL 1999 Core standard, Read Stability is called Repeatable Read.

DB2 UDB for IBM i supports read stability through COMMIT(*ALL) or COMMIT(*RS).

Cursor Stability

Like levels RR and RS, level Cursor Stability (CS) ensures that any row that was changed (or a row that is currently locked with an UPDATE row lock) by another activation group using a different commitment definition cannot be read until it is committed. Unlike RR and RS, level CS only ensures that the current row of every updatable cursor is not changed by other activation groups using different commitment definitions. Thus, the rows that were read during a unit of work can be changed by other activation groups that use a different commitment definition. In addition to any exclusive locks, an activation group running at level CS may acquire a share lock for the current row of every cursor.

In the SQL 1999 Core standard, Cursor Stability is called Read Committed.

DB2 UDB for IBM i supports cursor stability through COMMIT(*CS).

Uncommitted Read

For a SELECT INTO, a FETCH with a read-only cursor, subquery, or subselect used in an INSERT statement, level Uncommitted Read (UR) allows:

Any row read during the unit of work to be changed by other activation groups that are run under a different commitment definition. Any row changed (or a row that is currently locked with an UPDATE row lock) by another activation group running under a different commitment definition to be read even if the change has not been committed.

For other operations, the rules of level CS apply.

In the SQL 1999 Core standard, Uncommitted Read is called Read Uncommitted.

DB2 UDB for IBM i supports uncommitted read through COMMIT(*CHG) or COMMIT(*UR).

No Commit

✓ For all operations, the rules of level UR apply to No Commit (NC) except:

✓ Commit and rollback operations have no effect on SQL statements. Cursors are not closed, and LOCK TABLE locks are not released. However, connections in the release-pending state are ended.

✓ Any changes are effectively committed at the end of each successful change operation and can be immediately accessed or changed by other applications

Setting the Default Isolation Level

DB2 UDB for IBM i provides several ways to specify the default isolation level: You can use the COMMIT parameter on the CRTSQLxxx, STRSQL, and RUNSQLSTM commands to specify the default isolation level.

You can also use the SET OPTION statement to specify the default isolation level within the source of a module or program that contains embedded SQL. Another way is to use the SET TRANSACTION statement to override the default isolation level within a unit of work. When the unit of work ends, the isolation level returns to the value it had at the beginning of the unit of work.

Use the isolation-clause on the SELECT, SELECT INTO, INSERT, UPDATE, DELETE, and DECLARE CURSOR statements to override the default isolation level for a specific statement or cursor. The isolation level is in effect only for the execution of the statement containing the isolation-clause and has no effect on any pending changes in the current unit of work.

These isolation levels are supported by automatically locking the appropriate data. Depending on the type of lock, this limits or prevents access to the data by concurrent activation groups that use different commitment definitions. Each database manager supports at least two types of locks:

Share

Limits concurrent activation groups that use different commitment definitions to read-only operations on the data.

Exclusive

Prevents concurrent activation groups using different commitment definitions from updating or deleting the data. Prevents concurrent activation groups using different commitment definitions that are running COMMIT(*RS), COMMIT(*CS), or COMMIT(*RR) from reading the data. Concurrent activation groups using different commitment definitions that are running COMMIT(*UR) or COMMIT(*NC) are allowed to read the data.

Activation Group Sidebar -- Just what is an activation group? Activation groups are clearly a critical and confusing aspect of IBM i Integrated Language Environment (ILE) technology. The Integrated language Environment is IBM's supercharged programming model that replaced an offering today referred to as the Original Programming Model or OPM. Though we use them in all ILE programs, activation groups are difficult to define, however. The simple answer is that it is a part of a job structure on IBM i. But admittedly that does not say much.

So, let's ay that an activation group is a container for things needed to run processes in a job. Resources such as memory and variables and other job substructures are some of the things inside the container. When a IBM i job comes alive, it may have a number of activation groups that are associated with it. To describe this phenomenon, the experts like to say that the job "owns" these activation groups.

An activation group per se is a logical storage container reference within a job. It holds pointers to storage allocation and references the runtime program binding activities that the operating systems perform when a program executes. As IBM i has been expanded to support more and more facilities and more currency and threading, the underlying operating system has had to become more complex to accommodate it.

The notion of activation groups has been in effect since the ILE environment was announced in the mid 1990's but most users care nothing about it because they use the invisible default activation group that automatically gets created in most compilation and binding processes.

Continuing with the analogy of the activation group to a container or a box of sorts, consider that a container can store various items, whereas an ILE activation group contains the resources needed to run a job (one or more programs). A container has storage space, whereas an activation group has a notion called heap storage. The " the "heap" refers to storage that can be dynamically allocated, reallocated and freed. The container also has static and automatic storage.

It is tough to relate an activation group to anything physical. In many ways, it is best defined by the resources it owns. So, we may say with certitude that an activation group is used to deal with a group of internal resources for an ILE application. The resources owned include the program static and automatic variables, heaps, Open Data Paths, and commit scope.

The notion of commit scope takes us all the way back to how we got here in the first place using the With Isolation Level clause of the SELECT statement. Given that all these resources are scoped to one activation group in ILE, this allows for optional isolation of applications, giving users control of how much sharing is to be done within and between applications.

Each job on the IBM i has a DAG, or default activation group, that is automatically created when it is started. Actually, two default activation groups are created. These two activation groups are where your system code and OPM (Original Program Model) programs run. ILE programs can also run in the default activation group.

Chapter Summary

SQL provides powerful rule-based capabilities using a notion called constraints. These are a very powerful capability of SQL that are enforced by the database manager to assure the integrity of the database. The types of constraints that are offered are as follows:

- ✓ Unique constraints
- ✓ Referential constraints
- ✓ Check constraints
- ✓ Triggers

A unique constraint is the rule that the values of the key are valid only if they are unique. They can be created using the CREATE TABLE and ALTER TABLE statements. They are enforced during an insert or update

A referential constraint is the rule that the values of any foreign key are valid only if they also appear as values of a parent key, or some component of the foreign key is null. These are enforced when INSERT, UPDATE, and DELETE statements are executed against the table with the constraint.

A check constraint is a rule that limits the values allowed in a column or group of columns. They are added using the CREATE TABLE and ALTER TABLE statements and they are enforced during the execution of INSERT and UPDATE statements.

SQL trigger constraints are tested before or after a database operation. Before triggers can stop an update and an after trigger can update a file based on conditions found in the trigger.

Isolation levels are used to give the developer control over the level of locking that is to take place when using commitment control under SQL It determines the degree to which rows retrieved by X and database changes made by X are available to other concurrently executing activation groups.

Programs just doing reads are basically unaffected. When you do a read for update, however, and SQL grabs a number of rows for update purposes, you probably want to lock those rows so that your changes are not merged with other changes.

So, isolation is only important where databases get modified by DELETE, INSERT, SELECT INTO, and UPDATE. Since a SELECT of data may be for update, it is important also. The actual level of isolation can be explicitly specified on a DELETE, INSERT, SELECT INTO, UPDATE, or SELECT-statement. If the isolation level is not explicitly specified, the isolation level used when the SQL statement is executed is the default isolation level.

IBM i supports five different isolation levels. For all isolation levels except No Commit, the database manager places exclusive locks on every row that is inserted, updated, or deleted. In other words, to protect records from being updated by other processes, the database manager locks each and every record that is included in the return set. This ensures that any row that a user or a program chooses to change during a unit of work is not changed by any other activation group in the meantime. The protection prohibits any other activation group (typically in another job) that uses a different commitment definition from updating the data that your process has read until the unit of work is complete.

Key Chapter Terms

Activation group
Adding constraints
Check constraints
Commit
Constraint
Create trigger
CRTPFTRG
Cursor stability
Delete Cascade
Delete No Action
Delete Restrict
Delete Set Default
Delete Set Null
Dependent table
Descendent table
Dropping
Rule Enforcement
Exclusive
External triggers
Foreign key
ILE
Isolation level
No commit
Parent table
Phantom rows
Primary key
Read stability
Referential constraints
Repeatable read
Rule-based capabilities
Set Option
SET transaction
Share
SQL 1999 Core
SQL triggers
SQLCA
Uncommitted read
Unique constraints
Unique key

Exercises

1. Define an activation group. Are activations groups only in ILE objects?

2. Why would you use a unique constraint on a file?

3. What makes a primary key different from a unique key?

4. Describe the notion of referential integrity

5. How is referential integrity implemented?

6. What are the Delete options for a dependent file with a referential constraint? Explain.

7. What is a check constraint and why would you use one?

8. What is an SQL trigger? Is it the same as an RPG Trigger program?

9. What two types of triggers exist?

10. What is meant by the term isolation level?

11. Why are the IBM terms for the levels of isolation different from the
ISO standards?

12. What does the notion of isolation levels have to do with record locking for update or delete?

13. What is a foreign key and what role does it have to play in referential integrity?

This page and the next page intentionally left blank for future material

Chapter 18   Re-engineering PF & LF Objects to SQL DDL.

IBM Likes SQL

Throughout this book we have used the notion of DDS and native IBM i objects as a teaching vehicle for those who may today be running on a IBM i and performing data base tasks in the traditional native fashion – with DDS. From the beginning of this book I have discussed the notion of Why SQL and Why now?

And the answer has not changed despite the copious research I have done in between the first page and this last chapter. From my perspective, the most compelling reason for a IBM i professional to learn SQL and to begin to use it in an IBM i stop is portability of skills within the shop.

I have read extensively IBM's rationale for IBM i professionals making the trip to SQL and though IBM has a number of other bullets in its list than the one item I have, and most of the bullets have worth, they are not compelling. Portability of skills in your own shop, however, that is a compelling argument. In the IBM list you will find the following:

1. Portability of code & skills
2. Strategic database interface for industry & OS/400
3. Faster performance delivered by new Query Engine
4. Required for certain middleware such as distributed data processing.
5. The J2EE architecture based on SQL interfaces

6. Certain data types BLOB, CLOB, Datalink not supported in DDS
7. Auto incrementing table constructs
8. Sequence & Identity column attributes
9. Column level triggers
10. Encryption & Decryption functions
11. Better and faster indexes (Encoded Vector Indexes)
12. Better positioning of IBM i as a Database Server
13. SQL as a programming language can reduce total Lines of code
14. DB2 SMP - parallel database processing for the big shops.

IBM places a high value on portability of code for IBM i yet, "not to pontificate but" I don't see code coming from the IBM i to other shops – SQL or no SQL. Big Blue does not make its best database with native DDS and its RPG language available on other platforms. For non-IBM i users that means that IBM is not porting its main IBM i business language with IBM i specific function to other platforms.

The porting is all about applications coming to the IBM i but when they come today, they run under AIX or Linux. Thus, in many ways, application portability notion of SQL is somewhat bogus at an IBM i/OS level since applications are not coming to IBM i/OS. . I see more code being expunged from the IBM i environment as it is being rewritten for Windows because certain business partners want a share of the Windows wealth.

It would be good if IBM could port its whole RPG/DDS/CL environment notions to other platforms. Supposedly none of this has much to do with SQL anyway but it does provide a perspective that it is not IBM i code portability that is the value here; it is IBM i professionals being able to port their SQL skills to other platforms.

IBM has had over twenty years to make DDS a portable language and has chosen not to do so. Many of the reasons on the list above are because IBM has chosen to invest in SQL and not DDS even though its user base is and has been DDS and not SQL oriented. Here's another "I think" for you. I think IBM should invest in DDS and the physical file and logical file notions as product differentiators. It would be nice to see Big Blue make these available at least on other IBM platforms (PowerX-based) if not the non-IBM world.

Others such as California Software are making a business out of it. While they are at it, why not take the slick interactive interfaces for externally defined files and bring out an RPG and a feature-rich COBOL for other platforms. Business computing is not dead. The techno wizards have just had too much fun playing with spinning globes and dancing bears over the years to want to get serious with real business programming tools.

The fact is there is nothing wrong with DDS--- especially if you know it. The other facts in IBM's list are true, however. Most of them are under IBM's control and IBM has chosen to beef up the interface that its customers do not use so that they will switch to a "better" database interface.

People with a non-traditional IBM i outlook in IBM seem to be making the decisions about what IBM i technology survives and when they find things that are unique to the IBM i platform, they seem to have a deep compunction to remove these so that the interfaces are the same as what others are using. I don't know if we can change that no matter what we do. Therefore, IBM's SQL direction and lack of support for what many are using may actually be another compelling reason to look at SQL more seriously. The good news is that it is not Java and it is not Java-like. It's actually not a bad little language. As such, however, it ought to be able to sell itself.

Hoping to prove that SQL will not bring your IT shop down, IBM has done some analysis on the implications of tables vs. physical files and indexes vs. logical files, views vs. logical files and it has come to some conclusions

Advantages of Tables vs PFs

- ✓ More data types
- ✓ Constraint definitions can be included in object source
- ✓ Faster reads
- ✓ Longer, more descriptive column names
- ✓ Data modeling tool support
- ✓ DB2 attempts to automatically journal tables

Disadvantages of Tables Vs. PFs

- ✓ Slower writes
- ✓ No DDM, BUT SQL can utilize DRDA connections
- ✓ Multi-member files
- ✓ --SQL ALIAS provides solution:

CREATE ALIAS JanSales FOR SALES (JANUARY)

> Note: IBM acknowledges that one past disadvantage was that SQL tables did not support field reference files. IBM fixed that in V5R2 with a facility called CREATE TABLE LIKE

Advantages of SQL Indexes v. Logical Files:

- ✓ New Encoded Vector Index Structure
- ✓ 64K Logical Page Size for SQL-only

> Note: IBM made this change to improve the performance of SQL queries that scan many key values in an index. The 64K I/O operations bring many more keys into memory at one time. Larger logical page size can lend itself to more efficient index maintenance. Record at a time processing (most RPG shops today) even with SQL single key lookups in index may not be as efficient as the old way. Moreover, such large index pages may strain memory-starved IBM i environments.

Another issue is that SQL Indexes that are journaled explicitly or implicitly (System Managed Access Path Protection--SMAPPP) will increase the size of journal receivers. To help alleviate this IBM suggests you use RCVSIZOPT(*RMVINTENT *MAXOPT2) and that the Journal Receiver Threshold should be at least 6.5 GB

Disadvantages of Indexes v. Logical Files:

✓ 8K Logical Page Size for DDS
✓ No support for Select/Omit filtering or join logical files
✓ Not built into the new index structure for SQL

Note: Recognizing that there are still issues in converting to DDL from basic DDS, as noted previously, IBM has built its SQL index object as a keyed logical file such that SQL Index "DDS" includes all of the underlying table's fields into the logical file. This may help record at a time processing

Advantages of SQL Views v. Logical Files

✓ More flexibility in terms of selecting & processing data
✓ CASE expressions & Date/Time functions
✓ Grouping & more advanced Join processing
✓ Can be used as logical files to enhance native functionality

Disadvantages of Views v. Logical Files

Views cannot be keyed/ordered

Commentary

IBM's analysis of changing to SQL views from DDS logical files suggests that it does not mean that SQL views have slower performance. It does mean that switching may bring a change in performance to certain applications that are unexpected.

However, IBM believes that, assuming you have the right set of indexes/statistics in place for the query optimizer to use, an SQL View may be just as good as a logical file.

A View is used by SQL just to transform data. It is the query optimizer's job to find the best way to access the data. The data access speed is assisted by the use of indexes for selection or sorting. Though just about all AS/400 / IBM i shops rely heavily on keys to perform routine processing in programs, IBM offers that the fastest method may not be a keyed access method.

However, that would mean to gain any SQL speed that a data redesign would provide, a redesign of major applications would be needed and that is something a little more difficult than merely making the SQL switch. In our Y2K efforts several years back we got a taste of just how easy it was to switch from a two digit year to a four digit year. A DB redesign would be substantially more difficult.

DDS to SQL Conversion Tool

In 1994 IBM began working on Operations Navigator as a possible GUI for the AS/400. Always a little too unstable and way too bulky for the sized PCS on which it was deployed, the "Navigator" saw limited use. In 2000, IBM changed lots of names and in the process, the company re-christened the "Navigator" as the IBM i Navigator. Over these past six years, Navigator developers have given some very nice function to this tool, especially in the network and database areas. In V5R1, the Navigator team came out with a bona fide IBM i Navigator Generate SQL Task that is implemented internally by the QSQGNDDL API.

This tool does not convert DDS to SQL's DDL. However it does one better. It converts PF and LF objects to SQL. So, if you lost your DDS file, here is away of almost getting the source. This tool is very useful if yo wish to convert DDS to SQL for data definitions. The tool supports both physical and logical files but not all DDS features (e.g. EDTCDE) are converted because there is still not full compatibility between the function sets of the two offerings. It does do a great job, however, and what it does not covert, it explains why with messages embedded as SQL comments in the generated DDL. So, at the very worst, you get to learn moe about SQL's DDL.

Though IBM has announced support to define a table with a table reference file (as in the DDS field reference file), this generation of the tool has not yet been updated to support creating DDS with a reference file. In other words, if you created your file with a reference file, the link to the reference file is not preserved in the SQL generation. PF objects using reference fields and files store the reference data within the object structure. Thus, this certainly is something that IBM can add to this aid in good time if it chooses to do so.

Let me show you how it works. You first get your IBM i Navigator pointing to your system of choice. Then you open up the Database Area until you see all objects as in Figure 18-1 below:

Figure 18-1 IBM i Navigator – Select All Objects from Database

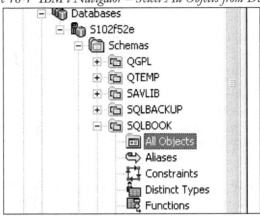

The tool can convert a single object or a group of objects. As you are about to see, output can be brought into an editable PC window or it can be placed right into a special source file that you may choose to call QSQLSRC in your favorite library or schema. Notice the chain down to the SQLBOOK library in Figure 18-1. Click on All Objects, and you will get a list of all the DB objects in your selected library. Notice that in Figure 18-2 the tables are listed before the views.

Figure 18-2 Double Click JOINTEST object

WUTSTPC	Table	BKELLY
WUTSTPD	Table	BKELLY
EARN_PROJECTION	View	BKELLY
JOINTEST	View	BKELLY
VENDORV	View	BKELLY

Databases tasks

Select schemas to display
Run an SQL script
Map your database

To demonstrate the utility of the Navigator, just click on the JOINTEST view and watch what happens on your screen. It actually runs the query and sends back a nicely shaped panel to your PC screen. So you can see it, I put it into a more narrow package for viewing at which time I squeezed the left and right sides on top of one another. It actually looks lots nicer than the result of my activities as shown in Figure 18-3. But, this is about as good as I can make it with a 4 inch text width.

Figure 18-3 Join Access Performed from Navigator

Contents of SQLBOOK.JOINTEST - 192.159.104.53(S102f52e)

	VNDNBR	CITY	STATE	VNDCLS	VNDSTS
1	7030	Cambridge	MA	20	A
2	7040	Scranton	PA	20	A
3	7060	Tampa Bay	FL	20	A
4	7080	Austin	TX	20	A
5	7120	Portland	OR	20	D
6	7140	Lancaster	PA	20	A

BALOWE	SRVRTG	VOUCHER_NUMBER	VCHDUE
352.56	A	4	6.00
.25	A	5	0
4.99	G	6	50.00
9.65	G	8	0
0	P	20	6.00
.25	G	40	.25

In this simple exercise, you can see how capable the "Navigator" has become. Let's set up for some object to SQL reverse engineering now. Go back to the panel in Figure 18-2

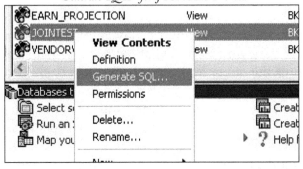

There are two options at the left bottom of Figure 18-5.

Figure 18-5 Select Where SQL Should Be Generated

If we picked a number of objects or if we chose to select all of
the file objects, they would appear in the panel in Figure 18-5
in a scrollable window. I did this a number of times in
preparing for writing this book. When you click the second
option of writing to a file, the file you select exists on your
IBM i, not the PC.. So, I alternately picked the SQLSTMTS
source file or the QSQLSRC source file depending on what I
was doing. The aid produced its output in one member with
all of the Create Tables and Create Views that I requested for

the file objects that it converted to SQL form. It worked first time and every time that I called it up with the RUNSQLSTM command. The aid is really convenient and powerful.

In this example for better viewing, let's bring the results of this generation to the PC window as we have selected in Figure 18-5. From the panel in Figure 18-5 just click on Generate and you will get the panel shown in Figure 18-6. That's the SQL plus a lecture on some things it did not do.
.

Figure 18-6 Generated SQL

```
Untitled - Run SQL Scripts - 192.159.104.53(S102f52e)

File   Edit   View   Run   VisualExplain   Monitor   Options   Connection   Help

Examples

-- Generate SQL
-- Version:              V5R3M0 040528
-- Generated on:         12/02/05 18:13:33
-- Relational Database:  S102F52E
-- Standards Option:     DB2 UDB iSeries

CREATE VIEW SQLBOOK.JOINTEST (
-- SQL1509   10   Format name INNERR for JOINTEST in SQLBOOK ignored.
-- SQL1505   20   Number of members for JOINTEST in SQLBOOK not valid.
-- SQL1506   30   Key or attribute for JOINTEST in SQLBOOK ignored.
           VNDNBR ,
           CITY ,
           STATE ,
           VNDCLS ,
           VNDSTS ,
           BALOWE ,
           SRVRTG ,
           VOUCHER_NUMBER FOR COLUMN VCHNBR      ,

Connected to relational database S102f52e on 192.159.104.53 as Bkelly - 016
```

I took the SQL as generated and copied it to my word processor so I could show you the whole specification for the Create View that it generated. This is shown in Figure 18-7.

Figure 18-7 All the Generated SQL

```
--  Generate SQL
--  Version:                V5R3M0 040528
--  Generated on:           12/02/05 18:13:33
--  Relational Database:    S102F52E
--  Standards Option:       DB2 UDB IBM i

CREATE VIEW SQLBOOK.JOINTEST (
--  SQL1509  10   Format name INNERR for JOINTEST in SQLBOOK ignored.
--  SQL1505  20   Number of members for JOINTEST in SQLBOOK not valid.
--  SQL1506  30   Key or attribute for JOINTEST in SQLBOOK ignored.
   VNDNBR ,
   CITY ,
   STATE ,
   VNDCLS ,
   VNDSTS ,
   BALOWE ,
   SRVRTG ,
   VOUCHER_NUMBER FOR COLUMN VCHNBR        ,
   VCHDUE )
   AS
   SELECT
   Q01.VNDNBR ,
   Q01.CITY ,
   Q01.STATE ,
   Q01.VNDCLS ,
   Q01.VNDSTS ,
   Q01.BALOWE ,
   Q01.SRVRTG ,
   Q02.VOUCHER_NUMBER ,
   Q02.VCHDUE
   FROM SQLBOOK.VENDORP AS Q01 INNER JOIN
   SQLBOOK.VOUCHRP AS Q02 ON ( Q01.VNDNBR = Q02.VENDOR_NUMBER )
   WHERE
   Q01.VNDCLS = +20 ;

LABEL ON TABLE SQLBOOK.JOINTEST
   IS 'LFVIEW of VENDORP, VOUCHRP' ;

LABEL ON COLUMN SQLBOOK.JOINTEST
( VOUCHER_NUMBER IS 'VOUCHER            NUMBER' ,
   VCHDUE IS 'UNPAID            BALANCE' ) ;

LABEL ON COLUMN SQLBOOK.JOINTEST
( VOUCHER_NUMBER TEXT IS 'VOUCHER NUMBER' ,
   VCHDUE TEXT IS 'UNPAID BALANCE' ) ;
```

Notice that it did not like the fact that I had a select omit view and it dropped the key. Also, it did not like the fact that I had a different format name and it complained about that. There is no place to specify a format name in SQL. I haven't figured out the "number of members" message yet and I want to get this revised book to the printers in a day or so. Send me an email and ask me about it and I'll be glad to respond.

That's it.

There is no Chapter summary here and there are no key terms and there are no review questions. This is more or less a state of the state on where the IBM i SQL product is headed. I think SQL will continue to improve and one day IBM will definitely be able to say in all respects that it is better than DDS. Then, maybe it will be an even easier sell.

Additional Information Sources

Through the course of this book I have given sources for various materials that would be helpful in your further research. I found an IBM presentation on the Web that was very well done and it had source information that I am presenting below to you as given to me by IBM.

DB2 UDB for IBM i home page
-http://www.IBM i.ibm.com/db2

Newsgroups

USENET: comp.sys.ibm.as400.misc, comp.databases.ibm-db2

Education Resources - Classroom & Online

http://www.IBM i.ibm.com/db2/db2educ_m.htm
http://ibm.com/servers/enable/education/i/ad/db2/recentin
dex1.html
DB2 UDB for IBM i Publications

Online Manuals: http://www.IBM i.ibm.com/db2/books.htm

Porting Help:
http://ibm.com/servers/enable/site/db2/porting.html
DB2 UDB for IBM i Redbooks (http://ibm.com/redbooks)
Stored Procedures & Triggers on DB2 UDB for IBM i (SG24-6503)
DB2 UDB for AS/400 Object Relational Support (SG24-5409)
Advanced Functions & Administration on DB2 UDB for IBM i (SG24-4249)

LETS GO PUBLISH! Books by Brian Kelly:

(Sold at www.bookhawkers.com; Amazon.com, and Kindle.).

LETS GO PUBLISH! is proud to announce that more AS/400 and Power i books are becoming available to help you inexpensively address your AS/400 and Power i education and training needs: Our general titles precede specific AS/400 and other technology books. Check out these great patriotic books which precede the tech books in the list.

Seniors, Social Security & the Minimum Wage
The impact of the minimum wage on Social Security Beneficiaries

How to Write Your First Book and Publish It With CreateSpace
This books teaches how to create a book with MSWord and then publish it with CreateSpace. No need to find a traditional publisher.

Healthcare & Welfare Accountability The Trump Way
Why should somebody win the Lottery & not pay back welfare?

The Trump Plan Solves Student Debt Crisis. .
This is the Trump solution for new student debt and the existing $1.3 Trillion student debt accumulation.

Take the Train to Myrtle Beach The Trump Way.
Tells all about the Donald Trump Plan to restart private passenger railway systems in America while it tells you how to get to Myrtle Beach by Train.

RRRRRR The Trump Way.
This book represents the overarching theme of the Trump campaign with verbs ready to reign in the excessive policies of the Obama Administration. These are the six verbs for the RRRRRR plan: Reduce, Repeal, Reindustrialize, Raise, Revitalize, Remember

Jobs! Jobs! Jobs! The Trump Way!
All about the jobs mess we ae in along with a set of Trump solutions

The Trump Plan Solves the Student Debt Crisis
Solution for new student debt and the existing $1.3 Trillion debt accumulation

101 Secrets How to be a High Information Voter
You do not have to be a low-information voter.

Why Trump?
You Already Know… But, this book will tell you anyway

Saving America The Trump Way!
A book that tells you how President Donald Trump will help America so that Americans wind up on top

The US Immigration Fix
It's all in here. Finally an answer to the 60 million interlopers in America. You won't want to put this book down

I had a Dream IBM Could be #1 Again
The title is self-explanatory

Whatever Happened to the IBM AS /400?
The question is answered in this new book.

Great Moments in Penn State Football
Check out the particulars of this great book at bookhawkers.com.

Great Moments in Notre Dame Football
Check out the particulars of this great book at bookhawkers.com or www.notredamebooks.com

WineDiets.Com Presents The Wine Diet
Learn how to lose weight while having fun. Four specific diets and some great anecdotes fill this book with fun and the opportunity to lose weight in the process.

Wilkes-Barre, PA; Return to Glory
Wilkes-Barre City's return to glory begins with dreams and ideas. Along with plans and actions, this equals leadership.

The Annual Guest Plan.
This is a plan which if deployed today would immediately solve the problem of 60 million illegal aliens in the United States.

Geoffrey Parsons' Epoch... The Land of Fair Play
Better than the original. The greatest re-mastering of the greatest book ever written on American Civics. It was built for all Americans as the best govt. design in the history of the world.

The Bill of Rights 4 Dummmies!
This is the best book to learn about your rights. Be the first, to have a "Rights Fest" on your block. You will win for sure!

Sol Bloom's Epoch ...Story of the Constitution
This work by Sol Bloom was written to commemorate the Sesquicentennial celebration of the Constitution. It has been remastered by Lets Go Publish! – An excellent read!

The Constitution 4 Dummmies!
This is the best book to learn about the Constitution. Learn all about the fundamental laws of America.

America for Dummmies!
All Americans should read to learn about this great country.

Just Say No to Chris Christie for President two editions – I & II -- Discusses the reasons why
Chris Christie is a poor choice for US President

The Federalist Papers by Hamilton, Jay, Madison w/ intro by Brian Kelly
Complete unabridged, easier to read, annotated version of the original Federalist Papers

Companion to Federalist Papers by Hamilton, Jay, Madison w/ intro by Brian Kelly
This small, inexpensive book will help you navigate the Federalist Papers

Kill the Republican Party!
2013 edition and edition #2)
Demonstrates why the Republican Party must be abandoned by conservatives

Bring On the American Party!
Demonstrates how conservatives can be free from the party of wimps by starting its own national party called the American Party.

No Amnesty! No Way!
In addition to describing the issue in detail, this book also offers a real solution.

Saving America
This how-to book is about saving our country using strong mercantilist principles. These same principles that helped the country from its founding.

RRR:
A unique plan for economic recovery and job creation

Kill the EPA
The EPA seems to hate mankind and love nature. They are also making it tough for asthmatics to breathe and for those with malaria to live. It's time they go.

Obama's Seven Deadly Sins.
In the Obama Presidency, there are many concerns about the long-term prospects and sustainability of the country. We examine each of the President's seven deadliest sins in detail, offering warnings and a number of solutions. Be careful. Book may nudge you to move to Canada or Europe.

Taxation Without Representation Second Edition
At the time of the Boston Tea Party, there was no representation. Now, there is no representation again but there are "representatives."

Healthcare & Welfare Accountability
Who should pay for your healthcare? Whose healthcare should you pay for? Is it a lifetime free ride on others or should those once in need of help have to pay it back when their lives improve?

Jobs! Jobs! Jobs!
Where have all the American Jobs gone and how can we get them back?

Other IBM I Technical Books

The All Everything Operating System:
Story about IBM's finest operating system; its facilities; how it came to be.

The All-Everything Machine
Story about IBM's finest computer server.

Chip Wars
The story of ongoing wars between Intel and AMD and upcoming wars between Intel and IBM. Book may cause you to buy / sell somebody's stock.

Can the AS/400 Survive IBM?
Exciting book about the AS/400 in a IBM i World.

The IBM i Pocket SQL Guide.
Complete Pocket Guide to SQL as implemented on IBM i. A must have for SQL developers new to IBM i. It is very compact yet very comprehensive and it is example driven. Written in a part tutorial and part reference style, Tons of SQL coding samples, from the simple to the sublime.

The IBM i Pocket Query Guide.
If you have been spending money for years educating your Query users, and you find you are still spending, or you've given up, this book is right for you. This one QuikCourse covers all Query options.

The IBM I Pocket RPG & RPG IV Guide.
Comprehensive RPG & RPGIV Textbook -- Over 900 pages. This is the one RPG book to have if you are not having more than one. All areas of the language covered smartly in a convenient sized book Annotated PowerPoint's available for self-study (extra fee for self-study package)

The IBM I RPG Tutorial and Lab Guide
Your guide to a hands-on Lab experience. Contains CD with Lab exercises and PowerPoint's. Great companion to the above textbook or can be used as a standalone for student Labs or tutorial purposes

The AS/400 & IBM i Pocket Developers' Guide.
Comprehensive Pocket Guide to all of the AS/400 and IBM i development tools - DFU, SDA, etc. You'll also get a big bonus with chapters on Architecture, Work Management, and Subfile Coding. This book was updated in 2016..

The IBM i Pocket Database Guide.
Complete Pocket Guide to IBM i integrated relational database (DB2/400) – physical and logical files and DB operations - Union, Projection, Join, etc. Written in a part tutorial and part reference style. Tons of DDS coding samples.

Getting Started with The WebSphere Development Studio Client for IBM i (WDSc).
Focus is on client server and the Web. Includes CODE/400, VisualAge RPG, CGI, WebFacing, and WebSphere Studio. Case study continues from the Interactive Book.

The IBM i Pocket WebFacing Primer.
This book gets you started immediately with WebFacing. A sample case study is used as the basis for a conversion to WebFacing. Interactive 5250 application is WebFaced in a case study form before your eyes.

Getting Started with WebSphere Express Server for IBM i
Step-by-Step Guide for Setting up Express Servers
A comprehensive guide to setting up and using WebSphere Express. It is filled with examples, and structured in a tutorial fashion for easy learning.

The WebFacing Application Design & Development Guide:
Step by Step Guide to designing green screen IBM i apps for the Web. Both a systems design guide and a developers guide. Book helps you understand how to design and develop Web applications using regular RPG or COBOL programs.

The IBM i Express Web Implementer's Guide.
Your one stop guide to ordering, installing, fixing, configuring, and using WebSphere Express, Apache, WebFacing, IBM i Access for Web, and HATS/LE.

Joomla! Technical Books

Best Damn Joomla Tutorial Ever
Learn Joomla! By example.

Best Damn Joomla Intranet Tutorial Ever
This book is the only book that shows you how to use Joomla on a corporate intranet.

Best Damn Joomla Template Tutorial Ever
This book teaches you step-by step how to work with templates in Joomla!

Best Damn Joomla Installation Guide Ever
Teaches you how to install Joomla! On all major platforms besides IBM i.

Best Damn Blueprint for Building Your Own Corporate Intranet.
This excellent timeless book helps you design a corporate intranet for any platform while using Joomla as its basis.
4
IBM i PHP & MySQL Installation & Operations Guide
How to install and operate Joomla! on the IBM i Platform

IBM i PHP & MySQL Programmers Guide
How to write SQL programs for IBM i

Joomla! books and many of the tech books above are only available at www.bookhawkers.com. Most books are available at amazon.com, Kindle, and other fine booksellers online and in the stores.

www.ingramcontent.com/pod-product-compliance
Lightning Source LLC
Chambersburg PA
CBHW071059050326
40690CB00008B/1062